F

The author: Patricia Dickson was born the only daughter of the late Richard Dawson – a distinguished political and literary figure of the early days of this century – and Isabel, née Campbell-Fletcher, of Jura, Argyll. She has travelled in many parts of the world as broadcaster, journalist and teacher. For the last few years she has been dedicated to research on the Duke of Argyll.

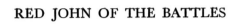

RED JOHN OF THE BATTLES

John, 2nd Duke of Argyll, from the painting by W. Aikman
in Her Majesty the Queen's Collection at Holyrood Palace

Red John
of the Battles

John, 2nd Duke of Argyll and
1st Duke of Greenwich
1680–1743

Patricia Dickson

SIDGWICK & JACKSON
LONDON

First published in Great Britain in 1973
by Sidgwick and Jackson Limited

Copyright © 1973 by Patricia Dickson

ISBN 0 283 97978 X

Printed in Great Britain by
John Sherratt and Son Limited, at the St Ann's Press, Park Road,
Timperley, Altrincham, Cheshire WA14 5QQ

for Sidgwick and Jackson Limited
1 Tavistock Chambers, Bloomsbury Way
London WC1A 2SG

Contents

List of Illustrations

Acknowledgements

My task as biographer of John, 2nd Duke of Argyll (1680–1743), has been greatly facilitated through encouragement from certain persons and entry to various libraries and archives.

The first acknowledgement is for 'The gracious permission of Her Majesty Queen Elizabeth II' to reproduce two documents, in photostat, of letters written by James III – the Pretender – found in the Stuart Papers at Windsor, and also the photograph of John, 2nd Duke of Argyll by W. Aikman – the portrait of which hangs in the Palace of Holyrood, Edinburgh.

Secondly, I acknowledge with gratitude the courtesy of the French Ministry of Foreign Affairs in allowing me access to the *Correspondence Politique et Diplomatique – Angleterre – 1700–1743.*

Thirdly, I have grateful memories of the many hours that I spent at Inveraray Castle, examining folios in the muniment vaults, and writing in the library. His Grace the late Duke of Argyll encouraged me at the start of this work.

Then, to His Grace the Duke of Buccleuch go my thanks for having given me the opportunity to transcribe a number of letters – mostly written by the 2nd Duke of Argyll's mother. These came into His Grace's family through the marriage of Lady Caroline Campbell – eldest daughter of the 2nd Duke – with the Earl of Dalkeith.

His Grace the Duke of Atholl allowed me to examine certain unpublished documents in the muniments of Blair Atholl : to him I am able to say that these Papers have thrown interesting light on certain passages in Duke John's life.

I am indebted to His Grace the late Duke of Marlborough for access to the muniments at Blenheim Palace.

For the Marquis of Bute, a very special esteem as he not only placed at my disposal his collection of Argyll family papers, but allowed me to work at his residence in Charlotte Square, Edinburgh.

In expressing thanks to the official sources whence documentary evidence has come, I would begin with the House of Lords library, and the immense help received from the librarian – Mr C. S. A. Dobson.

Next, I turn to the Scottish Record Office where I put in so many days when the work was in the embryo stage, and met great kindness from members of the staff. To them all – thank you.

The National Library of Edinburgh has also afforded me splendid assistance which I gratefully acknowledge.

At the Bedford Record Office I discovered the complete collection of the 2nd Duke's correspondence when he was Ambassador and Commander-in-Chief of the British Forces in Spain (1711–1712). To Miss Godber – the curator – very many thanks.

Researches have led me to the British Museum; Public Record Office; Hague archives; Vatican library; National Gallery of Edinburgh. To members of the staff whom I have met on my visits to these places, my deep appreciation for the help granted.

Sincere acknowledgement to Oxfordshire County Council for supplying information about Adderbury House.

To Colonel A. I. D. Fletcher, O.B.E., lately commanding Her Majesty's Scots Guards, I express gratitude for the interest he has taken in advising on the Sheriffmuir section.

Finally, I sincerely thank Sir Charles Petrie, Bt, O.B.E., for having read the manuscript.

Preface

'Red John of the Battles', his popular name in the Gaelic, has long deserved a full-length biography. The *Dictionary of National Biography* accords to him nine columns, and many references at the end of the article. The only serious attempt at a record of his achievements in politics and the field was written in 1745, only two years after Duke John's death, by one of his clansmen, Robert Campbell. Now a rare book, it only deals in a fairly perfunctory way with his military career. Both John Campbell and his younger brother Archibald, Earl of Islay, who was popularly known as 'King of Scotland' in the early Hanoverian days, have never received their due from historians.

John had five daughters, Archibald one (illegitimate) son. The elder brother was impetuous, impatient, ambitious, and certainly anxious to prove the iniquity of his grandfather's and great-grandfather's executions. But he was a Highlander at heart, and when Queen Anne bestowed on him the Barony of Chatham, the Earldom, and later Dukedom, of Greenwich, he chose as his motto 'VIX EA NOSTRA VOCO'.

Mrs Dickson has spent eight years of devoted research. She has travelled far and wide in the course of her work. She has taught me much, and I am most grateful for all she has discovered about my collateral namesake. May her book have all the success it well deserves!

Argyll.

Inveraray, 21 June 1971.

xi

(Attributed to John, 2nd Duke of Argyll)

Argyll is my name, and you may think it strange,
To live at a court, yet never to change;
A' falsehood and flattery I do disdain,
In my secret thoughts nae guile does remain.
My king and my country's foes I have faced,
In city or battle I ne'er was disgraced;
I do every thing for my country's weal,
And feast upon bannocks of barley meal.

Adieu to the courts of London town,
For to my ain country I will gang down;
At the sight of Kirkaldy ance again,
I'll cock up my bonnet and march amain.
O, the muckle deil tak' a' your noise and strife,
I'm fully resolved for a country life,
Where a' the braw lasses who ken me weel,
Will feed me wi' bannocks of barley meal.

I will quickly lay down my sword and my gun,
And put my blue bonnet and my plaidie on;
With my silk tartan hose, and leather heel'd shoon,
And then I will look like a sprightly loon.
And when I'm ance dress'd frae top to toe,
To meet my dear Maggie I vow I will gae,
Wi' target and hanger hang down to my heel;
And I'll feast upon bannocks o' barley meal.

I'll buy a rich garment t' gie to my dear,
A ribbon o' green for Maggie to wear;
And blawer than that I declare,
Gin she will gang wi' me to Paisley fair.
And when we are married, I'll keep her a sow,
And Maggie will milk when I go to plow;
We'll live a' the winter on beef and lang kail,
And feast upon bannocks o' barley meal.

Gin Maggie should chance to bring me a son,
He'll fight for his king, as his daddy has done;
He'll hie him to Flanders, some blooding to learn,
And then hame to Scotland, and get him a farm.

NOTE

Since the earliest days when the name was spelt 'EARRADH GHOIDAEL' (boundaries of the [Irish] Gael) the successive Earls and Dukes have used 'ERGYL', 'ERGYLE', 'ARGYL', 'ARGYLE', and now it is standardized as 'ARGYLL'.

Therefore, with the exception of quotations or correspondence in which the old spelling appears, I have used the standard version.

PART ONE

The Fateful Years

Introduction

HAM HOUSE – 1680

In Westminster Abbey, there is a monument inscribed with the words:

In memory of an Honest Man, a Constant Friend – John – the great Duke of Argyll & Greenwich, A General and Orator exceeded by None in the Age he lived.

The birth of the man thus described took place on 10 October 1680, at Ham House, Petersham – residence of the Duke and Duchess of Lauderdale. In the Yellow Satin Room he uttered the first challenge to life. For the mother, lying upon the great bed with its four posts surmounted by cups containing stiff feathers known as 'Spriggs', it was a supreme moment when the physician smacked the arse of the babe he had delivered and exclaimed 'a fine boy'. Even in the midst of her anguish, she wept for joy. After three years as wife of Archibald, Lord Lorne (eldest son of the ninth Earl of Argyll), Elizabeth – daughter of the Duchess of Lauderdale by her first husband – Sir Lionel Tollemache, Bt, of Helmingham – had borne a son.

John Campbell entered the world in a year which found his birthplace renowned for a magnificence unequalled in that Restoration age. His grandmother – first as Countess of Dysart (in her own right) and later as Duchess of Lauderdale – had gratified an avarice for pomp by extravagantly creating her residence a palace.

The enchantment began from the moment of passing from the Riverside Avenue to the central forecourt amidst which the statue of Father Thames presided upon a pedestal representing rocks and engraved with the arms of the City of London. Beyond was the

B

red-brick Jacobean mansion and, on either side, cloistered arcades where, set in circular niches, were busts of the Roman emperors.

Within the house, an unusual opulence prevailed. From Holland and Italy, artists skilled in various crafts had come to Ham and each, after their own fashion, endowed the rooms with a wealth of art in furnishings as well as decoration. Everywhere was a brilliance of colour.

To France the Duchess had turned for the exterior scene. The gardens and terraces were the design of Le Nôtre – famed as gardener at the court of Versailles. Beauty and stateliness formed the pattern. 'The very flowers are old-fashioned, none but flowers of the oldest time – gay, formal knots of pinks, solid cabbage roses and round Dutch honeysuckles.'[1]

Finally, there were the perspectives. To the north lay the Thames, to the south a lawn of two-and-a-half acres extended to the wilderness[2] at one side of which was a walk shaded by evergreen oaks and having in its centre a marble figure of Bacchus. A terrace – five hundred and thirty feet long and thirty feet broad – completed the view.

During John's infancy the era of lavish entertainment at Ham drew to a close. The Duke of Lauderdale's waning health cast a gloom which culminated with his death in 1682.

That year also brought another birth in the great bed of the Yellow Satin Room. Lady Lorne became the mother of a second son who would be christened Archibald, and eventually bear the title Earl of Islay.

She continued to live at Ham, so that it was there that John took his first walks and the infant brother came to toddling age. Then they were merely her 'poppets'[3]. Later years would see them as the sons of whom she would proudly write : 'My sons has made all the use as is thought for their successes.'

While life thus flowed tranquilly beside the Thames, there came a darkening of the cloud which had hung over the House of Argyll since 1681 when the estates fell forfeit to the crown and the name was attainted.[4] Upon news of Charles II's death (1685), Lord Lorne's father – the Earl of Argyll, then a refugee in Holland – plotted with other Scottish exiles to make a bid for restoration of Scotland's liberties and thus avert the popish impact of the new monarch – James II. The Duke of Monmouth was to raise rebellion in England and the Earl would command an invasion of Scotland.

Spring 1685 brought the hour of destiny for both the elder Argyll and his son. The invading force embarked from Holland. Lord

Lorne,[5] aware of the hazard to his own interests and family, proceeded to the English court and offered allegiance to the king.

As events happened, the attempted coup proved abortive. The Earl was captured and taken to Edinburgh Castle.

That same spring found John near Edinburgh on a visit to his aunt – the Countess of Moray.

EDINBURGH – 1685

The twenty-first of June was a day of importance for the populace of Edinburgh. It was also a day of destiny both for Scotland and England; but that belonged to the future. Meanwhile, as the hour approached two o'clock of the afternoon, citizens were thronging the streets leading from the Council House to the Market Place. A clash of emotions was manifest. In one quarter could be heard the clamour of the mob; in another, the murmurings of people stirred to compassion.

Within the Council House, Archibald, 9th Earl of Argyll, prepared for a martyr's end. He had taken leave of friends, sent messages to relatives, and now spoke freely of 'the dangers of Popery'; the reverses of his own fortunes; the injustice of the death sentence passed upon him; the mercy that should be shown to the Highlanders who had supported him merely as the consequence of being forced into military service.

So the moment arrived for departure to the place of execution. Mr Annand – Dean of Edinburgh – and Mr Charteris – an Episcopalian minister – took their places on either side of the Earl who was unshackled because of his privilege as a peer. They were followed by eight persons clad in deep mourning. In that order, the procession passed out to the multitude eager for the spectacle of witnessing a nobleman die for his faith. To both partisan and foe there was something remarkable in the Earl's attitude. Throughout the walk to the scaffold he maintained a bold step and stately deportment. In the centre of the square, where, on other days, the same humanity bought and sold, bargained and gossiped, the instrument of death – a rude guillotine – loomed starkly.

On arrival there, the Earl, after discourse with the ministers and an interval of prayer, looked out to the crowd and unfolded a paper in preparation for speech. A sudden hush ensued.

Among his words certain ones predominated: 'I pray God continue to increase the glorious light of the Gospel and restrain a spirit of oppression, Popery and persecution. I would pray that there might never want one of the royal family to be a defender of the true, ancient, apostolic, Catholic and Protestant faith . . . '

Upon conclusion of the address, he turned to the south side of the scaffold: 'Gentlemen, I pray you do not misconstruct my behaviour today. I freely forgive all men their wrongs and injuries done against me as I desire to be forgiven by God.'

The Dean of Edinburgh repeated those words in a louder tone, and the Earl moved to the opposite side for a similar pronouncement. The Dean repeated it, then, after a pause, added: 'This nobleman dies a Protestant.'

Argyll was inflamed to a final challenge: 'I die not only a Protestant, but with a heart-hatred of prelacy and all superstition whatever.'

He turned to the executioner.

In the moment when the blade descended upon the Earl's head, his grandson – John Campbell – fell out of 'a three pair of stairs window' at the Countess of Moray's residence. To the astonishment of attendants who rushed to his aid, he was uninjured.

This extraordinary incident caused the belief that the five-year-old child whose fair, graceful, yet commanding countenance predicted the capacity of leadership, would one day restore the name of Argyll to a place of honour in the land.

Meanwhile, there lay before him boyhood with his brother and two sisters – Ann and Kathryn.[6] In that time he was to make discoveries.

Chapter I

BOYHOOD YEARS

JOHN's first discovery concerned his brother. Instead of finding companionship he found discord. This sad truth had early become evident to those who had charge of them. Except for the fact of having been born in the same bed, there was no point of agreement between them either in character or as brethren. John had 'genius with all the lights and shades thereto appertaining. He was warm-hearted, magnanimous, but fierce-tempered, rash, ambitious, haughty, impatient of contradiction.'[1] On the other hand, Archibald displayed characteristics which would develop to shrewdness and an argumentative disposition. It was the latter that largely contributed to the friction, because John's forthright nature abhorred argument. Whenever the signs of dispute showed, he merely turned his back and strode disdainfully away. 'I wanted to discuss such an affair with my brother,' Archibald said in days to come, 'but all went wrong. I saw the Tollemache blood rising and so I e'en quitted the field.'

During that span of boyhood so susceptible to impressions and influences, his father – Lord Lorne and Master of Argyll (as he styled himself) – restored the fortunes of his House with right to the title of Earl. The tide turned from that hour of 1688 when he was deputed to offer Scotland's Crown to William, Prince of Orange. Acclaimed 'One of the politest men of the time and of great capacity', he arose to more than one department of State.[2] The polish of the diplomat, the subtlety of the politician, the initiative of a man of action, the boldness of a leader, were facets of a many-sided character capable of adapting itself readily to the particular circumstance, whatever its character. With equal ease he could be the courtier beside the king; the soldier creating a regiment to bear his name and constitute Scotland's first standing army; and the Scotsman of whom King William declared: 'I got more truth from

Argyll than from all the rest of my servants in Scotland because he had the courage to speak out what others durst not venture to speak.'

As John came to learn of these facts, he captured certain lights destined for reflection in his own career – ability to place a nation's interests before personal sentiments; loyalty to religious doctrines; fearlessness in approach to mankind; the very qualities which brought his father to eminence during an era of revolution would emerge in John and dictate his actions at a time when monarchy again became the supreme issue.

After restoration of the Argyll estates, the Campbell domain – Roseneath – on the Argyll shore of the Firth of Clyde by Gareloch, was used as a residence by the Earl and his family. During those times among his clansmen, John's outlook was so shaped as to promote a 'penetrating judgement' in matters relating to the Church. The religious controversies of the age governed conversation. From all entrusted with his upbringing came the same injunction: To remember that he belonged to one of the staunchest Presbyterian families, and loyalty to the Kirk must always prevail. He was also constantly reminded of the fact that the name of Campbell evoked awe as well as respect among the inhabitants because the Earl of Argyll was powerful with King William.

John's education began under the Reverend Walter Campbell of Dunoon and continued under John Anderson[3] who, besides being an old family friend, was the Duchess's most trusted adviser. In course of time, the usual subjects were joined by the Classics and Philosophy. Learning, however, did not blend with a high-spirited, ever restless quest for pursuits demanding vigour, hazard and initiative. He studied merely as a duty. On the other hand, all forms of athletic exercise found him a keen student and splendid physique gave him superiority.

When John attained the age of fourteen, his father approached King William with a request. On a spring day of the year 1694 came the reply: 'John, Lord Lorne, to be Colonel of the Regiment of Foot whereof Archibald, Earl of Argyle, was late Colonel, and likewise to be Captain of a Company in the same Regiment. Dated at Whitehall – 7th April 1694.'

Thus read the commission that brought the young Lord Lorne to the threshold of the army. For some time to come he would not assume official duties, but continue his education with no difference save developed studies. It was only an honorary appointment granted by the King's grace. As the custom of that day allowed, the

Earl had invoked royal prerogative on behalf of his heir who, so clearly, personified the born soldier. By authorizing transfer of the regimental command from father to son, King William conferred the strongest proof of his favour. For the Argylls it constituted a signal honour.

The final stage of Lord Lorne's progress from youth to manhood became the responsibility of a Scotsman who had been beside the Earl at the time of the Revolution. Both were members of the party that accompanied the Prince of Orange to England. Alexander Cunningham, appointed tutor and travelling companion, could be relied upon to guide his pupil along the right course of religious doctrine and political principle.

Scholar, courtier, diplomat: such was the pattern of Cunningham's activities, with the starting-point at Leyden – then regarded as centre of European culture. Like so many contemporaries of his age, he had been caught in the web of events and spun to other orbits. Acquaintance with William as prince; a strengthening of the friendship with William as King; a man who had set forth to pursue scholarship, found himself being employed on confidential missions both by Monarch and Parliament.[4] First, however, he was scholar devoting time to the preparation of noblemen's sons for their place in the world of affairs.

Under his tutor's guidance, Lord Lorne read more widely and as great works in the classics were introduced to him a taste for literature awakened. The benefit would be realized when the hour arrived for him to command by oratory rather than the sword.

He was sixteen when an event broke the domestic circle. His parents separated.[5]

After that, the ways of the family diverged. John's father went on to advance his position in the state by becoming Colonel of the Royal Horse Guards and Extraordinary Lord of Session (1696). He also took an interest – as shareholder – in the enterprise known as the Company of Scotland Trading to Africa and the Indies.[6] His mother removed to Campbelltown to live in retirement though not in idleness. Besides management of her property there and, later, the Argyll estates throughout the county, she would preside over the local community. The daughters went, for a time, to Roseneath. Archibald, Lord Islay, destined for law, pursued his studies, first at Eton and then at Glasgow University. For John, Lord Lorne, it was departure to the Continent.

Chapter II

THE YOUNG COLONEL

1697–1701

THE Earl of Argyll's Foot was on campaign in the Spanish Netherlands – central theatre of operations in the War of the League of
Augsburg[1] against France. They had experienced all the vicissitudes
of a struggle destined to cost King William, as Commander-in-Chief,
many moments of anguish, and yet to prove his triumph as a soldier.
When Lord Lorne joined them, the only Allied victory of the seven
years' conflict had been gained at Namur, and there was report of
the end to hostilities. As 1686 drew to a close, the gleam of truce
became real. A year later, through the Treaty of Ryswick, it
expanded to the dawn of peace and the western world rejoiced.

Diplomatic relations between England and France were resumed
soon afterwards with the appointment of embassies. Marshall
Tallard was accredited to London and the Earl of Portland to
Paris. Among those who attended the English ambassador's entry to
Paris was Lord Lorne, and the great ceremonial which distinguished
it must have impressed him in this first introduction to a foreign
court.

An extract from a letter addressed by the Earl of Argyll to
Alexander Cunningham alludes to the occasion:

Edinburgh, August 3rd 1697

Sir,

    I am twice in your debt. I thank you for giving me an account
of my son. I have heard from himself since, but not of his being
with Earl Portland which I long for an account of from himself . . .

While London and Paris celebrated, military minds – and Lord
Lorne's was one – assessed the truth. They judged it not as victory
to either nation, but certainly a triumph on King William's part.

In the field, commanding the army; in international negotiations, all his energies had been directed to a single cause: to curb Louis XIV's dominion. He had succeeded in curbing his rival's power. Only one thing further was required to guarantee the day that this dawn promised. The maintenance of land and sea forces would secure the world from the incessant conflicts which had troubled it for several centuries – and always with the roots in France.

Unfortunately, William's ministers lacked the foresight of their Monarch and the captains who had been associated with him in the active prosecution of the war. To them – enclosed in their insular limits which merely showed expenditure and taxation – armed strength in peacetime represented unwarranted extravagance. So they met the King's plea for the preservation of his forces with a negative answer, and thus abandoned England to her fate. Although he mastered his emotion and bowed to the will of the narrow-minded assembly at Westminster, a permanent scar remained. His honour as a soldier had been mortally hurt.

The Commons were resolved upon redundancy of the armed forces. To them, basking in the sunshine of peace, it seemed absurd to maintain a strong army and navy. The initial cut in national expenditure would fall in this quarter.

A letter addressed from Alexander Cunningham to William Carstares throws interesting light on Lord Lorne's feelings on the subject of Parliament's decision:

Bruges – October 20th 1697

Revd. Sir,

I had the honour of your's before I parted from Brussels, and I find by it that upon all occasions you are ready to oblige your friends. I do not yet know whether I shall go to Paris or not before I return to London. My Lord Argyle has not yet written anything concerning his son; he was gone from this place to his regiment before I came here, which I was glad of for I know his Lieutenant-Colonel will take care of him. He is mightily concerned for his regiment. Everybody tells him it will be broken. I have assured him that you will do your utmost for him . . .

Lord Lorne's concern for his regiment was only too well founded. It suffered the fate that befell the standing army; disbandment and officers placed on half-pay. As for the rank and file, they were cast adrift to sink or swim.

The tragic spectacle was not lost upon the young Colonel. His magnanimous nature reacted through a deep compassion not only

for the men themselves, but for the King who had led them so
valiantly in the fight. The soldier within him understood the folly
as well as the selfishness of the Tory and Whig politicians who
refused to consider Britain's security and, instead, indulged in their
own petty feuds.

An interval at home followed the break in military duties. The
years 1699 and 1700 took him abroad again for a further term of
education. Accompanied by Alexander Cunningham, he visited
various European capitals, among them Rome.

Europe moved onward not to the peace which everyone desired;
but to a renewal of the storm. Although a spirit of pacifism prevailed
among peoples economically exhausted by the struggle, the har-
monies of that condition were absent. When they looked towards
Spain their minds became tense. In her death-tremors both as a
nation and a monarchy, she had drawn forces dangerous to the
progress of Anglo-French relations. Besides Austria and Bavaria,
each with a candidate for the throne of the dying King, stood
Louis XIV on behalf of his grandson Philip. The situation caused
uneasiness and this sentiment was aggravated by another disturbing
element. Jacobite intrigues were ever energetic with their mainspring at Versailles.

The turn of the century brought optimism. There were signs that
the diplomatic structure of Louis and William to preserve Europe's
stability at all costs might succeed. Treaty by treaty their negotiations had advanced and the cardinal stage of agreement was
imminent. At the same time, Louis had reached a cross-roads where
he must make a choice of the gravest kind. One pointed to '*Le Roi
Soleil*' (Louis XIV) as master of Europe and therefore open to
antagonisms. The other to '*Le Soleil*' distributing his sunlight for
the benefit of mankind. Personal ambition or international welfare?
Which would it be? On that question the world entered 1701.

A YEAR OF DESTINY – 1701

Besides the importance of 1701 to English politics[2] and international
affairs, it proved fateful for the House of Argyll. John's father
received a dukedom. 'By patent dated 23rd June, the Earl's services
to the State were rewarded by elevation to the rank of Duke with
right to the titles – Marquis of Kintyre and Lorne, Earl of Campbell and Cowal, Viscount Lochaw and Glenila, Lord Inveraray,
Morven, and Tiree.

It might well have been this June month when the new-created

Duke came to London to attend at Court, that from his house in
Holborn he sent a communication to Lord Lorne – then back in
England:

To my Sonn of Lorne
Sonn,
   The bearer hereof – Mrs Wright – is the party to whom my
wife was a debtor to for her wages £4:10: which I desire you
may pay her at the sight hereof without further scrouple, for if I
bee found to be a debtor to the executors I shall repay it you, and
keep you from all dangers that way,
         Subscrived
            with my hand
               Argyll

at my house in
holborn
the 21 of June

Send her not bak to me for she is a railing wyf.

For Lord Lorne, destiny also had something in store. Aged
twenty-one he had much to recommend him – good looks, position
and a warrior's deportment. It was therefore inevitable that he
should be one of society's most sought-after figures. Parents with
eligible daughters were especially anxious to have him in their
company. Although attracted by the feminine sex and always ready
to make a conquest, he had hitherto treated flirtation lightly and not
allowed himself to be conquered. Then one autumn day all was
changed.
   How and where he met Mary Browne can only be surmised.
Besides the absence of facts, there is even a confusion about her
antecedents. In the Scottish peerage she is described as 'daughter of
Thomas Browne (afterwards Duncombe) Receiver-General of the
Excise'. According to another source, Thomas Browne belonged to
the parish of St Margaret's, Westminster, and married Ursula Duncombe – sister of Sir Charles Duncombe,[3] a politician who held high
offices in the City. At the end of May 1700, Sir Charles was
nominated Lord Mayor of London, and Mary acted as her uncle's
Lady Mayoress.
   Gossip of the day reported that the Duke of Argyll was strongly
drawn to her, or believed it to be so at the time. His wooing –

passionate and influenced by an impetuous nature which, on occasions, could prove his worst enemy – led to a speedy marriage. On 30 December 1701, the contract was signed.

The sequel to this rash action was tragic for the young couple. In the early days of their married life, they awoke to the realization of being quite unsuited to one another. The shock of disillusionment affected John more severely than Mary, who was even then in delicate health. As the flame that had so irrevocably scorched him flickered out, he experienced a chill equally powerful. It was the revelation of dislike. Without delay they separated. Fortunately for the embittered husband, there would soon come a call to his best-loved sphere.

The period of truce in Europe was almost at an end. Louis XIV's choice of course had precipitated the breakdown of diplomatic relations with England. By establishing, through devious stratagems, his grandson Philip as Spain's new king, he commanded not only a greater part of the European stage but the Spanish dominions in South America and the Indies. As a master stroke he proclaimed the exiled James III (the Pretender) at Versailles as England's future monarch.

Under these circumstances, King William, with Marlborough beside him as chief architect of policy, emerged with a bulwark to oppose the French peril. It was the Grand Alliance of Britain, the States-General (the Netherlands), Russia, and the Empire.

In England, the army's reconstruction became the 'Order of the Day'. Disbanded regiments were re-formed, and officers on half-pay recalled. For John, Lord Lorne, there came (by favour of King William) the colonelcy of his own regiment of Foot, to serve under the Dutch Command.

Chapter III

CAMPAIGN

1702-3

In February 1702 King William died, leaving his sister-in-law, Anne, as Queen. A few weeks after her succession – on 11 March – she met her Parliament.

Her Majesty – being seated on her Royal Throne, adorned with her crown and royal ornaments, attended by her officers of State : the Peers being all in their robes, – commanded the Gentleman-Usher of the Black Rod to let the Commons know – 'It is Her Majesty's pleasure that they attend her presently into the House of Peers', who being come with their Speaker, Her Majesty was pleased to say as follows :

'My Lords and Gentlemen,
    'I cannot too much lament my own unhappiness in succeeding to the Crown so immediately after the loss of a King who was the great support not only of these Kingdoms, but of all Europe, and I am extremely sensible of the weight and difficulty it brings upon us.
    'The present conjuncture of affairs requires the greatest application and dispatch; and I am very glad to find in your several Addresses so unanimous a concurrence in the same opinion with us that too much cannot be done for the encouragement of our Allies to reduce the exorbitant power of France.'

When spring returned to Europe it was to find the Armies marshalled for campaign in the Low Countries. Belgium and Holland would again be the central theatre of war. The French, with their chain of fortresses controlling the rivers Scheldt, Meuse, and Rhine, enjoyed strong strategic advantage. While they held these formidable barriers the Dutch were deprived of movement.

Allied military policy therefore concentrated upon an offensive of sieges to liberate the waterways from enemy domination.

On 16 April, the Allies invested the Rhine fortress town of Kaiserwert. Among the regiments assembled there was the Duke of Argyll's under its colonel – Lord Lorne – and for the first time his exploits in action received official mention. 'He is fearless of danger and manifests a natural courage' stated a dispatch. On many occasions during the two months that elapsed before the town's capitulation, he displayed remarkable initiative.

Towards the end of June, Marlborough assumed command of the forces, and some weeks later – in August, the siege of Venloo, the strongest of the three fortresses north of Maestricht – opened. Although surrender came after four weeks, the struggle, while it lasted, was fierce. Fort St Michael at Venloo constituted the vital target and demanded men of dauntless spirit to lead the attack. According to record, 'When the fighting Lord Cutts – in command of the Anglo-Irish Brigade – led the victorious assault, Lord Lorne served as volunteer.'

The fall of winter brought a halt in operations. The army moved into quarters and a new phase of activity began. Much time was devoted to the drill which the elaborate line tactics of the day required. For colonels – as virtual proprietors of their regiments – these months enabled a 'breathing space' in which to reorganize the regimental strength and commissariat. Trusted officers were delegated on missions for this purpose.

Beyond such routine duties was life in the camp – the times when Lord Lorne could forget both rank and politics and meet his fellows in the raw. The coarseness of language and morals must have been sharp contrast for one reared in the circles of God-fearing strictures and elegance. However, with the same graceful manner that made him so charming in society, he adopted the rough modes of speech and behaviour. He could sleep with a woman who followed the army as easily as with a courtesan of the fashionable world. The rank and file idolized him. His brother officers venerated him. He was a splendid companion – always ready with the right word spoken in a voice that impressed by reason of its eloquence. So rare too in commanders, he did not lose the common touch and understood how to mix with the motley crowd found in the Allied armies. Like Marlborough, he recognized not the station of the man; but the man himself. The mercenary – if he proved worthy in the field – occupied as high a place in Lord Lorne's esteem as the regular soldier.

Before another phase of warfare resumed, Lord Lorne went on a very special mission to the court of Hanover. The order apparently emanated from his father who, at that time, was among the Commissioners nominated by the Queen to design a Treaty of Union. As the Hanoverian Succession was opposed in Scotland, yet strongly favoured by the Dutch and Whig statesmen, stratagems to win Scottish adherents were resolved.

To quote Colonel Hooke, agent for the Court of France to the Jacobites: 'I have a letter from that Court [Hanover] which assures me that Lord Lorne, son of the Duke of Argyll, has arrived there and that he has made the journey by order of his father, and it is perhaps in consequence of his instructions that the Duchess Dowager of Hanover has recently sent £10,000 sterling to some friends there [Scotland].'

Marlborough's arrival at the Hague in March 1703, and the reviews of troops and garrisons that followed, set the pace for renewed hostilities. The chief consideration was the plan of campaign. Should it be an offensive launched by the 'Grand Army' – or a continuation of siege warfare? Had the decision rested with Marlborough alone he would have chosen decisive action aimed at the sea-ports of Antwerp and Ostend. This freedom did not belong to him. The States-General had to be consulted, and they were adamant for sieges. So, in deference to them, a scheme of operations amidst the fortress zone was determined. While Marlborough proceeded to invest the Rhine town of Bonn, the Dutch Commander – Overkirk – guarded the line of the Meuse between Maestricht and Liège. It was under his command that Lord Lorne served.

Meanwhile, the French marshals, Villeroy and Boufflers, had received orders from Versailles to recapture Liège – with expectations of making this the first victory of the new military year. At the beginning of May they advanced towards that fortress. On the 5th their vanguard reached Tongers – an entrenched position held by two Battalions, one Dutch, the other Scottish, forming part of the Duke of Argyll's regiment. For twenty-four hours the Allied contingent heroically countered an attack by superior forces. Although ultimately forced to surrender, their long resistance contributed, in large measure, to Liège's salvation. The delay allowed Overkirk the time that he needed to strengthen his positions. This, besides the fact that Marlborough had sent strong reinforcements, dissuaded France's marshals from further siege of a fortress so solidly entrenched.

The rest of the summer passed unsatisfactorily for captains of Lord

Lorne's calibre – who recognized the wisdom of Marlborough's so-called 'Great Design': a battle striking at liberation of the coastal region. At one moment, in June, after Bonn's fall and the French retreat from the Maestricht area, it seemed that the way lay open to such a course. The enemy apparently thought so too, and an atmosphere tense with apprehension governed armies as they waited, only leagues apart, for developments. These came on the part of the Dutch who made certain unwise moves and precipitated a series of reverses for the Allied cause. Every British soldier shared the frustration that befell Marlborough.

Lord Lorne was in this humour when news arrived which recalled him to England and, for a time, ended active service. By his father's death on 25 September[1] he had succeeded to the Dukedom and Earldom of Argyll.

As Duke he was received in audience by the Queen, who honoured him with the appointment that his father had held: Colonel of the four Scots Troops of Horse Guards.[2] He was also admitted to the Privy Council.

During these days, the campaign in which he had played so conspicuous a part came to a disappointing conclusion. The fault belonged chiefly to the Dutch High Command whose policy it was to hold Marlborough in 'leading strings' rather than encourage him to follow his own initiative. To make a dismal situation gloomier, everything pointed to the French launching a full-scale offensive in the new year.

The thought of being absent from the war at that critical stage displeased the twenty-three-year-old soldier Duke. Nevertheless, he had to resign himself to the duties of his inheritance.

INHERITANCE

There was a feature in his father's life that John had never approved. So on taking possession of his estates, he acted in drastic fashion by 'turning all his father's mistresses out of doors and seizing their ill-gotten goods by his own authority according to the Highland custom.'[3]

A host of responsibilities faced him.[4] Both for the young Duke and his mother, there was a legacy of legal as well as financial confusions. The late Duke's will, which had been made at Inveraray and bore the date 26 September 1690, was produced in Edinburgh on 2 October 1703. Due to the involved state of affairs as the result of debts and family circumstances, two years were to elapse before it was proved. Meanwhile, Argyll began a correspondence with his kinsman – Ronald Campbell. The first of these letters[5] was written at the turn of the year 1703/4.

Ronald,

I have heard from my Mother in answer to the letter I writ her to beg she would be pleas'd to clear the affaires of Kintyre to inable my Managers to pay me quickly the thousand pounds I should have from the Esteat. She tells me she will make her accounts and contribute all she is able that the payments may be speedy. So Ronald I expect to have that Thousand Pound very quickly. I am sure my want of it is most extream. I have sent down Saunders Campbell that was in Holland, and so soon as he arrives I expect that without delay you fall to work to put my Peapers in order. It is a work of absolute necessity so pray let it be gon about immediately –

I have nothing else at present –

Argyll

Expectation of a speedy settlement was, however, doomed. Time passed without sign of progress. Argyll's mother, who played so remarkable a part in the management of her son's affairs, wrote in anxious tone to Mr Anderson (the family lawyer) and the Duke of Somerset.[6] Meanwhile, the late Duke's creditors claimed payments and even the funeral expenses could not be met.[7]

Argyll became more and more exasperated. He did not conceal the fact from Ronald Campbell.

I cant imagine how you can think I live here and I dair assure you if I havena that thousand pounds with the answer of this letter and am not for the future pay'd, surely to a day I shall alter my method for by God Almighty I will not starve for the saik of my Family or any thing on earth.

Besides financial crises there was still another problem. It related to the future of the ancestral seat – Inveraray. For this purpose, Argyll found it necessary to compose a lengthy document of instructions to his managers.[8]

Succession to the Dukedom had certainly brought trials almost beyond the endurance of a temper which flared at the slightest provocation. On the other hand the early days of 1704 were to bring him his first recognition from Her Majesty.

C

Chapter IV

THE BATTLE OF POLITICS — SCOTLAND

In February 1704 the Queen conferred the Order of St Andrew with a green riband of the 'Thistle' upon the Duke of Argyll.[1] He had turned his attention to Scottish politics and proposed to attend the summer session of the Estates.[2]

During the last year of the late Duke's life two important events had occurred. The first was a conference of Commissioners appointed by the Queen to 'treat of an Union between the two Kingdoms of Scotland and England'. The second came in sequel to the defiance of Scots politicians towards the Hanoverian Succession. As the Duke of Hamilton had expressed it: 'Upon the death of the Queen without issue or without successor appointed by Herself and the Estates, Parliament should, after twenty days, nominate a successor of the royal line of Scotland and of the Protestant religion who should not be successor to the Crown of England, unless in this or in some subsequent Parliament such conditions of Government had been enacted as should secure from English or from foreign interest the honour and independence (sovereignty) of Scotland.'

The Act of Security was thus passed, and in course of the next years it formed material for the duel of antagonisms to be waged against a background of Jacobite intrigue.

While these political moves were in progress, Scotland was steadily moving towards a crisis.

In the Scottish Highlands and among many of the oldest families there was a strong affinity with France. Their veneration for liberty fortified a determination to risk everything in order to secure independence. Even the Presbyterians, who opposed the cause of the exiled James III (Chevalier St George), were in agreement on that score. The existing state of affairs provided a strong motive for Scotland's detachment from dependence upon England. Yet because of diverse factions with different views, there was no one willing to begin by display of open force. Nevertheless, lands were rendered barren through taxes and peasants were taken away as recruits to support a war in which they had neither taste nor interest.

In England too there was a marked narrowness of opinion in regard to the north. Argyll had often been impelled to contradict statements spread by the exaggeration of travellers' tales that the Scots were as inclement as their Highlands – dour, uncouth and only capable of warfare. During his days on the Continent he had made it known that Scotsmen possessed qualities unsuspected by their English contemporaries and which, once fostered, could make strong impact upon the world at large. In his vision as a military man, he saw beyond insular boundaries. Internationalism was greater than nationalism, and when both parties – English and Scots – were freed from their nationalist strictures, then the creation of a new Britain would be open to give them its commerce and receive from them the values of tradition.

A few days before the opening of the Scots Parliament the Duke of Argyll arrived in Edinburgh. During the slow progress of the drive to the palace of Holyrood where, as hereditary Master of the Household, he had apartments, there was opportunity to observe the people of every sort and condition who thronged the 'Mile'. The majority appeared to be sightseers and either strolled or loitered idly so as not to miss personalities. He saw many of the faces close at hand and, being trained in the art of observation, discerned something more than mere curiosity. It suggested a tenseness. Had they caught the flame of unrest which subversive forces were trying to fan? These, in the form of the rebel, the conspirator, the religious fanatic, found fertile soil in the capital as the heart of Scotland's political life. Only one section of the crowd appeared to be aloof from the evidently prevailing mood. They were the civic guards armed with Lochaber axes. Their deportment was disciplined and their countenances were stolidly set as they patrolled in that efficient manner which enabled them to maintain a fair measure of order.

As the hour drew near for Parliament's opening, the atmosphere of tension mounted. Everyone realized that critical days lay ahead. In all ranks of Edinburgh society the conversation centred upon one subject: Scotland and her leaders. At Holyrood, Argyll entertained friends, and over glasses of wine and exchanges of snuff, discussed the prospects.

'Crisis is certain; Tweedale and his "Squadrone" will find themselves in a minority as the result of Queensberry's move to the side of Hamilton and Atholl.' 'How can they honour their pledge to Godolphin to steer the Succession the way of Hanover?' 'They are too "light-weight" to stand against the storm that awaits them . . .' 'In all likelihood the Opposition will try to force the issue by urging Her Majesty's signature to the Act as it stands.' 'What then of Scotland?'

On these lines they argued. Argyll, a man of honourable principles, did not mince words when speaking of either the Marquess of Tweedale or his Independent Whig associates – the Earls of Rothes and Roxburgh, Baillie of Jerviswood, James Johnstone. In his opinion they merited their title – 'The Flying Squadron'. Swift changes of course to suit the wind's temper: of such calibre were the men who had veered from being Jacobite patriots and become Court proselytes within the narrow margin of two sessions.

Argument then transferred to Queensberry. He, too, had changed direction in order to be in a strong position to defeat the Marquess of Tweedale who had so meanly supplanted him as Commissioner. Yet, in Argyll's view, his action could be condoned on the grounds that he was zealously bound to Scotland's cause and did not wish to see the delicate affair of the Succession mishandled by men lacking both stamina and sincerity.

On a day in the first week of June, the Estates members walked in procession to the Parliament of which they were so justly proud. Few could pass to the well-paved square courtyard with the equestrian statue of Charles II in the centre and the fine buildings which bordered it on the west without a sense of inspiration. It was the noblest spot in Edinburgh. Dignity and majesty were both present – the one in the precincts, the other in what was portrayed above the entrance of Parliament House: Scotland's arms supported on either side by Mercy and Truth with the inscription – *'Stant has Felicia Regna'* (By these kingdoms stand happy') – while beneath were the words *'Unio Unionum'* ('Union of Unions'). Within the hall, stately through its loftiness and the magnificent arched roofs of Scots oak, the Duke of Argyll's place was among the dukes and earls who occupied the upper tier of benches lying to the right of the Commissioner's throne on the south side. Below them sat representatives of the shires. To the left where seats also rose in tiers, were the viscounts, barons and burgh delegates.

After the traditional prayers, the Lord Clerk Register read Her Majesty's Commission to John, Marquess of Tweedale. Then the Duke of Atholl, Lord Privy Seal; the Marquess of Annandale, Lord President of the Council; and the Earl of Cromarty, Lord Secretary, were sworn into office. The Duke of Argyll, together with certain others – took the oath of allegiance and oath of Parliament. The rest of that day's business was devoted to the conferring of titles – more numerous than usual – on members of the Scottish nobility.

A week later – on Tuesday 11 June – Parliament again met, this time to hear Her Majesty's message: 'Nothing has troubled us more since our accession to the Crown of these Realms than the unsettled state of affairs in this our ancient kingdom.'

Thus it began and went on to mention the 'divisions which have proceeded to such a height as to prove a matter of encouragement to our enemies beyond the sea to employ their emissaries among you in order to debauch our good subjects from their allegiance . . .'

There followed reference to the Marquess of Tweedale as Commissioner, 'He being a person of whose capacity and probity or qualifications and dispositions to serve us neither we nor you can have any doubt.'

Argyll, listening to those flattering phrases, felt both angry and ashamed that the man of whom they were spoken should so little deserve them. He looked towards Tweedale who was almost in line with him because the throne's height reached the level of the uppermost benches. His countenance showed no sign of what surely he must be feeling, in the knowledge that the majority of the assembly were against him.

Then came the principal theme of the Queen's message. It drew Argyll's attention from the Commissioner to the body of the hall where stood the long table on which lay the honours of Scotland – crown, sceptre and sword.

The main thing we recommend to you and which we recommend with all the earnestness we are capable of is the settling of the Succession in the Protestant Line, as that which is absolutely necessary for your own peace and happiness as well as our quiet and security in all our Dominions and for the reputation of our affairs abroad, and consequently for the strengthening of the Protestant Line everywhere . . .

Matters are now come to that pass by the undoubted evidence of our enemies that a longer delay of settling the Succession in the Protestant Line may have very dangerous consequences and a disappointment of it would anfallibly make this our kingdom the seat of war.

We are now in a war which makes it necessary to provide for defence of the kingdom, the time of the funds that were lately given for maintenance of Land Forces being expired and the said funds exhausted, provision ought also to be made for supplying magazines with arms and ammunition repairing the Forts and Castles, and for change of the Frigates that prove so useful for guarding the coast.

Lord Justice Clerk's voice ceased. He folded the document. A murmur passed around, but only for a moment. Silence renewed when the Commissioner arose to make his speech in reply.

The Earl of Seafield, who as Lord High Chancellor sat directly beneath the throne, was the next speaker. He stressed the danger of divisions and animosities and then in tones that rang sincere urged the assembly to employ 'your thoughts for promoting what is for the security and Advancement of the Kingdom . . . Succession to the Crown in the Protestant Line will be the surest foundation for the security of your religious liberties . . .'

In conclusion he appealed to them all to comply with the imperative need; Supplies for the maintenance of the Armed Forces. 'It is to be regretted that the Nation is in so low a condition; but what we give is necessary for our own defence and will circulate within the kingdom.'

Those words took Argyll's thoughts far beyond that hall. He was back with the men of his regiment in those tragic days of 1697 when the army was allowed to disintegrate. As a soldier he realized only too well the values of strong defences and the folly of letting these decline.

The final speech came from the Earl of Cromarty, Lord Secretary, whose place was on the left of the throne, that of Baillie of Jerviswood as the Lord Treasurer Depute being on the right. Like the preceding ones, its keynote was the Succession and Supply. Unless these questions were solved without delay the whole of Britain would be in a perilous situation.

Two days after the speeches, the Duke of Hamilton took the initiative by presenting a resolve to the effect that, 'This Parliament will not proceed to nomination of a Successor until we have had a previous treaty with England in relation to our Commerce.'

At the next meeting of the Estates on 17 July, he re-introduced it; and on this occasion the Earl of Rothes also presented a resolution: 'That Parliament will, in the first place, go into their conditions and regulations of Government as may be proper to rectify our constitution and vindicate and secure the Sovereignty and Independence of the Kingdom and this Parliament will take into consideration the Resolve offered for a treaty previous to a nomination.'

A debate followed and it was then decided that no successor would be nominated until there had been a previous treaty with England and further resolved that Parliament 'will proceed to make such limitations and conditions for the rectification of our Constitution as may secure religious liberty and Independence of the nation before they proceed to the said nomination.'

The Opposition were determined to steer matters their own way. This could only be achieved by forcing the more vital issue of the country's economy. Funds were desperately needed and to negotiate these with England when the Act of Security was still undecided meant the release of rebellion's forces.

Once more the Duke of Hamilton took the lead by expanding his original resolve to another: 'That this Parliament will name Commissioners to treat with England for regulating commerce and other concerns with that previous to all other business except an Act of two months' Supply first of all to be granted for the present subsistence of Her Majesty's Forces.'

A day or two later, both the Acts of Supply and Security received a first reading and were then debated. The outcome was a resolution introduced by the Earl of Roxburgh: 'That a first reading be inscribed on the Act of Security and both this Act and the one of Supply should not be proceeded on until the Commission receive instructions as to the Act of Security. Then Parliament could be free to proceed to these Acts either jointly or separately.'

During these days, Queensberry, the subtle diplomat, had been busy behind the scenes. A word was dropped in Jacobite circles to the effect that Her Majesty 'did not so much care about the Crown's passage to Hanover as having it positively settled'. So in the debates the Independent Whigs, who had set out to arrange matters the way which they believed to be Godolphin's desire, found themselves at an impasse. In the debates there was no other option than to follow the flow of the tide. The fact that they were in a minority gave them no chance to break away; and not even the able James Johnstone could find an opening.

The crucial stage was at hand and with it Queensberry's opportunity to regain prestige. His influence stimulated Hamilton's action of an ultimatum to Godolphin. 'In the event of Her Majesty's refusal to sanction the Act of Security no further taxes would be voted and the Scots army of three thousand strength would disband.'

The circumstances of the hour suited these tactics to bring pressure upon the Queen and her ministers. The war in Europe had deteriorated for the Allies. Marlborough seemed unable to surmount the series of reverses which his army had encountered. France, jubilant at the promise of conquest, was planning her supreme coup – the invasion of Britain.

Those last days of July were indeed dark for England and ominous for Scotland. The Queen – carrying the additional burden of ill-health – was torn between personal feelings which spurned the Act decreeing Scotland's independent sovereignty, and her duty as monarch in a grave crisis.

Then one morning in the early part of August, Edinburgh's citizens awoke to news. Royal assent had been given to the Act of Security. While they rejoiced, there came other tidings: Marlborough had won a great victory at Blenheim.[4]

Now that the way lay clear, the Estates could proceed to the urgent question of Supply. The following act was decreed: 'The Estates of Parliament taking into consideration the danger that still threatens the kingdom by reason of the continuance of the present war which visibly requires the keeping up of standing Force and Supplies necessary for their maintenance; and frigates employed for defence of our coasts, make offer to Her Majesty of the sum of £432,000 Scots, extending to six months less which new Supply will be raised out of Land Rent of this kingdom.'

Appended to this act was a list of Commissioners who would make themselves responsible for the collection of this rent. Argyll's name figured among them.

The session was nearly at an end. On 28 August it closed with an address presented by the Estates of Parliament to the Queen.

When Argyll left Edinburgh it was not to return immediately south. There would be a journey to the Highlands. For him the most agreeable part of a visit to the west was to be among his own clansmen and join them at their hearth-sides. It revived memory of evenings around the camp fire when men shed the mask they wore before the world and became human. Thus it was in the Highland homes where character had been formed by living close to the land with all the struggles for existence. Domestic habits were of the simplest; yet the attitude towards life was based upon the solid foundations of staunch religious principles and loyalty to traditions. Conversation alternated between the serious and gay – tales of distress arising from humorous anecdotes – and invariably of valiant deeds.

On a day in mid-September after various visits, Argyll set out for London.

THE BATTLE OF POLITICS
ENGLAND 1704

Argyll returned to a London where talk of politics had succeeded thanksgiving for Blenheim. People were conscious that days promising political excitement approached. In a few weeks – at the end of October – Parliament was due to reassemble. Then, two questions which the High Tories[5] intended to use as their challenge to Godolphin and Marlborough threatened a crisis for Britain. One was the Occasional Conformity Bill[6]. The other – and more important issue – touched the Crown: the Act of Security. Tory partisans were not inactive on the eve of the Session, particularly as public sentiment showed signs of a drift towards Whig sympathies. Scotland, shrouded in mist for the majority of Englishmen, provided good propaganda material. They made it their business to emphasize England's danger if 'those wild Northerners' became independent. Thus national interest in the Scottish problem was aroused.

Of Scots politicians then in London, the New Party (Squadrone) chiefs were busy fermenting a campaign aimed at a man whom they had reason to fear. The Duke of Argyll's frequent attendance at Court was not missed by men with so much either to gain or lose during the next months. They attached great significance to the fact that 'His High and Mighty Grace' was beside the Queen at Kensington, Windsor, or wherever she happened to be in residence. Hitherto, he had played the role of spectator rather than actor. Now, it seemed that he intended to reverse this and emerge to the foreground of affairs. In their knowledge of his contempt for them, they began a feverish energy of manoeuvre and intrigue calculated to destroy Argyll's prestige. At the same time, for the sake of personal interests, it was necessary to coerce him.

In writing to the Earl of Mar[7] on 7 October, Secretary James Johnstone reported the latest rumours. He had heard that all Union opponents were to be dismissed. 'Roxburgh is to be a Secretary of State and one of Queensberry's people the other. What Tweedale and others will be neither they nor I know. The Whigs say that I and others were in a juggle with the Dukes and you and Dupplin[8] and nothing can be invented that is not said of us all. As to yourself, if the Court and I can serve you, you may depend on it we will do it and Coulter tells me that Argyll will joine, which if he do we will prevaile . . .'

At about this time, the Duke of Queensberry who was one of Argyll's friends also wrote to the Earl of Mar.

London, 12th October
Parliament will meet at the time which is appointed; and I beg therefore that your Lordship may make hither. Our enemies are gathering and so its high time for us to begin to be active here. I have very good hopes of matters if we be unite and diligent, for to my certain knowledge the eyes of certain people are opening.

The struggle for power knew no restraint. To Argyll this was the most distasteful side of politics. Ambition compelled a place in the conflict. He did, however, take an independent line which exasperated enemies. As an individualist he left no loophole for either persuasion or compromise. The essence of his purpose beside the Queen was to press her consent to a party sincerely bound to the creation of a United Kingdom. Those who sought to interfere, especially by underhand means, were nothing more than 'unfaithful friends' to Her Majesty and their fellow men. On this account, the petty methods of 'the gentlemen who had disappointed the Queen's measures' [9] at the last session affected him merely by sharpening his resolve to get Scotland's affairs established 'on a Revolution foot'.

It was the end of November when the anxiously awaited hour of debate on the Scottish Act of Security arrived. Through the murk of a wintry day, Her Majesty drove to Westminster. Although this constituted a breach of precedent, she was determined to attend. Thus would Ministers have proof of her sincerity 'to take care of her Ancient Kingdom.' [10]

The stage was the House of Lords, then the crucible of political power. The first day's business took the form of a prologue to the drama destined to evolve during the next two weeks. The Act of Security was read and the Lord Treasurer, Godolphin, pronounced words which he would often reiterate in stronger tone: 'The passing of the Act of Security was absolutely necessary.'

The House then adjourned until Wednesday 2 December. Despite the bitter cold, which forced her to remove from the Throne to a bench by the fire, the Queen was again present. Lord Haversham led the debate on behalf of the High Tories. His theme was accusation. 'By yielding to the Scottish will, the Ministry had betrayed the Crown's interest in favour of Hanover.' Godolphin refuted the statement. He had no other choice than to advise the

Act of Security. It was the only medium between peace and war. Now, to counter-balance its effects, the course should be 'Union without delay'.

Argyll, who attended in the capacity of a 'distinguished stranger', experienced a profound emotion as he heard those words. His hour was most surely at hand.

The next phase of the debate belonged to the lords of the Whig Junto who controlled the balance of the House. Halifax, leading for them, launched a scathing attack. 'Many warm things were said and the Scottish Acts of the two Sessions were accumulated. How was it possible that any Englishman would consent to them? It became the greatness of a Queen of England to refute their advices.'

In the face of such animosity, matters looked ominous for the Government. It was then that Lords Somers and Wharton arose from their places on the Junto benches and moved to the side of Godolphin. For some moments the three conferred in whispers. To the audience this sudden intervention suggested that a compromise had been found to save a desperate situation. This proved correct.

Lord Somers proposed that the Queen should authorize the appointment of Commissioners to advance the cause of Union. Meanwhile, in order to show Scotland how much she stood to lose by adhering to her policy of isolation, a form of Sanctions should be imposed.

The proposal appeased the Government's opponents. For several more days the Lords' debate continued and the Alien Bill was conceived. Then these decisions were passed to the Commons for review.

Secretary Johnstone writing to Baillie of Jerviswood on 21 December reported: 'The Lords have sent their Bill to the Commons who are upon it. It gives a power to the Queen to name Commissioners to treat about an absolute Union, and makes you aliens and forbids your cattle from the last day of the next Session in case neither the Succession nor the Union be settled then.'[11]

In that very moment when the tempers of England's leaders began to moderate, there arrived news which plunged everyone into a turmoil of agitation. By order of the Privy Council in Edinburgh, Captain Green (Master of an East Indian vessel, the *Worcester*, which, for some months, had been detained on Burntisland[12]) was under arrest charged with having seized a Scots trading vessel, the *Speedy Return*, and murdered her captain, somewhere on the high seas. 'The East India Ship makes a great noise here ... It is certainly a great misfortune. What will become of our affairs between the House of Lords and the House of Commons is very uncertain; but I am thoroughly convinced that if we do not go into the Succession or Union very soon, Conquest will certainly be upon the first Peace . . .'[13]

It was generally felt that Scotland stood on the threshold of great change; for good or ill none could predict, although Argyll himself took a hopeful view. 'There will be alterations in our Scots' business and they must be better because they cannot be worse', he wrote to the Earl of Mar.

The first sign of that change occurred shortly afterwards. Mr Cockburne of Ormiston – a sincere Whig and staunch Presbyterian – was delegated to Scotland in the capacity of an unofficial ambassador. His mission would take him among various people to seek their opinions with regard to a treaty.

The early days of the New Year found Argyll and Godolphin much in consultation. While the Lord Treasurer recognized in Argyll the qualities most needed for Scotland of that hour, and had actually marked him as Commissioner, he adhered to a policy of preserving the balance with all parties. On this point they disagreed. Argyll declared that he would accept the Commissioner's appointment only upon his own terms. These touched the future of the New Party, as well as the measures most likely to stimulate more cordial Anglo-Scots relations. Godolphin chose a non-committal response. He preferred to 'talk Argyll into things'.

By the beginning of January, reports referring to Argyll as the next Commissioner were in circulation. From the Earl of Roxburgh who, of all the Independent Whigs, had sound sense[14], there came the comment: 'Since the Scottish Parliament must meet so soon and since success is so uncertain, I am very clear for Argyll being Commissioner and for Annandale being Secretary.'

Members of the Squadrone party were filled with alarm. They saw themselves being ruthlessly displaced. Consequently, in a final bid to prevent inglorious decline, they set out to put the 'Nation [Scotland] in a flame', and so raise 'stores of opposition' against the Duke whom most men envied because they could not emulate him.

Certain letters that passed between Baillie of Jerviswood and James Johnstone illustrated the character of the intrigue afoot.

I am much vex'd for Argyll's business [Baillie wrote]. What do we pretend there are but four ways possible; first – by time which cannot be granted; or second by Queensberry whom neither we nor greater folks are for; or third by Argyll, and such when it seems we will not have neither; or fourth by Hamilton who will not have us. To become ridiculous is the worst figure that any sect of men can make.

On his part, Johnstone had this to say: 'Roxburgh is mighty nice to have it known that he is either for Argyll or Annandale. I have prevailed upon Roxburgh to be more frank with Argyll as I have been myself; but you'll be surprised to hear that the Queen is mightily against Argyll, and works upon Seafield to be the man, which, I hear, has made an impression which in my opinion will be ten times worse. Argyll knows all this and if he be capable of prudence can hinder it . . .

'I have seen the Act about Scotland which is very different from what any of us ever heard it to be. The preamble mentions the necessity of a nearer and even more complete Union. The powers are to treat of such an Union and other matters, clauses, and things as the Commissioners in their wisdom, shall think fit.'

How to manage Argyll so that he would not have it all his own way? That was the perplexing question. Quest for an answer found men playing one off against the other through abuse, slander, rumour, each of which were treated as lightly as a game of battledore and shuttlecock.

Argyll has been spoken to. He asks many things and particularly alterations and has got such answers it seems as please him. March-mont's affair is agreed to, and Roxburgh has orders this night to write to him of it. Montrose's business too is as good as done; but Argyle knows of neither. Seafield is very uneasy, which will keep him firm to Tweedale. Leven is not satisfied but will needs have more than he has and he'll get it. Hamilton is incomprehensible; he tempers on but never concludes.

Towards the end of February, Argyll moved nearer the Commissioner's office. On the 27th Her Majesty received him in audience. 'I am just come from the Queen with Seafield and Argyle,' wrote the Earl of Roxburgh that same day, 'so the ceremony of kissing hands is over. I must say Argyle has whipt it off having harangued the Queen upon Annandale's being in place of Marchmont – with abundance of zeal.'

Besides the Earl of Roxburgh there were others to report the event and embroider it with either comment or speculation. James Hamilton addressed a letter (3 March) to the Duke of Hamilton: 'Doubtless your Grace knows the Duke of Argyle is declared Com-

missioner to the Assembly, and the Marquess Annandale Secretary
& that Tweedale is to be President of the Council. All these things
are very firmly talked and credited. The Commissioner's Secretaries
have been this day in the royal appartment and office house. I have
trusted them to see all against Monday next. He is a very young
Commissioner.'

When, however, the Duke of Hamilton wrote a week later (10
March) to Lord Belhaven, he had another account to give.

> Argyle was no sooner named than he desired all those who brought
> him in to be turned out; I mean Tweedale's friends, for Rox-
> burgh has been the principal negotiate of this affair by Queens-
> berry. How he'll answer this to his friends let him and them see,
> for I assure you they have effectually undone themselves and
> Baillie will find this ere long. This has been a refined piece of
> Johnstone's continuance tho he'll suffer for it. I confess I think
> they are happiest who have least to do with them, for Lord
> Stair will show them what it is to have play'd the fool, and Argyle
> will lord it as they deserve. If our country were not to suffer, I
> should have pleasure to see what I know will fall out.

The 11th March found Anne, Duchess of Hamilton, writing to
the Duchess of Atholl:

> When Argyle kissed the Queen's hand, he asked a favour which
> was that she should make Annandale Commissioner to the
> General Assembly. My Lord Roxburgh being by remembered
> the Queen that she was alreadye ingadged, upon which 'tis said
> the Duke of Argyle replyed it was not then for his power to serve
> her and offered to demit [resign] on which its said he and
> Roxburgh fell a littell warme together and the Queen recommen-
> ded good agreement to them. Seafield interposed that Her Majesty
> would take it to her consideration. So it ended for that time . . .
> Roxburgh and Johnstone may be out and Philiphaugh in it
> again, and the Duke of Queensberry may come to assist Argyll . . .

Five days later (16 March) Ann, Duchess of Hamilton, wrote
again to the Duchess of Atholl: 'Argyle is certainly Commissioner
and setting in on a very high foot and has proposed the turning out
of all the sett that came in last.'[15]

To the Duke of Atholl similar news was conveyed in letters written
by Patrick Scott – the first, addressed from Edinburgh on 13 March –

informed that 'Report of Argyle as Commissioner has been received in Edinburgh. He has accepted on condition that Johnstone, Belhaven, Jerviswood, and Sir John Hume are putt off and that Alex Cumming should replace Mr Wedderburn as Secretary.'

The second, dated 19 March, and also with Edinburgh as the address, stated: 'Annandale's Commission is come down to be Commissioner this year's Assembly and Seafield to be Chancellor. I do not yett know if any agree or if D. Argyle's be yett come.'

Meanwhile, Godolphin still persisted in his wary attitude towards Argyll's demand for the New Party's dismissal. He believed such a move to be imprudent and attached more value to Seafield's opinion that 'unity of all parties was essential to execution of the Government's policy'. However, circumstances urgently required a strong man in Scotland. Only one person could claim that title. He was the Duke of Argyll.

Chapter V

A STRONG MAN FOR SCOTLAND

On 13 March the Alien Bill had become law.[1] It was an ill-timed hour. In the Tolbooth, Captain Green and fourteen members of the *Worcester*'s crew awaited trial on the charges of piracy, robbery, and murder. To Scots' temper agitated beyond the point of control, these men presented targets for retaliation against the harsh measures imposed on them by London's politicians. When, seven days later, they faced their judges, matters had been so framed that their fate was virtually decreed. Evidence based on mere supposition and not fact was distorted in such a manner as to convey no doubt of their guilt. They were condemned to death, the executions to take place in batches during successive weeks.

The verdict divided public opinion throughout the realm. In the north, almost every Scot upheld the sentence. In the south, Englishmen unanimously denounced it as an act of gross injustice. The English Cabinet met. At the end of a session lasting several hours, one of the members, Lord Somers, stated that in his opinion the whole proceedings bore the taint of illegality.

To those whose work was for the creation of a greater Britain, this incident could become the instrument of defeat. Upon one in particular it had a profound effect. Argyll venerated justice, and that it should be dishonoured by his own countrymen was like a stab in the back. He was convinced that a grave error had been committed in the name of the law. 'If anything can be done to save the lives of men who are innocent until there is certain proof that they have committed the crimes imputed to them, I shall do it to the extent of my power!'

In manner characteristic of him when firmly resolved, he did not hesitate to take the strongest course. It led him to the Queen.

The interview must have been both dramatic and poignant. Being a devoutly religious woman, Ann's compassion was deeply stirred. As ruler over a kingdom torn by discords, she came into conflict with her womanly sentiments. If she allowed the sentence to stand, the English people would rise against her. If she conceded to the English will and granted a reprieve, all her hopes of Union were gone. While she listened to her young Commissioner pleading from the depth of his heart for the exercise of her prerogative, she was in struggle with womanhood demanding mercy and duty towards the nation. Argyll well understood what she suffered during those moments and his heart went out to her. Here was a woman who personified all that he most admired – courage, prudence, virtue. When he had concluded his plea, there was a pause before she replied. Her answer authorized him as Commissioner to write to Chancellor Seafield ordering that the executions should be suspended until the case had been more thoroughly investigated.[2]

His enthusiasm at having scored this victory with Her Majesty might well be imagined. In that mood he notified Seafield of her order. Upon the Chancellor it had a negative effect. He regarded its tone as too flamboyant to warrant serious credence. The matter did not rest there; New Party members of the Privy Council were quick to make a show of the letter against the one man whom they most feared.[3]

Cockburne of Ormiston, on a mission of 'reconnaissance' to ascertain the views of the leaders, related an episode in his report, dated 7 April, to Godolphin : '. . . I went to the country for some days and on my return I understood there was a great flame against the Duke of Argyle; the occasion for it was taken from a letter he wrote to the Chancellor of Her Majesty's order about a reprieve to Captain Green and his crew.'

Cockburne supported Argyll.

> However this letter might be written not altogether agreeable to our form, yet I cannot think so great occasion needed be taken to expose his Grace in an affair so popular as this is, as altogether tends to ruin his interest, especially whilst he stood under the character of Her Majesty's Commissioner; and ever anything looked like an escape in form, would have been overlooked was it not that those got the management of affairs the beginning of winter, easily hearken to imputations, as that the Duke of Argyle will not be satisfied till he has a thorough change in the Ministry. Of this they are acquainted by one who was sent down last summer by Her Majesty and is now at London still in possession of a good post of this kingdom; his advices do not tend to beget a good understanding.

D

The person in question was James Johnstone, and he too had a
report to make on the same subject. While writing to Baillie of
Jerviswood, there arrived:

A flying packet from my Lord Argyle by Her Majesty's order,
signifying to the Chancellor that it was Her Majesty's pleasure
that all executions of sentence be dropt till the whole process be
laid before Her Majesty and that she had given her orders about
it . . .
   This step of Argyle will, I fear, do him no good. I understand
that he is advised for this not to keep to words but to get all done
before he pairt, and in a letter which the Advocate showed me
today, he says that he hopes to have the Government put more
upon the Revolution foot before he pairted.

The slight given to her Commissioner's authority did not pass
unnoticed by the Queen. She personally wrote to sanction a reprieve.
At a meeting of the Privy Council on 3 April her letter was read.
An order was then issued that the first group of men due to die on
the following day would be granted a week's respite.
   News of Her Majesty's intervention threw Edinburgh's citizens
into a frenzy. This was another instance of England's interference
and it must be resisted. While reports on the affair were being
examined in the two capitals, clamour for vengeance upon all who
sought to meddle with the course of justice filled the Edinburgh air.
   Thus the week passed and the day of the 10th arrived. Seafield,
who inclined to Argyll's view of a great wrong being done to
fellow-men, urgently summoned a Privy Council. He entered the
Council Chamber to receive a shock. Instead of the full complement
of councillors who should have been present, a number were absent
including the Earl of Roxburgh and New Party colleagues; they
had retreated at the crucial hour. For the Chancellor, it was a
desperate situation. In London, as he knew, the Queen and Argyll
were both busily engaged on study of his report. How was it possible
to help them if they lacked the Privy Council's unanimous support?
The tumult of the rioting mob reached him as he presided over the
meeting and he, himself, began to quaver. A further postponement
of the executions would jeopardize the lives of all Her Majesty's
servants then in Edinburgh. However, he decided on a final effort
and again called a Council for the next day. On this occasion eleven
members only took their places at the table. To aggravate matters
and heighten the tragedy, there had just arrived affidavits from two

sailors who had given evidence at the trial. It absolved the *Worcester* crew from all charges brought against them. In a few hours, Captain Green, Simpson, chief mate, Madder, gunner, and Jeigle, carpenter, were to hang. Should the executions be stopped or allowed to proceed? The Councillors answered by terminating their Session on a note of indecision.

Before that unhappy day closed, the bodies of two Englishmen, Captain Green and Simpson, and a Scot, Madder, hung from the gibbets on Calton Hill. Eighty thousand rioters had hounded them to their fate.

Argyll's departure for Scotland was imminent; yet he had not received satisfaction in regard to his demands. The only answer that came from Godolphin was: 'The Queen will do nothing so long as you stay in London, but what you represent for her service in Scotland will be done.'

To be placed in this uncertain position must have been gall to a humour which spurned half-measures. Indeed more than once he had intimated a desire that Her Majesty should appoint another Commissioner; but was persuaded by Godolphin's conciliatory words.

Neither the Queen nor her Treasurer could afford to lose so loyal a servant. Argyll was aware of the value that they placed upon him. He also knew that whatever the future might bring his duty lay in Scotland. The Green tragedy had made that fact clear.

To Chancellor Seafield went three letters dated 7, 8 and 9 April, each with allusion to Argyll's plans.[4]

The first was from Godolphin: 'I have nothing more to trouble you with but that the Duke of Argyle says he has sent away his coach upon the Northern road and will certainly be at Edinburgh himself before the 28th. I wish you may find him inclined to hearken to the advice of his friends there for much will depend upon that . . .'

The writer of the second was the Early of Roxburgh – then at Floors Castle: 'I have sent your Lshp. on the Queen's letter to the Council but have nothing worth your Lsp's while in my letter save that the Duke of Argyle gives out that there cannot but be changes now upon what the Council did in relation to his letter and that your Lsp. and all of us here set ourselves on a foot of opposition to the Queen.'

The third letter, written by Mr Wedderburn, gave news of Argyll's departure:

My Lord,

Nothing has occurred since my last on Scots affairs worth you Lsp. reading save that the Duke of Argyle parted from hence yesterday about noon. He went privately and some say resolves to go post part of the way. His Grace carried with him the papers past the Queen's hand whereof a list is enclosed. He left me noe directions except an order to deliver to Sir David Nairn all letters and pacquets for him, and also to receive from Sir David a letter he shall have to despatch for His Grace by ordinary or flying pacquets. There appears little on the disposition here, to give credit to the guilt proved against Captain Green and confessed by one of his men. It seems necessary for the reputation of our country and of the Government in particular a full relation of the proceedings in this matter and that it be clear upon what motives any of the accomplices have confessed. Otherwise it will be spread to our dishonour that those poor men have either been forced by torture or induced by promises of life, to confess anything they perceived would soon be most desired, such base informations are very uneasy to those that have a concern for the honour of their country and the reputation of those in the management, but I can not say all Scots men here feel it alike . . .

On the eve of setting forth to a mission of the greatest responsibility, Argyll addressed a letter to Mr Carstares, an old family friend and the first Principal of Edinburgh University.

15 *April* 1705

Sir,

I received your's. I'm sure you'll easily believe me when I tell you nothing could be more pleasing to me than the Assembly's letter, and I assure you your being Moderator is a satisfaction to all honest men and particularly to myself. In relation I must tell you one piece of news that will not be displeasing to you. Yesterday, the Queen was pleased to lay aside Mr Johnstone[5] as a proof of her deciding to make some other steps. So soon as I come to Scotland, Lord Philiphaugh is to have his post again and I am hopeful to persuade the Queen to allow his Commission to be sent down tonight. I desire to go from hence this night and therefore shall say no more, but that you shall always find me,

Your faithful friend
and humble servant,
Argyll

On 23 April John, Duke of Argyll, crossed the borders near Berwick-upon-Tweed. The fact that the premier chieftain of Scotland came as Her Majesty's Commissioner was a reason for his arrival to be honoured by conspicuous ceremonial. A squadron of the Marquess of Lothian's dragoons, clan chiefs, and lords were awaiting to escort him on the final stage of the journey.

They took the Dunbar road and in the late afternoon made their first halt. This occurred at a spot some three miles or so from that Burgh. There, to receive the Duke, was the Lord Provost of Glasgow, magistrates, town councillors, and chief burghers of that city nearly fifty miles distant. They had travelled thither in token and evidence of long and uninterrupted good understanding between His Grace's noble family and Glasgow and their sense of gratitude for the many favours and kindnesses they had received.

A mile farther on, officials of the Burgh of Dunbar welcomed the Duke to their town which he entered towards six in the evening. A night of receptions and entertainment ensued.

Next morning brought many visitors to wait upon his Grace and accompany him on his progress to the capital. By ten o'clock he was ready to depart and the townspeople gathered to watch that spectacle. The pomp of the procession led by Argyll mounted on horseback, impressed the crowd. Their applause rang forth and continued until the cavalcade had passed through the town to the highway. Some miles beyond Dunbar a squadron of horse, the Lord Provost and magistrates of the city of Edinburgh, and a number of noblemen met the company.

Whatever their feelings were and would be in the future, Edinburgh's citizens had decided to make this a day of celebration. They thronged the streets, in apparel usually reserved for the sabbath, and their appearance was orderly. Faces too wore happier expressions, though these might be merely assumed to accord with the festival mood.

Argyll's arrival at Holyrood was announced by a salvo of cannons fired from the Castle. Then the guns in the parks and aboard the men-of-war – both Scottish and Dutch – lying in the Road of Leith, boomed out salutes. When evening came, fireworks illuminated the city; people paraded with flambeaux; drums, fifes and pipes of the Castle garrison played martial airs; and in fashionable homes men drank the Commissioner's health while their womenfolk enjoyed the dance.[6]

Meanwhile, at a session of the Privy Council held in the Royal Apartment of Holyrood Abbey, Her Majesty's letter appointing

new councillors was read. There were three : the Earl of Glasgow;
Lord Philiphaugh; and Lord Archibald Campbell (the Earl of
Islay).

The time had come for Argyll and his brother to combine their
remarkable powers in a manner that could serve the interests of the
state. The younger was as brilliant in the finesses of law and state-
craft as the elder in military stratagem. He had a trained legal mind,
swift to discern the crux of a subject, then argue and reason it until
his point was gained. In politics, this would give him the ascen-
dancy and there were to be times when he played Cato to his
brother's Caesar. In private life their relations could never change
by virtue of such wide diversities in character. On the stage of
public life, bound to the same cause, they were both to wield great
influence. John, the commander with the force, charm and eloquent
oratory which captured an audience; Archibald, the lawyer and
politician with his shrewdness, industry, and ability to scheme. Thus
these two men would eventually appear before the world. Meanwhile, this first association was to find them 'doing much more to
the vigour of their measures and the high reputation of their names'.

Chapter VI

COMMISSIONER

THE day after his arrival (Wednesday 26 April) the Commissioner received calls from various persons.[1] He was fully resolved to make matters plain regarding the men who had acted so unmercifully in the matter of Captain Green and his crew.[2] However, he had promised the Queen that he would take the views of others. This, together with the more important task of consulting about affairs in general, became his immediate aim. By 6 May, he was able to report to Godolphin:

> I have obeyed the Queen's commands by consulting with such of Her Majesty's servants whom I could trust about her affairs in this Kingdom, and I find them perfectly of the opinion that the Government would never recover its strength, but be ever feeble so long as it was not of a piece . . . We unanimously agreed that it was impossible the Queen's service could be carried on by any other method than by Her Majesty being pleased to lay aside the New Party as they are pleased to call themselves, consisting of half a dozen, and put their place in the hands of men as have always been firm to a Revolution and who have ten times the interest and fifty times the inclination to serve Her Majesty.

The Queen's sense of loyalty and a desire to preserve a balance between all parties caused her to hesitate. She could not bring herself to consent to her Commissioner's advice. To Argyll this was a defeat, and for members of the New Party an incentive to renewed effort against their foe. As Johnstone in London said:

> Argyle is losing himself. The New Party must be patient to give him time. The Queen reckons it not for her service to have this Party out.

Others too were busy with report. The Duke of Hamilton, writing on 6 May to the Duke of Atholl, stated: 'My nephew tells me that he thinks the Duke of Argyle already wearies of his post. I am persuaded he'll meet with difficulties, but I don't see our nation is fully apprized of their danger, though its upon the very brink of ruine.'

At about this time, Colonel Hooke informed the Duke of Perth, '. . . there is no fear of this Parliament, nor of my Lord Argyle, for not only the Country Party will maintain what they have done; but the Duke of Queensberry and the Marquess of Annandale having not succeeded in serving the Court, they do all they can to hinder a boy's having better success.'

During these days, Scotland was in a dangerously inflammable state. The friction between the leaders had repercussion upon the masses desperate for a return to order. Despite the presence of a Commissioner who, as Chief of the Campbells, could, on the least provocation, put six hundred or more Highlanders into the field, the atmosphere remained sultry. Uncertainties were prejudicial to so critical a situation, and Argyll, still without complete authority, was in a dilemma. His impulsive temper dominated him at this time and dictated resignation.

> May it please your Majesty, [he wrote on 13 May] when in obedience to your commands I undertook this post it was in the hopes of being serviceable to your Majesty in the great and good designs you had of settling this nation, and now that I am perfectly persuaded I can be of no use to your Majesty in it, in all humility beg your Majesty will be pleased to permit me to deliver the Commission to your Council which so soon as I am honoured with your Majesty's allowance I shall do.
>
> I hope your Majesty will not think I resign my post of Commissioner in order to persuade you to make the alterations I proposed. I assure your Majesty it is out of no such design . . . This nation will never be persuaded to believe that your Majesty has withdrawn your favour from them, which will make it much the same thing as if they were confirmed. I must indeed own I am perfectly of opinion that if your Majesty had done what I proposed relating to your Government here at the time I proposed it, your affairs would have gone well; but that is over, and I can now as Duke of Argyle only present to say that as long as I live I shall act for the Protestant succession and as far as in me lies, to the last drop of my blood, support your Majesty and your Government. . . .

To Lord Godolphin he wrote in the same strain, but gave an even clearer picture of the situation which had been allowed to develop as the result of Her Majesty 'declining to determine'. It had become common talk in Edinburgh that the Queen favoured the New Party. The fact afforded them such encouragement that even were they to be laid aside, the harm was already done. This 'together with the irrecoverable loss of time, makes it improbable we should be able to do the Queen's business, therefore I shall say no more.'

While Argyll waited for a reply to this letter resigning his appointment, he turned to a subject of grave concern to him not only as a soldier, but because it concerned Scotland's security. It was the state of the armed forces. On 13 May he addressed a letter to the Earl of Mar:

> I have advice from the Court that St Paull is come out of Dunkirk with five or six men-of-war, having on board arms. ammunition, and money to be landed in Scotland. Therefore, I desyre your Lordship will immediately to Stirling Castle and put things in the best posture may be and remain there till you hear from me. If you have any officers of your Regiment absent, pray order them to the post.
>
> I am, my dear Lord, your most obedient humble servant,
>
> Argyll

Besides issuing orders for a full investigation[3] of that most strategical stronghold,[4] he informed Lord Godolphin of his own findings in regard to the armed strength in Scotland. 'I think it my duty to acquaint your Lordship that the Arms of all the troops in this Kingdom, Except the Horse Guards are very insufficient and we have almost no ammunition so that unless the Queen is pleased to send down some arms and ammunition troops here will be of little use.'

On the same day (16 May) as the despatch of this letter, Patrick Scott was writing from Edinburgh to the Duke of Atholl at Huntingtower. He had no further news of Government changes, but was able to give report of Argyll. 'On Monday night, the Commissioner, Chancellor, Leven, and Glasgow drunk only coming till betwixt 6 and 7 in the morning and went then to bed.'[5]

The 18 May brought a courier from London with news from Lord Godolphin. The Queen had dismissed the New Party. It was a measure forced upon her by the powerful Whig ministers who unanimously supported Argyll's opinion that such 'light-weights' as

May it Please your Majesty

I send your Majesty enclosed the Coppies of all the papers, delivered me in Presence of some of your majesties Servants, by one Mr Daniell, an Irishman, perfectly unknown to every body here, who pretended to make a discovery, we all thought it our only since such papers were delivered to us, that they should be

laid before your Majesty, though indeed we are all of Opinion that it is highly probable that that this fellow is a Rogue and Impostor, who has contrived this story out of hope of getting a reward, the Great number of Considerable Noblemen and Gentlemen of good reputation he accuses, the simplicity of the cypher'd Letters, his Letter wherein he talks so much of a reward, Steward who he mentions in his papers not coming as he positively asserted he would before last Night, and lastly his not appearing these two days are all arguments against

there being credit given to what he sayss, we
humbly think it absolutely necessary for your Maj
esty service that your Majesty would be pleased
not to let the names of those he pretends to accuse
be known unless there should appear much stro
nger reasons to believe what he sayss than doe
att present I am

May it please your Majesty

your Majestys

most dutifull and

most Obedient Humble

Subject and Servant

May it Please your Majesty I am just
now informed that this Mr daniell is run
away So those of your Majestys servants
show are now present believe it is
all a Cheat

to the Queen
May 2 1705

Edinburg May the seven
1705

the Squadrone had twice proved were unworthy of office. However, in his letter, Godolphin placed the onus for Her Majesty's
decision upon Argyll. He had assured her of success if this step were
taken.

The Commissioner used tact in his reply. 'I am far from pretending to give the Queen assurances of success; it were by no means
serving her faithfully if I did, for nobody here will be persuaded but
that the Queen may be prevailed withal to make another change at
the end of the Parliament, if our faithful endeavours fail of
success . . . Opinion encourages the opposing party so much and dis-
courages ours that if there was nothing else to confound business this
alone would be in danger to do it.'

Argyll chose this hour which brought him full power[6] as Commissioner to refer to the favour which he had asked of the Queen
before leaving London.

I do hope your Lordship will do me the favour to intercede with
the Queen that I may have the Peerage of England now which
your Lordship knows was the only favour I presumed to ask of
the Queen and which I had hopes from your Lordship and My
Lord Duke of Marlboro I should have. I shall not desire to have
the patent immediately, since your Lordship was pleased to tell
me it was not for the Queen's service the matter should be made
public so long as I was Commissioner; I only intreat her Majesty
would be pleased to let me have the warrant which I shall upon
my honour not produce till after the Parliament.

A purpose governed the request. He desired an English peerage
so that when the time came for Union his voice could be heard in
the House of Lords' debates.

The response brought him satisfaction. In his words, 'It is matter
of great joy to me that Her Majesty is pleased to have any confidence
in my affection to her interests. I am deeply sensible of the extraordinary mark of Her Majesty's favour in this of the Peerage of
England.'

The first claim upon Argyll settling to work as Commissioner was
the choice of colleagues. In presenting a list for the royal approval,
he recommended the Duke of Queensberry as 'one who may be able
to advance the Queen's service'.

That name did not appeal to the Queen.[7] On the other hand she
realized that after the Commissioner, Queensberry was the most ably
qualified for the conduct of affairs; Argyll had the energy and

force; whereas the other possessed the diplomat's tact and winning manner. A coalition of these two might be valuable, especially with the neutral Seafield to hold the balance. Anne knew that she must reconcile herself to Queensberry's return to office; but because it was distasteful to her principles chose to defer the affirmative answer. This caused Argyll some anxiety. 'After its being known that I proposed his being employed, if Her Majesty should slight him by not taking him into her service, it will make his influence here so small as to render him of very little use to the Queen's affairs. On the contrary, if Her Majesty is pleased to employ him, and let him have her countenance, he may be able to do Her Majesty considerable service.'

Meanwhile, another matter demanded speedy settlement. It related to policy. 'As for the measures we are to propose, Her Majesty has but one of two to choose, either the Succession or a treaty. The treaty is certainly the most easy to obtain, and the Succession much the most desirable, but which of the two we are to go upon we must be dictated in by Her Majesty.'

Correspondence was also passing between Godolphin and Chancellor Seafield on this subject. It pointed to the fact that Argyll still stood 'on trial' before the Queen and her Chief Minister :

May 31st 1705.

My Lord,

I have the honour of two letters from your Lordship, one by the ordinary and the other by the flying packet. The Queen will not make an answer till Saturday. In the meantime I would not delay to acquaint your Lordship that the Duke of Argyll was told plainly that if the Queen were sure her measures would succeed in his hands, yett she was not in circumstances to make use of his services just now, nor indeed ever hereafter till he would be pleased to make one step towards Her Majesty which the present occasion of a Treaty makes very nattural since it was always his own principle and there does not seem to be much reason to depart from it now, but for the pleasure of opposing Her Majesty.

I wish my Lord Commissioner could have been prevailed with not to have made so totall a change, and particularly that My Lord Roxburgh had continued who seemed to me to want neither inclination nor capacity to serve the Queen.

I have not yett spoken with the Duke of Queensberry since these letters came, nor doe I know how farr he will be inclined to goe down and assist the Commissioner, tho' I think his friendship to him ought to engage him to doe it, as well as his duty to the Queen, but whether his presence would be a reall assistance I am not able to judge.

I shall trouble your Lordship again next Saturday with an answer to your Lordship by the flying packet and am always

My Lord, Your Lordship's most humble & obedient servant,
Seafield[8]

During these days of preparation for the Session, every communication to and from the Commissioner's office in Holyrood Abbey was observed. The *Edinburgh Courant,* printed by James Watson in Gray's Close and sold at the Exchange Coffee House, published this paragraph on the back page of their four-sheet newspaper: 'On Saturday June 7th about four in the morning came a Flying Packet addressed to His Grace the Duke of Argyle, Lord High Commissioner, the contents of which are not yet known. The same evening about two o'clock, there went one from His Grace to Her Majesty.'

Today, such an announcement would give rise to enquiry. So it was then; readers of the *Courant* became busy with gossip. 'There is something of consequence afoot.' 'What can it be?' 'Perhaps we shall know in a day or two.' ''Tis said the Commissioner called the Lord Chancellor, Lord Register, Lord Justice Clerk, and Lord Annandale, to his office.'

That was true. On Saturday the 7th, Argyll had summoned them in order to discuss two letters from the Queen to the Parliament – one relating to the measures of the Succession; the other to those of the Treaty. As he afterwards informed Godolphin, 'I desired they might give their opinion which of the two was most proper for the Queen to propose. They did declare their opinion but not agreeing, I have ordered Lord Register to give your Lordship an account of what passed at the Conference. I beg the Queen will be pleased to send her positive command which of the two she will have me proceed upon and I shall dutifully obey . . .'

He could make no move without notice being taken in a manner designed to give it significance. The Duke of Hamilton writing on 8 June to the Duke of Atholl remarked: 'I hear that the Commissioner was yesterday to make a visit to the Duchess of Gordon and stayed some hours with her; but I as little understand that part of the politicks as the rest'.

On the morning of 9 June, the death of the Lord President of the Session and Criminal Court occurred. In consequence, Argyll immediately wrote to Lord Godolphin recommending that Sir Gilbert Elliott be appointed. 'He is and has been long a Lawyer in perfect good repute, has always been firmly on the Revolution Foot, and hath the courage to act as such in the very worst of times . . .'

In this letter, he once more stressed that 'it was of great concern for Her Majesty's service that the Duke of Queensberry be imployed . . .'

On 10 June a further development occurred. The Privy Council met in the Royal Apartment of Holyrood Abbey. According to the *Edinburgh Courant* :

> There was read Her Majesty's letter signifying that it was her royal pleasure to remove the Rt. Hon. the Marquess of Tweedale from his office of President of the Privy Council; the Earl of Rothes from Keeper of the Privy Seal; the Earl of Roxburgh from Secretary of State; George Baillie of Jerviswood from Lord Treasurer-Depute; the Earl of Selkirk and Lord Belhaven from being Lords of Treasury, and all the other Lords from the Privy Council and Exchequer. And two Commissions under the Great Seal were read – the one creating the Rt. Hon. Earl of Loudoun Lord Secretary of State; the other to the Rt. Hon. the Earl of Glasgow to be Treasurer-Depute – And their Lordships qualified themselves accordingly . . .

In sequel to this Privy Council meeting the Duke of Hamilton reported (14 June) to the Duke of Atholl :

> Tis talkt as a great secret that Queensberry is not to come down, but I am become St Thomas. I believe only what I see and feel. Tis certain the Parliament will sitt at the time appointed and I am told the measure is the nomination of the successor – the Commissioner, Annandale, the Justice-Clerk are for pushing it off score and if they don't succeed in that they don't care for success in any other thing – I have been told Stair and that sett were for pushing the Treaty and Tweedale was still with his friends for the nomination of the Successor upon 'the old cant' of their Limitations, so they have catcht them for notwithstanding they have been turned out they fancy they can't goe back so far as to be against the measure. They themselves were pressing as if they doe there's are exclusion of them for ever . . .

During the next three weeks, Argyll was engaged with business of an official as well as a private character. In the first place he had colleagues and friends to consider. Accordingly, he requested Her Majesty's authority to 'give Green Ribbons' to the Marquess of Lothian, the Earl of Mar, the Earl of Haddington, my Lord Chancellor, and my best friend Lord Orrery.'

Then there was his brother – 'I also intreat Her Majesty would be pleased to let my brother have the Commission of Dumbarton Castle. I do not mean that it should be now made public unless there should be some disorder in the county happen which might require somebody to act in that post, but that he should keep it private till after the Parliament.'

Each day too found him in consultation with one or another of those who were to form his ministry. His chief concern was to discover every shade of opinion, and so he invited several members of the opposing party to join his conversations. 'They all say almost in the same words they would have gone into a treaty if the measures of the succession had been put off till next session of Parliament and if in the Treaty England had granted anything that was reasonable, they would then have gone in to the succession; but since Her Majesty has pressed the succession before a treaty has been set on foot to regulate matters between the two Kingdoms, they will go into neither.'

In reporting to Godolphin a situation which raised a deadlock, Argyll's own reaction was one of resolution to force the would-be defeatist into the field. Thus, his mood when, on the morning of 28 June, he led the procession to Parliament House where a deputation of city officials awaited to receive him. According to the minutes of Edinburgh Town Council for that date: 'The Counsell appoynts the Deans of Gild and his Counsell to admit and receive His Grace *John*, Duke of Argyll, Lord Archibald Campbell brother-german to his Grace the Duke of Argyll, Sir James Campbell of Auchinbreck, Mr James Campbell of Ardkinglass, Mr Patrick Cram of Heugh-head, Andrew Lockhart of Kirktoone by rights of his father; and to admite Sir Alexander Cuming of Culter, Andrew Allan – gentleman to the Duke of Argyll, and Mr David Campbell – merchant in London . . .'

After prayers, Sir James Murray of Philiphaugh – Lord Clerk Register – read Her Majesty's Commission to John, Duke of Argyll, for representing her in the session.

The Laws and Acts made by the Third Session of the First

Parliament of our most High and dread Sovereign Anne by grace of God Queen of Scotland, England, France and Ireland, Defender of the Faith – Holden and Begun at Edinburgh the 28th day of June One thousand Seven hundred and Five years by His Grace, John, Duke of Argyle; Marquis of Kintyre and Earl of Campbell and Cowal, Viscount of Lochawe and Glenisla, Lord Inveraray, Mull, Morven and Tiree; Heritable Justice-General and Lord High Lieutenant of the said share; Her Majesty's great Master of the Household in the Kingdom of Scotland; one of the Lords of her Majesty's honourable Privy Council and Extra-ordinary Lord of Session; Brigadier-General and Captain of Her Majesty's Life-Guards of Horse; Brigadier-General and Colonel of a Regiment of Fusiliers in the service of their High Mightinesses the States-General, and Knight of the most ancient and noble order of the Thistle; Her Majesty's Commissioner for holding Parliament. By virtue of a Commission under the Great Seal.

Lord Clerk Register resumed his place at the long table in the centre of the hall. Then Rolls were called and, the absence of certain members being noted, the Commissioner adjourned the House without the reading of Her Majesty's letter.

Five days later – Tuesday, 3 July – there was a full attendance to hear that message memorable for its tribute to the man who sat on the Commissioner's throne with the silken purse before him.[10]

My Lords and Gentlemen,

It hath been our great care and concern ever since our Accession to the Crown to preserve the peace and promote the interest and advantage of that our Ancient Kingdom, and above all to have your present Establishment so secured that both you and after ages may reap the benefit thereof . . . In your last meeting we recommended to you with great earnestness the settling of the succession of that our Ancient Kingdom in the Protestant Line. And several things having since happened which shows great in-conveniency of this matter continuing in suspense. We cannot but at present most seriously renew the recommendation of this settlement as being convinced of the growing necessity thereof both for the preservation of the Protestant Religion and th peace and safety of all our dominions . . . And therefore we must still leave it upon you as most necessary for all the ends above-mentioned that go to settlement of the succession before all other business.

E

We are fully satisfied and doubt not but you are that great benefit would arise to all our subjects by an Union of Scotland and England, and that nothing will contribute more to the composing of differences and extinguishing the fears that are unhappily raised and fermented by enemies of both nations than the promoting of everything that tends to the procuring the same. Therefore, we earnestly recommended to you to pass an Act for a Commission to set a Treaty afoot between the Kingdoms as a Parliament of England has done for effectuating what is so desirable and for such after matters and things as may be judged proper for our honour and the good and advantage of both Kingdoms for ever. In which we shall most heartily give our best assistance.

There followed a reference to the need for providing supplies adequate to the maintenance of the armed forces and then came the outstanding feature of the message.

We have named John, Duke of Argyll, to be our Commissioner to represent our Person in this Session of Parliament as one of whose capacity and zeal for our service and the Kingdom is good and advantage. We are sufficiently assured and no less hopeful that he will be to you acceptable. We have fully impowered him to declare our firm resolutions to maintain the Government both in Church and State as by Law established, and likewise to consent to such further Laws as shall be thought needful for that end.

We have also impowered him to give Royal Assent to such good laws as shall be concluded for the advancement of piety and the discouragement of immorality; for the better encouraging and improving of trade and conveyances, and for promoting the more easy and speedy administratives of Justice and generally for what may be found for the good and advantage of the Kingdom. In all which and whatever else may contribute to the happiness and satisfaction of our people you shall have our ready and cheerful concurrence. And so we bid you heartily farewell.

The voice of the Lord Justice Clerk ceased. There was a stir of movement among the assembly. Then silence renewed as the Duke of Argyll arose to make his speech as Commissioner:[11]

My Lords and Gentlemen,

Her Majesty has in her most gracious letter expressed so much tenderness and affection towards this nation in assuring you that she will maintain the Government as established by Law both in Church and State: and acquainting you that she has been pleased to give me full power to pass such Acts as may be for the good of the nation that were it not purely to comply with custom I might be silent.

Her Majesty has had under her consideration the present circumstances of this Kingdom, and out of her extreme concern for its welfare has been graciously pleased to recommend to you two expedients to prevent the ruin which does but too plainly threaten us: In the first place your settling the succession is to the Protestant Line as what is absolutely and immediately necessary to secure our peace to end those fears which have, with great industry and too much success, been fermented among us, and effectually disappoint the designs of our enemies: In the second, a Treaty with England, which you yourselves have shown so great an inclination to form that it is not to be supposed it can meet with any opposition.

The final part of the Funds which were appropriated in your last meeting for the Army are now at an end. I believe everybody is satisfied of how great use our Frigates have been to our trade and it is fit to acquaint you our Forts are ruinous and our magazines empty. Therefore I do not doubt but your wisdom will direct you to provide suitable supplies.

My Lords and Gentlemen, I am most sensible of the difficulties that attend this post and the loss I am at by want of experience in affairs. But I shall endeavour to make it up by my zeal and firmness in serving Her Majesty, and the great respect I shall have to whichever may be for the good of my country.

There was no falsehood in that voice so irresistible to any audience. The final phrase represented his life's allegiance, and one which he pursued until very near the last hour.

Immediately after the session's inauguration, the Commissioner summoned his colleagues – Lord Archibald Campbell, Lord Annandale, Lord Seafield, the Earl of Mar, the Earl of Glasgow, Sir James Murray of Philiphaugh, and Sir David Nairn. The purpose was to form the plan of action. In his opinion they should move ahead of their opponents; and he advocated tactics based upon knowledge of the course that the opposition were likely to adopt.

We shall offer a proposal to the House in these words – 'Proposed that the Parliament go in to consideration of such limitations and conditions of Government as shall be judged proper for the next successor to the Protestant Line. You, my Lord Annandale, as being Her Majesty's first Secretary of State, I make choice of to deliver our proposals . . .' As I know they are to do, the Opposing Party will offer a resolve – 'To proceed, before all other business, to the consideration of the state of the nation in relation to trade and coin.' Then my Lord Annandale will speak against resolves in general, but if the House incline to proceed on our lines, he shall change the proposal to a change in this manner – 'Resolved that the Parliament go in to the consideration of such limitations and conditions of government as shall be judged proper for the next successor in the Protestant Line, and we will immediately remit the State of the Nation in relation to coin and trade to a Committee.'

This proposal received approval, and accordingly their side of the stage was set for the first phase of the political drama due to open in three days' time. During that interval, the Commissioner dealt with business requiring a communication to Lord Godolphin.[12]

On Friday 4 July, Parliament assembled. The events of that day are best described in Argyll's own words:

My Lord Annandale offered no proposal and my Lord Mareschal offered the Resolve of the Opposing Party. I must say my Lord Annandale managed the affair most abominably for he never added the change at the end till before the vote so that a great many had not time to comprehend it, as the rest did not so much as hear it, by which mismanagement it proved of no effect, whereas otherwise it might have gone a great way towards taking away the force of their popular Resolve. The debate lasted betwixt four and five hours, and was managed by the Opposing Party with a great deal of calmness. At last the House determined that the Lord Mareschal's Resolve should be two votes; first, which of the proposals should be received, which was put to the vote, and the Lord Mareschal's was carried; next, by way of overture excluding no other business, or if it shall be by way of Resolve, excluding all other business till it was entirely finished; we carried it should be by way of overture only.

To Argyll, presiding over that assembly, a fact had emerged to cause him both anger and disappointment. Among his colleagues was a Judas. Duty forced him to enlighten Lord Godolphin. 'I warn your Lordship not to have great regard to what advices may be offered by my Lord Annandale : I know not what they may be but in general I know perfectly well he has no other aim but to promote the mis-carrying of Her Majesty's affairs, hoping that if this Parliament should rise in confusion, he might find his own account in it. I have taken no notice of him that I have found this out, but so soon as we meet before your Lordship, I shall let him know what I have to say against him.'

Meanwhile Lord Godolphin was writing to the Earl of Seafield.

Windsor, 14 July 1705

Butt the Duke of Queensberry being now on the road to Scotland, I should be glad to know very particularly from your Lordship how he fares himself and his friends there, towards the Queen's Service in the present conjunction of Affairs according to his earnest professions here at parting.

I might also acquaint Your Lordship that I find misunderstanding betwixt My Lord Commissioner and My Lord Annandale are come to a great height, which I am very sorry for, because I doubt it must needs have an ill effect at this time for the Queen's Service. Your Lsp. will best judge how farr the Duke of Queensberry may be useful in reconciling them.

I shall think, My Lord, you must find some opportunity of telling the Duke of Hamilton or my Lord Roxburgh soe, as occasion offers that either of them have it much in their power to doe themselves a great deal of right to the Queen and to their Country, the former, in case the Parliament inclines to a treaty, by making it practicall and not stopping it with insuperable difficulty ; the latter in case they proceed on limitation, by not insisting upon such as are unreasonable in themselves and inconsistent with the Monarchy.

These are the men in whose power this seems most to rest and consequently the men most worth the managing at this time. I am always sincerely my Lord

Your Lordship's most humble & obedient servant

Godolphin

The next move in the battle belonged to the Duke of Hamilton who, on Tuesday 17 July, raised a resolve similar to the one which he had proposed and carried the previous session: 'That this Parliament will not proceed to the nomination of a successor till we have had a previous treaty with England in relation to our Commerce and after concerns with that of the nation. And further it is resolved that this Parliament will proceed to make such limitations and conditions of Government for rectification of our Constitution as may secure the Liberty, Religion, and Independence of this Kingdom before they proceed to the said nomination.'

According to Parliamentary minutes of this date, the resolve was put to the vote – 'Approve or not and carried Approve'.

The Commissioner immediately called his ministers to discuss the line that their reply should take. 'They were of opinion', he wrote after the meeting 'that an Act should be brought in for a Treaty which, I believe, will be done on Friday.' The Earl of Mar was deputed to draft the text.

By that Friday – 20 July – the man who would play so vital a part in influencing the way of affairs had arrived. The Duke of Queensberry – as Lord Privy Seal – was present to hear the Marquess of Lothian read the draft for an Act of Treaty with England.

Before the month closed, the Government had pressed a first reading to the Act, while the Opposition was adamant upon Parliament going for limitations.[13]

The beginning part of August found the Commissioner ill, so much so that he could not attend to business and had to delegate Sir David Nairn to keep Godolphin informed of parliamentary affairs. Towards the end of the month he was recovered and ready to put the Treaty and Cess to a trial. 'What their fate will be I am not able to determine. Some think they will succeed, others think otherwise . . .'

The Opposition were certainly out to hinder progress. The method by which they sought to do this aroused Argyll's temper and caused him to declare, 'Most part of the people here are stark mad and not themselves know what they would be at.' As illustration was an incident which he regarded as 'something extraordinary' and therefore fit for report to Lord Godolphin.

Some proposed t'other day in Parliament to limit the successor by a claim of right which they pretended a vote of Parliament was sufficient to finish without Royal assent; this the Duke of Hamilton went violently to do, and said we could have no other security for our limitations, for that we had never so many Acts of Parliament, English influence and English bribery would take them off; and when they found the House did not go into so absurd a proposal they then proposed the limitations should take

place in the Queen's own time; these proposals I believe your
Lordship will think were sufficiently disrespectful to her Majesty
though couched under the civilest words . . .

As August drew to a close Parliament returned to serious consideration of Union. Some weeks earlier the Earl of Mar – on behalf
of the Government – had raised proposals for a Treaty. Then, however, the House had been toying with the alternative of succession
and the Limitation scheme of the Nationalist element led by Fletcher
of Saltoun. These had since collapsed due to the reluctance of the
majority to come to a decision on the subject of the Crown until
relations between the two countries were set upon a more solid
foundation. So in the last few days of the month, the Acts of Cess
[Supply][14] and Treaty were introduced to the House. With regard
to the former 'a proposal was offered that the House should agree
to give the Act of Cess a first reading, but that it should not have a
second till the affair of the Treaty was settled.'[15]

The Treaty question brought bitter argument. To quote Argyll –
'The Opposing Party were divided; some were against treating upon
any terms and others were for not treating until the English [Alien]
Act should be rescinded.'

The debate which ensued on the subject of how the Scottish
Commissioners should be appointed to negotiate with their English
contemporaries provoked fierce argument. At the same time, it
brought the first bold pronouncement of the Session. Andrew
Fletcher, Laird of Saltoun – whose nationalist principles were as
sincere as those of the Duke of Argyll to Union's cause – presented
the draft of an address to Her Majesty.

We – your Majesty's most loyal and faithful subjects – the
Noblemen, Barons and Burgesses convened in Parliament –
humbly represent to your Majesty that the Act lately passed in
the Parliament of England containing a proposal for a Treaty of
Union of the two Kingdoms, is made in such injurious terms to
the honour and interest of this nation that we who represent this
kingdom in Parliament can no wayes comply with it, which we
have the greater regret to refute because any Treaty of Union
has, in this Session, been recommended to us by Her Majesty.

But out of the great sense of duty we owe Your Majesty we
are ready to comply with any such proposals from the Parliament
of England whenever it shall be made in such terms as are always
honourable or advantageous to this nation.

These concluding words reflected the opinion of all wise thinking men. They were wearied of so much confused talk and no definite action. Unless something happened soon, the Alien Act would be enforced. For the first time there was suggestion of a more rational attitude. Argyll determined to take advantage of it in such a way that the Government would emerge victorious from an intensely difficult session.

Three days after the address presented by the Laird of Saltoun, Parliament proceeded to deliberation on the Treaty Act and the clause relative to powers to be conferred on Commissioners received especial attention. During the discussion on this delicate subject, the Duke of Hamilton arose to move that there be an addition to the said clause in these terms: 'The Union to be treated on shall not derogate any wayes from any fundamental laws, ancient privileges, rights, dignities, and liberties of this Kingdom.'

Following debate, the proposal was put to the vote and defeated by two votes.

To the proud Hamilton, whose defiance in face of opposition matched that of Argyll, this defeat must have been a sharp disappointment. The fact too of shadows in his private life aggravated a sense of ill-luck. He fell into a mood open to whatever light might show. It came from the most unexpected quarter. His arch-rival – the Duke of Argyll – invited him to the side of Union.

There is no evidence to show how these two ambitious Dukes entered into an agreement of so secret a character that not even Hamilton's closest friends suspected any change of policy. Indeed, at the very moment when other plans were being laid, rumour was circulating to the effect that Hamilton – descended from the royal line of Stuarts – had designs upon the Crown if its reversal to Scotland could be achieved.

Parliament sat again on 1 September. It was moved that 'the Act for Treaty be plain and simple – and the sentiment of the nation regarding the clause in the English Act for declaring the Scots to be Aliens be considered in a separate way.'

The Duke of Atholl immediately arose to present a Protest,[16] after which voting on the Alien Act proceeded. As the hour was late when it approached conclusion, the day's business appeared to be at an end. A number of members were certainly under that impression and prepared to leave. On the other hand, Government supporters remained as if expectant of something about to happen. They were not mistaken. There came an announcement: 'Parliament will now consider the way of nomination of Commissioners for a Treaty –

Whether the same shall be left to Her Majesty or be done by the Estates of Parliament.'

Following these unexpected words, the atmosphere of crisis predominated. A murmur among the assembly was succeeded by a significant hush. In this moment the Duke of Hamilton arose. Addressing himself to the Chancellor he pronounced, in that majestic and pathetic tone which commanded respect, the most sensational words of the Session : 'The nomination of Commissioners should be left to the Queen'.

A stunned silence ensued. Then, as the shock passed, there came loud cries of dissent. Andrew Fletcher did not hesitate to call 'traitor'. Others ran from the House and exclaimed as they went 'Tis no purpose to stay any longer since the Duke of Hamilton has deserted and betrayed us.'[17] Those who remained began a debate in which they contested their leader's action by hurling back at him the arguments that he had so often used against the Crown having a say in the nomination.

> What! Leave nomination to the Queen! No, she is, in a manner, a prisoner in England, and the Estates of Scotland has taught us a duty in a case nearly related to this during the captaincy of King James I. Our Queen knows none of us, but as introduced by our English Ministry and recommended by our inclinations to serve that Ministry. . . . Our Queen never had an opportunity to know the true interest of our country and though she did, yet, as she was circumstanced, could not show her true regard for it. Who then so proper to nominate Scots Commissioners to treat on Scots affairs as a Scots' Parliament.[18]

The Duke of Hamilton made no attempt to vindicate himself. Instead, he insisted that the vote be taken – leave the nomination of Commissioners to the Queen or to Parliament.'

Accordingly, the vote was taken and due to the absence of Opposition members, carried – 'To be left to the Queen'. All the Ministers supported the Duke who had so unexpectedly swerved from defence of Scotland's nationalism to favour of Her Majesty's interests.[19]

Sir John Clerk of Penicuik, in his memoirs, throws some light on Hamilton's startling action. 'The proposal on the nomination of Commissioners by the Queen came from the Duke of Hamilton who, from that piece of independence, expected the honour of being appointed by the Queen . . .'[20]

'I know that the Duke was so unlucky in his private circumstances that he would have complied with anything.'

On the strength of the Government's triumph, the draft of the address by Parliament to Her Majesty was prepared[21] and on 4 September presented to the Estates – 'Approve or not and carried Approve'.

The Treaty Act paved the way for several other acts to pass the House[22] and by 22 September Argyll was able to inform Godolphin that 'after consultation with Her Majesty's servants', he had adjourned Parliament to the twentieth of December. 'It ended with all the decency imaginable, which has been very unusual of late.' In that same letter, he alluded to the general satisfaction felt at Her Majesty's consent to 'remove Lord Annandale from his post as Secretary of State, but I assure your Lordship if it be not done without allowing my Lord Annandale to go to London it will prove more uneasy to Her Majesty and your Lordship than you can possibly imagine.'[23] 'I design to stay here till I am honoured with an answer because I think it is of the greatest consequence to Her Majesty's service that my Lord Marr have his commission here . . .'

October opened to find Argyll 'honoured with an answer'. He summoned the Privy Council and, according to a report dated 4 October in the 'Postman's log' of the *Edinburgh Courant*[24]: 'This day the Privy Council met on the Royal Appointment where a Commissioner in favour of the Earl of Marr to be Secretary of State in place of the Marquess of Annandale was read. Then they adjourned till the first Tuesday in November.'

On the day after this Privy Council meeting, Argyll wrote to Godolphin:

> I received your's from Newmarket and at the same time Commissions to the Marquis of Annandale[25] and the Earl of Marr. The Marquis refused his and said he design'd to go to London and wait on her Majesty. I acquainted the servants with his refusal and they are all of opinion that if he does go to London it will not be for her Majesty's service that he should meet with a good reception because that might make him insolent whereas if he be made sensible that Her Majesty is displeased with his behaviour in this affair your Lordship will find him very humble. I design to begin my journey on Monday or Tuesday at the farthest.

The date of a letter which brought State business to an end was Friday 5 October. Next day the Duke took leave of the Edinburgh world. 'Saturday, at five in the afternoon, John, Duke of Argyle, Her Majesty's Commissioner, set out from Holyrood Palace for Newbattle,[26] a seat of the Marquess of Lothian. And I am informed His Grace will part from thence this day for London.'[27]

EPILOGUE

At the outset of the Session, the Duke of Argyll had stood 'on trial' not only before the Queen and her Chief Minister, but also politicians accustomed to navigate the undercurrents of intrigue. There had been the moment when he doubted his capacity of experience to control the subtle factors within the Estates, and under the burden of that doubt sought retreat from the office of Commissioner. Yet when the Queen had left him without choice of resignation, he had adopted a tenacity of purpose by 'preaching every day Union's doctrines'. At the same time, in his relations with the Duke of Hamilton, he had shown signs of being accomplished in political craft. Above all, he was a 'most persuasive speaker' and absolutely sincere for the Queen's interests.[28]

Chapter VII

RETURN TO LONDON

London – October 25th

Yesterday His Grace the Duke of Argyle arrived here from Scotland, as did the Rt. Hon. the Earl of Seafield, Lord High Chancellor of the Kingdom.[1]

On the eve of a Parliamentary session with Godolphin's coalition ministry of naturally-inspired Whigs and Tories in power, the nation's strength loomed to the public mind. In bold perspective there stood forth a kingdom united so that peace could be maintained at home while the Duke of Marlborough advanced war on the Continent. Men capable of promoting that unity were to be applauded, and one of them was John, Duke of Argyll, who had 'Maintained the character of Lord High Commissioner with a degree and propriety and firmness greatly beyond what could have been expected from one of his years.'[2]

From Scotland had come reports which gave him the highest reputation. As his former tutor, Alexander Cunningham, wrote: 'For in the first place he resolutely restored the declining authority of the Parliament. Then, thoroughly informing himself of the parties, he gained many of them to his interest; and being once gained, united them together for promoting the Queen's service; the offer disunited Hamilton's attempts and broke the power of his faction.'

Thus it was that from the hour of arrival at his residence in Bruton Street the Duke received congratulations from friends and Whig political chiefs. In turn he met them with that courtesy of manner which charmed even his most hardened foes. There could be no doubt that 'His High and Mighty Grace' – as critics alluded to him – was in a humour for the pleasures of London : attendance at the play; making the round of coffee houses in the company of his young swordsmen acquaintances[3]; visits to his Dysart relatives at Ham.

Meanwhile to the day of 25 October and Parliament's re-assembly: as a misty dawn broke, there burst forth a sound that must have stirred Argyll's warrior spirit. Upon London's citizens and members of the Lords and Commons riding in from the country to attend at Westminster its effect was to arouse memories of Blenheim a year ago. Guns firing salvoes of salute from the Tower and Hyde Park proclaimed victory. Soon the news was known. Barcelona had fallen to the general commanding in Spain – Lord Peterborough.[4] 'Nothing can be more evident than that if the French King continues master of the Spanish Monarchy, the balance of power in Europe is utterly destroyed and he will be able in a short time to enjoy the Trade and the wealth of the World.'

While echo of those salvoes was still upon the air and the bells of Westminster and St Paul's were expressing the suddenly awakened sentiment of jubilation, the Queen had opened her address from the Throne.

In a voice that conveyed the emotion which all her subjects must then have been feeling, she went on to pronounce what would prove the strongest message of her reign.

No good Englishman can be content to sit still and acquiesce to such a project and at this time we have great grounds to hope that by the blessing of God upon our Arms and those of our Allies, a good foundation is laid for restoring the Monarch of Spain to the House of Austria, the consequences of which will not only be faire and advantageous, but glorious for England.

If we be not wanting in ourselves we shall see the next campaign begun effectively on all sides against our enemies in a most vigorous manner.

From that theme of war, Her Majesty passed to the one perhaps nearest her heart both as a woman and a Queen –

By an Act of Parliament passed this last winter I was enabled to appoint Commissioners for this Kingdom to treat with Commissioners to be empowered by Authority of Parliament in Scotland concerning a nearer and more complete Union between the two Kingdoms as soon as an Act shall be made there for that purpose. I think it proper for me to acquaint you that such an Act is lately passed there & I intend in a short time to cause Commissioners to be made out in order to put the Treaty on foot, which I heartily desire may prove successful because I am persuaded that a Union of the two Kingdoms will not only prevent many inconveniences which may otherwise happen, but must continue to the peace & happiness of both nations – and therefore I hope I shall have your assistance in bringing this great work to a good conclusion.

A pause at this point signified something more to come.

There is another Union I think myself obliged to recommend to you in the most earnest and affectionate manner. I mean an Union of Minds and Affections among ourselves. It is that which would, above all things, disappoint and defeat the hopes and designs of our enemies.

Through these challenging words, the Queen appealed to a spirit which would be reflected in the men elected to preside over the nation in this autumn hour of 1705.

Sidney Godolphin – First Minister with the purpose of a country united and enjoying civil liberty; Robert Harley – the House of Commons Tory with vision to realize that a policy founded upon moderation would embrace parties instead of dividing them; Marlborough – absent in Europe, yet towering above the senate because of his reverence for a monarch who disciplined personal inclinations for the sake of the nation's welfare. Under this triumvirate of patriot minds progress was inevitable.

Maximum support was voted to the Captain-General so that his organization of campaign on two fronts[5] could advance. As a gesture of the mellowness of mood towards the Scots people, Tories and Whigs alike cast their thoughts upon repealing the odious Alien Act. It was Harley who took the initiative by moving that the clause which described the Scots as Aliens should be removed! To this, several Tories added their voices – declaring that they had remonstrated against the Act last Session because they considered it a piece of unnecessary & unwarranted injustice done to Scotland and an irregular procedure towards persuading them to meet & treat in a friendly manner and with a disposition of agreement; but since the House was then of another opinion, they were obliged to submit. But they would gladly know what was the matter now and why the people who had proposed it last year as being absolutely necessary for England's honour and security should be the first to propose its repeal.[6]

Before the Queen would agree to repeal of the act, she wanted to be more sure of the mood that prevailed among her political chiefs. Yet on the day after Parliament's opening, the opinion of Englishmen was voiced in *The Observateur*. 'All People know a Union with Scotland is necessary and of great consequence and all that is spoken in one paragraph . . .'

Meanwhile, the ministry moved on to the most important issue in those early days of the session. The Regency Act was born through spontaneous manoeuvre rather than design. With the express purpose of creating a difficult situation for their Whig adversaries at a crucial period of natural progress, the High Tories raised the question of an invitation to the Dowager Duchess of Hanover to visit England. They well knew how delicate a subject it was with the Queen and how embarrassing for the ministry to refuse it and remain on good terms with the electoral heir's mother. Godolphin and his colleagues were, however, equally capable of subtle tactics. Instead of a visit from the Dowager Duchess during the Queen's lifetime, there would be an article establishing a Council of Regency to rule between the time of Her Majesty's death and the Prince's arrival.[7]

Of all Whig partisans, the Duke of Argyll had the strongest reason to applaud the ministry's brilliant strategy in the face of an Opposition seeking to stir agitation. Ever since his mission, in 1703, to Hanover, he had been a zealous supporter of the Hanoverian Succession. An act which safeguarded the Electoral Prince's accession came as a spur to his ambitions in that direction. The day was to come when he would be foremost to ensure the guarantee being honoured.

In the English political scene he had no part as yet; but there was promise of the reward most desired.

'It is certain the Duke of Argyle be made an English Peer' – wrote Anne, Duchess of Hamilton, to the Duchess of Atholl at Dunkeld on 25 November.

On that very day, the Queen created Argyll an English Peer with the titles Baron Chatham and Earl of Greenwich.

'*Vix ea nostra voco*' ('This is scarcely my own') he exclaimed upon being informed. These words became the motto which he chose for his coat of arms.

The closing days of 1705 found him both restless and dissatisfied. Besides a natural inclination to return to military duties and be off to Europe for the new campaign, he was aware of another's shadow across his path. The Duke of Queensberry had not only returned to power at Court; but consolidated his position with the Queen and

Godolphin. Apparently they attributed the successful turn of events at the end of the Scottish session to his diplomacy and so were disposed to the advice he had to offer on the subsequent course of affairs. For Argyll – still Commissioner in name[8] – this new circumstance came as a wound to his pride. There was justification. He had presided over a Parliament nursing elements almost impossible to reconcile: personal jealousies, intrigues, party struggle: but solely upon the ideal that governed each step of his career: 'As long as I live I shall act for the Protestant Succession and as far as in me lies to the last drop of my blood support your Majesty and your Government.'[9] Thus his attitude before that assembly of so many dissentient forces had been a positive one marked by speech which carried the accent of an indomitable spirit. The effect was a respect strong enough to break down the opposition at first so hostile. In the end he could count among his party men who had once been devoted to King James. Although persons of not very considerable interest to him, and only with hopes of high places and commands in the army, they were at least new allies to the Crown's cause.

The urge to resign his present course and return to military duties grew upon Argyll as time approached for the renewal of political business in which it was evident that Queensberry's voice would rule. He hinted this change of mind and there were persons quick with report. The Duke of Atholl writing from Dunkeld on 3 December to the Marquis of Tullibardine stated: 'The Duke of Argyle owned there is no reason for any lodgings [in Holyrood Abbey] as not designing to stay in Scotland . . .'[10]

By the turn of the year when selection of Commissioners to represent Scotland at the Treaty Conference loomed into prominence, the Queen, on whom the authority of choice had been vested by the Scottish Estates, passed it to her Chief Minister and the Duke of Queensberry. They would have the power of decision.

Although Argyll attended the talks held to discuss nominations, he was out of tune with the whole affair. The atmosphere of discord that prevailed at these conferences did not improve the situation. The sight of colleagues stabbing one another with arguments in their endeavours for appointment annoyed him beyond measure. Scotland and her future seemed to have taken second place. He began to wish himself out of this narrow circle of petty strife and this made itself apparent in bouts of ill-humour. It was not easy for him to attend those meetings of conflict. Loyalty to his nation and Monarch alone made it possible; but for how long?

Answer to that question which he must have asked himself many times during the last weeks of December and on into January came through the Duke of Queensberry. He advised against the nomination of the Duke of Hamilton to the Commission as being an injudicious proceeding; His persuasive speech won the Queen's approval.

For Argyll the hour of action had arrived. In justice to the promise by which he had gained the Duke of Hamilton's signal act before the Scottish Parliament, and also to his own honourable principles, he could no longer continue at the talks.[11]

> Queensberry went from this [Edinburgh] on Monday. Some believe there is no understanding betwixt Argyle and him because of the palace . . .

In the early part of the New Year, George Baillie of Jerviswood reported this news to the Earl of Roxburgh. At about the same time, a certain Mr Hall wrote to Colonel Hooke – a Jacobite Envoy:

> You'll have heard that the irresistible Arms of the Confederates have gained to the Arch-Duke Charles almost the whole Kingdom of Catalonia, and that many towns in other parts of Spain are revolted. We, in Britain, are resolved to support that Prince and establish him King of all the Spanish dominions; but at the same time we lay ourselves open to French invasion, or any that pleases to attack us.
>
> There goes shortly to Barcelona eight regiments – three out of Ireland, and two Scots regiments out of Holland – all to be commanded, under Peterborough, by the Duke of Argyll, who desires to be layd aside as to State affairs and have leave only to follow the Military. So the declining politick business and Annandale being disgracefully turn'd off without giving a reason why, none was more violent than he for all the Court's proposals for the succession of Hanover, so Queensberry is the only man now that rules well.[12]

These reports of Argyll were true – the field – not the conference table – would henceforth be his province.

F

NOTES

Introduction

1 Description by a lady who saw the gardens as left by the Duchess of Lauderdale.
2 In after years, Archibald, Earl of Islay (and 3rd Duke), planted the wilderness with lofty Scotch firs.
3 In one of her surviving letters, she uses the expression 'poppet'.
4 Following the Earl of Argyll's escape from Edinburgh Castle where he was imprisoned – under sentence of death – for refusing to subscribe to the Test Act.
5 In 1683, a grant from the forfeited estates was made to Lord Lorne.
6 Lady Ann Campbell became the wife of the first Marquess of Bute (1731) and later of Alexander Strichen of Aberdeenshire. Lady Kathryn Campbell died in 1699 and was buried at Petersham.

Chapter I

1 Memoirs of Lady Louisa Stuart.
2 First admitted to the Privy Council (1689), he later became Lord of the Treasury and one of the Extraordinary Lords of Session.
3 John Anderson was grandfather of the founder of the Andersonian Library, Glasgow (University of Strathclyde).
4 On one occasion it would be to provide William with a detailed account of the French military dispositions; on another, to proceed to the Continent for the purpose of undertaking certain political negotiations on behalf of the English Ministry.
5 A letter written by the Earl to William Carstares – Principal of Edinburgh University – explains the reason which dictated his action in this affair:

Edinburgh – March 30th 1696.
    I received your's dated the 24th instant . . . as to what you say in relation to myself and my own particular behaviour, I take it very kindly of you. I know it is the effect of your friendship and concern in my person besides my family. I do assure you my carriage shall be such as I shall give no just cause of scandal or offence; though I know some make it their business to render me criminal and at least censurable, even where there is the least ground . . . I need scarce hope to be free of censure should I lock myself up in a cage; daily they will be hatching something. There is one thing I know will be clamoured against, that I have sent my two daughters home to Roseneath designing to take the charge of them myself. My reason for so doing are, since they are mine, and that I am bound to provide for them, none can blame. I will endeavour that they be bred up with all duty and love to me as their father, which I cannot expect in the circumstances they have been in hitherto, living with a mother on those terms with me, and who never in her life showed them either the example of good nature or duty to their

parent, and who always carries herself to her children to an extreme one side or t'other, by too much fondness or too much severity. They are coming up to an age in which its presumable they will receive impressions; and I have not forgot the Latin – '*Quo semel est imbuta*' . . . But above all, my chief reason is she having had lately the charge of her sister Doune's daughter, some years older than any of mine, she did encourage her in things I would not for all the world be guilty of, when a parent especially, which was to encourage her to write little 'billets-doux' and letters to Carnwath – Sir George Lockhart's son and heir; and by the company she kept by her example; as the Countess of Forfar, Nanny Murray, etc., she had like to a been ruined, and came to that length of impudence that dancing with Carnwath in the dancing school she squeezed his hand. All which the youth told; and the girl was sent for home. As you are my undoubted friend I give you the trouble of all this; though I hope the envious world themselves must acknowledge a father can dispose of his children . . .

6   In 1695, the Company of Scotland to trade with Africa and the Indies was founded by twenty-one persons – eleven Englishmen and ten Scotsmen – among whom was the Duke of Argyll who invested £1,500. The first quarter of this sum was paid on 31 March 1696.

Chapter II

1   The League of Augsburg was composed of England and Holland (Maritime Powers), Germany and Spain.
2   Two bills destined to govern the policy of the next reign passed the House of Commons where the group of dogmatic Whig aristocrats had been replaced by Tories under the moderate Robert Harley. One was the Act of Settlement fixing the Crown on the Protestant House of Hanover. The other authorized William to proceed with international engagements, and thus pave the way to re-opening of the war.
3   Sir Charles Duncombe was a son of Mr Duncombe of Drayton Beauchamp, Burchigston. After his death in 1711, Jonathan Swift wrote: 'I hear he has left the Duke of Argyle 200,000 pounds. I hope it is true for I love that Duke mightily.'

Chapter III

1   The first Duke of Argyll's death occurred at Stourton (Chirton) House in the north of England.
2   Colonel Hooke in his correspondence alludes to the Scottish forces as existing in the year 1703/4: 'A Company of Horse Guards who should count a strength of 120, but is not more than eighty; of them sixty-one are staunch Jacobites who never retire to sleep before having saluted the health of the young King. The Duke of Argyle commanded them, but as he died after my departure, I do not know to whom they are given.'
3   Cunningham.

4   One of these responsibilities formed the subject of a letter addressed to the Marquess of Lothian on 15 March 1703/4:

> My Lord, I must beg the favour from your Lordship to permit my Father's Body to be laid in your Burial place at Newbattle till such time as I can eventually transport both my grandfather and him to their own burial place in the Highlands, this my Lord if you will please to consent to will be a favour dun to
> Your most obedient humble servant
>
> Argyll

5   For series of letters see Appendix I.
6   For these letters see Appendix I.
7   As illustration, is a letter dated 17 July, written by a claimant.

> *Edinburgh – 17 July* 1704
> May it please your Grace
> To pay to Mr. Joseph Young merch^t in Edinburgh the sum of one hundred and fifty five pound, eighteen shillings Scots money at his shop in lawn-mercatt of Edinburgh and that upon the twenty-first day of Jully instant, make thankfull payment which I shall allow in pairt payment of what is due to me for the funeral of your Grace's husband and his father which will singularly oblidge
> Your Grace's most humble servant
>   fit pub et vibitur
>   Jo: Patterson
> To Her Grace the Dutchess Dowager of Argyll
> Which Bill was presented to her Grace by a Nottar and protested eighteen day of August 1704 because of not acceptance and not payment.

8   See Appendix I.

Chapter IV

1   Duchess of Atholl to Duke of Atholl, 9/10 February 1704

> 'The having the Order of St Andrew with a green riband is thought Very rediculous and there can be no reason found out of it but the Duke Argyle has a mind to wear . . . livery. I hope you shall never be in it . . . There is many adherents yet not only . . . and the Court are for the Prince of Wales, but yet Her Majesty herself was for him as concerned in the reall plott.'

14 Feb. 1704. Hamilton writing to Atholl expresses anger that Argyll has received the Thistle before the others and considers that Atholl should not have accepted it. (A letter of 10 February from the Duchess of Atholl to the Duchess of Hamilton alluded to the fact that Argyll's acceptance of the Thistle was not approved by her brother, the Duke of Hamilton.

> 'The reason why the Order is given is because they say it was worn green before and that the thistle being green it is the proper colour,

but I believe the best reason is because the Queen being Governor can change it into what colour she pleases. On the first institution it was only a choice and afterwards a green riband as King James the 5th is painted on the Queen's.

2 'Estates' was the name given to the Scots Parliament.
3 The Earl of Seafield was also one of the Secretaries of State. The other was the Earl of Roxburgh.
4 The Act was signed on 5 August. In giving her assent to it, the Queen had yielded to the arbiter of Britain's fortunes. Yet had the despatch from Marlborough arrived on the *eve* instead of the *morrow* of 5 August, she could have followed her own inclinations.
5 The High Tory chiefs were the Earls of Nottingham and Rochester, and Lord Haversham.
6 Marlborough had shown hostility to this bill.
7 The Earl of Mar had attached himself to the Court Party and favoured Union. Later, he became a Jacobite.
8 Viscount Dupplin.
9 Argyll's own words.
10 Scotland.
11 Secretary James Johnstone (Lord Clerk Register) to Baillie of Jervis-wood, Lord Treasurer Deputy, Scotland.
12 Detained as a reprisal for the impounding by the English East India Company of a Scots ship, *Annandale*.
13 The Earl of Roxburgh to Baillie of Jerviswood — London, 26 December 1704.
14 Roxburgh stated: 'I do believe that the Union were the best thing for Scotland and England should yield all that's reasonable . . .'
15 Reference to Tweedale's set.

Chapter V

1 Under its terms, all Scotsmen not resident in England, Ireland and the Colonies would receive alien status. English horses, arms and ammunition were forbidden to Scotland, Scottish cattle, coal and linen were banned from England.
2 On 30 March, Patrick Scott wrote from Edinburgh to the Duke of Atholl: 'A letter has been received from Argyle saying that the Queen has commanded the sentence not to be put into execution until she had examined the evidence . . .'
3 'The letter of Duke Argyle is much taken notice of', Patrick Scott's report to the Duke of Atholl continued,

> They say it is a very good preliminary to the Parliament and brings to remembrance his first actions in all his three eminent advancements; first when he gott the Guards upon Her Majesty's promise of . . . He was pleased to send down his order before he gott his Commission which being read on the head of E Troop — They said they knew him. The next was being Extraordinary Lord of Session. The very first day of his admission he was pleased to vote in one of the most difficult dayes has been in the House — The Duke of

Buccleuch & Eildon without having a word in the debate, and next
day when a Bill was given in returning he made his speech that he
hoped the House had more honour than to do one thing to-day and
write it the next. And the third being of a . . . with the former two
has given people to expect we'll have a very pleasant Parliament. It's
talked that he says 'Tis a shame to think how the throne has been
invaded of late, but it will not be allowed any more . . .

I forgot to tell that the Commissioner [Argyll] gets Queensberry's
houses and the use of all his furniture notwithstanding £3,500 for his
Equipage.

4 Seafield Papers (unpublished).
5 Secretary James Johnstone.
6 On 4 May Sir Alexander Erskine, Lord Lyon, wrote to the Duke of
Atholl: 'No doubt your Grace has heard what a deale of pains was
taken to give him [the Commissioner] a glorious entry.' His letter
continued: 'I had not the honour to kiss His Grace's hand till yesterday, he had a very thin Court, but there's abundance of Campbells in
town to-night to make a Court themselves.'

Chapter VI

1 New Party members were among them. Afterwards James Johnstone
wrote to Jerviswood: 'This day we saw the Commissioner in the
presence, but he said nothing to either Tweedale or me; talks a little of
cock and bull to Roxburgh, I find that Tweedale resolved to trouble
him no more; and who can blame him. Roxburgh to-morrow is to
acquire his commands; for that he designs for the country – In short,
we that are here, desire nothing so much now that we should be laid
aside.'
2 They had failed to implement Her Majesty's policy during the previous
Session of the Scottish Parliament, and deserted the Privy Council in
the eleventh hour of the Green affair.
3 From Stirling Castle, the Earl of Mar wrote to the Earl of Seafield:

My Lord,
I had the honour of your's last night about five o'clock and also
the Commissioner's commands, and accordingly came here
immediately thereafter. I have given His Grace an account of the
condition of this place which hardly can be known. I trust something
may be asked about it . . .

4 Stirling Castle governed the central approach to the Highlands.
5 Atholl Papers (unpublished correspondence).
6 The Duke of Hamilton wrote to the Earl of Seafield (Lord High
Chancellor of Scotland):

My Lord,
You needed have laid noe introduction upon me not to communicate what you wrote to me for I protest I can't yet find out the
secret. Your great men get away of everything so mystically that a

plain country gentleman like myself will need plainer languag[e] before I can understand you. If the Commissioner has great powers allowed him, I suppose the publick will soon see it and when your Lsp. will be pleased to honor me with the knowledge of anything I begg it may not be in soe reserved a strain. All I desire to know is when the Parliament will certainly meet which I hope will not be made a greater myster of — for

Your Lsp's most affectionate cousine and humble servant

Hamilton

May 24th, 1705

7   The Queen had not forgiven the Duke of Queensberry's part in the 'Scotch' or Fraser plot.

8   Seafield Papers (unpublished).

9   The Order of the Thistle.

10 According to custom, a silken purse lay on a cushion before the Commissioner.

11 There were two texts of the speech, one — abbreviated in his own words — which is quoted in this chapter.

12 According to George Lockhart: 'the Duke of Queensberry pretended sickness and various excuses to avoid being present at the beginning of the Session, that he might see how affairs were like to go and whether or not he might venture in Scotland; and likewise let the world see that 'tho the Duke of Argyle was Commissioner, yet he was not able to oppose the Cavaliers unless he came down and by his presence and influence assisted and supported him.'

13 Argyll reported the concluding debate to Lord Godolphin in the following terms:

John Hume who is a lord of the Treasury, the Earl of Marchmont who has a pension of four thousand pounds a year, the Lord Tressichen who has a company in the Army, all voted against the Queen, and my Lord Lauderdale who has a post in the Mint of six hundred pounds a year, besides his post in the session and the Earl of Glencairn who is a Lieutenant-Colonel, would not come to the House and Mr Bennit, Muster Master which is a very profitable post, notwithstanding that I spoke to them three or four times in relation to this measure, thought fit not to vote.

Towards the end of the debate, in answer to some of the New Party who were bawling for the limitations, the Earl of Glasgow desired they would be pleased to explain themselves, much depending upon what the design was of bringing to the limitations at this time, that if they were to be put into an Act of Settlement and the Protestant successor named, he would willingly go along with them, but if the design was only to enact limitations without settling the succession, that then he hoped the House would rather proceed to a Treaty and so desired them to say if they designed to name the successor, to which they and the Duke of Hamilton answered with a loud 'no'.

In short, my Lord, I think yesterday's vote shows to a demonstration who are for the supporting of Her Majesty's government and maintaining the peace of the nation and who aim at nothing but confusion.

14 Maintenance of the forces.
15 Argyll.
16 The protest presented by the Duke of Atholl was recorded as follows:

> In regard that by an English Act of Parliament made in the last Session thereof intended Act for effectual securing the Kingdom of England from apparent dangers that may arise from several Acts lately passed in the Parliament of Scotland; the subjects of this Kingdom are to be adjudged Aliens born out of the allegiance of the Queen as Queen of England after the 25th December 1705; I do therefore protest for myself and in the name and behalf of all who do adhere to this my protestation that for saveing the honour and interest of Her Majesty as Queen of this Kingdom, and maintaining and preserving the undoubted rights and privileges of her Subjects – no Act for a Treaty with England ought to pass this House unless a clause be added thereto prohibiting and discharging the Commissioners that be nominated and appointed for carrying out the said Treaty to depart the Kingdom until the said clause be Repealed and Rescinded by the Parliament of England. And do therefore desire this my protestation may be marked and recorded in the records of Parliament.

17 Lockhart papers.
18 Ibid.
19 In letters dated 10 and 11 September, Ann, Duchess of Hamilton, wrote to the Duchess of Atholl expressing wonderment at her brother's behaviour in acting as he had recently done in Parliament. She alluded to a letter from the Duke explaining his conduct. In it he stated that this Parliament 'had been made for the country's good, and many were convinced that he was right to vote for the Queen choosing Treaty Commissioners'.
20 According to Trevelyan's *History of England under Queen Anne* (London; 1934). Hamilton's agreement with Argyll had been made on the assurance that were the choice left to the Queen, he would be one of the Commissioners.
21 May it please Your Majesty,
     We, your Majesty's most loyal and faithful subjects, the Noblemen, Barons, and Burgesses assembled in Parliament, do in all humility represent to your Majesty that in compliance with desire of your Majesty's royal letter whereby you earnestly recommend to us to pass an Act for a Commission to set a treaty on foot betwixt the Kingdoms of Scotland and England, and for a nearer and more compleat Union between them, and for such other matters and things as may be judged proper for Your Majesty's honour and the good and advantage of both Kingdoms for ever. We have by our vote agreed to the passing of the said Act in the most fair and open

terms that could be expected, leaving to Your Majesty the nomination of the Commissioners for this Kingdom and the time and place
of their meeting with the Commissioners of England.

But we have in that Act forborn to take any notice of a chance in
a late Act of Parliament of England intitled An Act for the effectual
securing the Kingdom of England from the apparant dangers that
may arise from several Acts lately past in the Parliament of England.
By which clause the natives of this your ancient Kingdom of
Scotland are after the twentyfifth day of December next to be
adjudged and taken as aliens born out of the allegiance of the Queen
of England. Yet we cannot but with all submission, signify to Your
Majesty as Sovereign of both Kingdoms, that we and the whole
Nation whom we represent are most sensible of the great injury done
us by that clause whereby we are denyed the right and privilege in
England which natives of England do injoy in Scotland, and which
we have constantly injoyed in England as a loyal and necessary
consequence of our being natural born Subjects of the same
Sovereign and hath always been sustained as a mutual priviledge in
Courts and judicatures of both Nations. For which reason We have
found it absolutely necessary for maintaineing the honour of this
Nation to agree and order unanimously – 'That the Commissioners
to be nominated by Your Majesty for this Kingdom shall not
commence any treaty with England until first the said clause in the
Engish Act be rescinded.

We must therefore in all humility intreat and hope from Your
Majesty's goodness and justice – 'That in your Royal Wisdom you
will take such course as the said clause in the Act of the English
Parliament may be repealed to the effect the aforesaid Treaty of
Union so much desired may commence and proceed with the wishes
of Success.'

22 These acts formed the subject of a report addressed by the Duke of
Argyll to Godolphin : The first related to Cess [Supply] which, for some
while, the Opposition had 'struggled with all their force' to hinder.
However, on 8 September – 'We brought in and carried six months
Cess for the Army and two Frigates formerly maintained, and a
seventh month to maintain an additional forty gunships and two small
vessels on the West Coast to hinder the importation of prohibited
goods. This was carried with very little opposition by reason of the
Opposing Party's being dispirited with their having lost every vote
since the Treaty was brought in, so your Lordship sees, notwithstanding
the infinite number of difficulties we have had to struggle with this
Session of Parliament will, I hope, end to Her Majesty's satisfaction.
There are two Acts passed since the Treaty, one for encouraging the
exportation of beef and pork, and another declaring linen and woolen
manufactures free of duty at exportation. These two Acts the servants
are unanimously of opinion should have the Royal assent; and there
are two more which will in all probability pass the House, one for
hindering the importation of foreign leather; and the other appointing
this Nation's having an Ambassador at all general Treaties . . . I hope

your Lordship will let me have Her Majesty's commands as to these four Acts.'

23 Lord Annandale was virtually dismissed because it was believed that he had held a private correspondence with the Squadrone.

24 The *Edinburgh Courant* was then printed by the 'Heirs and Successors of Andrew Anderson – Printers to the Queen's most excellent Majesty – City and Colledge'.

25 According to the 'Postman' in the *Edinburgh Courant,* the Marquis of Annandale had been sent a Commission to be President of the Privy Council.

26 It was probably during those hours at Newbattle that Argyll replied to a letter which had come from Ann, Duchess of Hamilton:

> *October* 8th
> His Grace received a letter from her Ma'dam in relation to the lodgings her Ma'dam has been pleased to offer me in the Abbey of Holyrood. I hope your Grace will be pleased to give your orders in the approved form that they may be delivered to me or whom I shall appoynt to receive them.

27 *Edinburgh Courant.* The announcement appeared in the 'Postman's Log' in the last issue of an edition which ran from June until 8 October.

28 Acts passed during the session:
    (1) Discharging importation of English, Irish, and foreign butter.
    (2) Advancing fishing trade in and about the kingdom.
    (3) Appointing a council of trade.
    (4) For treaty with England.
    (5) Encouraging export of beef and pork.
    (6) Declaring linen and woollen manufactures free of duty for export.
    (7) Supply of seven months' cess out of land rent.
    (8) In favour of town of Glasgow for imposition of two pennies on pint of ale and beer.

Chapter VII

1 *Edinburgh Courant* – the 'Postman's Log'.

2 Alexander Cunningham in his *History of Great Britain.* Similar words were used by Sir John Clerk of Penicuik who wrote in his *Memoirs* – 'John, Duke of Argyle, as Her Majesty's Commissioner, behaved himself in a manner far above what could be Expected from one of his years.'

3 According to Cunningham, 'he took a great delight in being attended by a number of swordsmen whom he retained for that purpose'.

4 *The Observateur,* in the edition that ran from Wednesday 24 October to 27 October reported – 'The Earl of Peterborough – he has got the possession of Barcelona and consequently of the province of Catalonia.'

5 Spain became the second theatre of operations. The objective was the restoration of the Spanish Crown to Arch-Duke Charles of Austria.

6 Lockhart.

7 Lord Wharton, a recent Hanoverian convert, proposed the measure. Lord Somers, the eminent Whig constitutionalist, afterwards translated it into terms of law.

8 Until relinquished by the Queen's consent.

9 Extract from a letter that he had addressed to the Queen.

10 Yet only a few weeks before, the Countess of Orkney in a letter to the Duchess of Atholl 'regrets that she cannot use her influence to recover the lodgings in the Abbey formerly used by Atholl as these are now being claimed by Argyle.'

11 According to Lockhart: 'And the Queen refusing to name the Duke of Hamilton as he [the Duke of Argyle] had promised, he resented it so far that he would not suffer himself to be named, and even threatened, at that time, to oppose the Union upon that account, though ways and meanes were fallen upon afterwards, to induce him to alter his mind.'

12 In sequel to this letter, Colonel Hooke reported the contents to Monsieur de Torcy:

2nd *Fevrier* 1706

Par l'ordinance d'Hollande, j'ay reçu deux lettres d'Ecosse. L'une de 29 Decembre est de Mr Hall que me mande que le Duc d'Argyle commandera les troupes que les enemys envoyent en Catalonia. Le Duc a demandé a n'être plus employé dans les affaires, et qu'on le laisse suivre le metier de la guerre, qui est plus de son gout. On lui donne huit regiments, dont trois partiront d'Irlande, trois d'Angleterre, et deux regimens Ecossais d'Holande. Mes lettres d'Irlande sont ceux de milord Dungannon, de milord Inchiguin, et de milord Mohun; celui de milord Windsor est du nombre de ceux qui sont commandé en Angleterre; on ne me nomme pas les deux autres. La Reine Anne va lever sept nouveau regimens.

PART TWO

Warrior — Statesman

Chapter I

CAMPAIGN — RAMILLIES

ONLY one with the military profession in his blood could understand the feelings that possessed Argyll when he sailed for the Continent and war. Liberated from a way of life which he disliked because of its falsities and insincerities, there would come revival of the finer side of his nature: the gay, open-hearted, intrepid spirit flashing courage and championship of his fellow-men. It was this side that endeared him to the soldiers who regarded him as a comrade rather than commander.

In this regained mood, he must have known an additional satisfaction: the fact of 'escape' from men ignobly engaged either in gossip or dispute for place in the Council Chamber. Report doubtless reached him of the 'noise' which prevailed among the Scots' leaders as the hours of 12 April and the opening of the Treaty talks approached. It no longer mattered, nor the fact that his name was still associated with intrigue[1]. Of far greater consequence was the forthcoming campaign and where the stage would be set.

For Marlborough – Captain-General – upon whom the decision rested, it was a critical moment. Unless he could achieve another Blenheim, the Grand Alliance was doomed and the might of France restored. In the dismal view of two years gone without advance towards reconquest of the Netherlands, the exaltation of 1703 had departed from the minds of the Allied rulers. Instead, they were governed by a sense of depression and stagnation. The outward effect was dissatisfaction with Marlborough. On the other hand, France's prestige, diminished since her defeat on the Danube, was in the ascendant. Among the generals and troops, morale, never wholly dead, had strengthened. They believed that Marlborough's power was near an end.

Confronted by this situation, the Captain-General planned his campaign to be beside Prince Eugene in Italy. Circumstances, however, intervened and he found himself forced to abandon the scheme. The only alternative was return to that quarter which had hitherto proved so barren of success. A despondent humour claimed him when, in the early days of May, he directed the armies of the Grand Alliance towards the Netherlands frontier. There seemed no likelihood of anything spectacular in that region. It would merely mean the renewal of a defensive to hold a zone of vital strategical importance.

Since his return to the Continent, the Duke of Argyll, appointed Brigadier-General in the British army,[2] had been commanding the Scots Brigade in the service of the States-General. They were among those forces that marched with Marlborough, and, as fortune ordained, to the event which caused the bells of Westminster to ring out again in applause of victory.

In the dawn of Whit Sunday – 23 May – the Allies saw through the mists lifting off the plateau near Ramillies[3] the army of France – sixty thousand strong. Their Commander, Marshal Villeroy, had decided to launch an offensive which, as he confidently believed, would avenge Blenheim. For Marlborough it was an act of Providence. His old resolution, dimmed by adversities, returned; so too his defiance.

The battle which bequeathed so valuable a legacy to the Alliance[4] was virtually won in the southern sector of the field where the open nature of the ground favoured cavalry manoeuvres[5]. There, the main Allied strength belonged to the States-General army of General Overkirk: the Duke of Argyll came under his command. According to a bulletin issued, by authority, from St James's on 26/27 May[6]: 'The Duke of Argyle's regiment was a British regiment in Dutch pay and was in the left brigade but one in the Allied Order of Battle.'

Posted in a key position just to the south of Ramillies, the Scots formed part of the infantry forces that the Dutch General led to the assault when the village became the last stronghold of defence for the enemy and the final obstacle in the path of victory for the Allies. According to eye-witnesses who left records, the most violent fighting of the day occurred among the narrow streets and byways thronged by the Swiss and French defenders with their cannon.[7] In those moments when the struggle was at its height, the Duke of Argyll, as Brigadier of the Scottish Infantry, displayed a signal act of valour. In the words of the French Colonel La Colonie: 'The Duke was himself the second or third man who, with his sword in his hand, broke over the enemy's trenches and chased them out of the village of Ramillies.'

The Earl of Mar wrote: 'I heartily congratulate with Your Grace upon account of the glorious victorie ye have had and the consequence of it, and the great pairt Your Grace had in it. We hope that it is so intyre [entire] that their armie will not again this campaign at least offer to give you any resistance.'

His letter, which took nearly two months to reach the Duke, continued:

> Our Treattie advances very well, in a little time I hope will come to a good conclusion.[8]
>
> Your Grace's friends here think on the theme of the Treattie that it wou'd be for your own interest and the advantage of carrying the Treattie throw in our Parliament which is all our interest as it is the nations in general, that Your Grace wou'd be pleased now to make an end of your campaign in Flanders and come home and serve with the rest of your friends in another where you will get more action tho' of another nature. Your Grace may be sure we wish it upon our own accounts, but because several of our friends with whom I've talk't realise that it is for your own interest too, and I wish with all my heart that Your Grace may be of our opinion. This day the Chancellor, Loudoun, Glasgow, and I spoke of it by the Treasurer who approves of it and said he wou'd wright [write] of it to the Duke of Marlborough. I am certain your coming wou'd be the surest way for Your Grace to obtain anything you want for yourself and your friends. And then consider of what great consequence it wou'd be to the affairs we have to do in which I doubt not but Your Grace is singularly concerned. I believe Your Grace will find more of your friends of this opinion and I intend you wou'd be pleased to think of it and be of the same mind with us. If I were not concerned upon our account I shou'd not be so earnest with you, not since it is my regard for Your Grace and your interest, I hope you'll pardon this freedome.

The aftermath of Ramillies was swift pursuit of the enemy, succeeded by a campaign dedicated to siege operations against the strongholds of Ostend, Dendermonde, Menin and Art.[9]

Five British regiments and a force of Dutch troops were detached from the main Army to besiege Ostend. Argyll was their commander, and again he won distinction both for himself and his

G

brigade. After the town's surrender, there followed an interval when he found himself in camp at St Louis le Père. Then it became possible to deal with correspondence.[10]

On 18 July, he replied to the Earl of Mar's communication:

> I should have received your letter before Ostend, but as it is I had it only this morning. I am extremely sorry that all my friends should desire me to doe what for aught I can as yet see I shall not be able to comply with. My Lord, it is surprising to me that my Lord Treasurer who is a man of sense, should think of sending me up and down like a postman from one country to another without even offering me any reward. Thier [There] is indeed a seartin [certain] service due from every subject to his Prince, and that I shall pay the Queen so faithfully as any body can doe; but if her Ministers think it for her service to imploy me any farder [further] I doe think the proposal should be attended with an offer of a reward. But I am so far from being treated in this manner that I cannot obtain justice even in the army where I doe flatter myselfe I have dun [done] the Queen so much service to say no more, as any body in my station. My Lord, when I have justice dun me here and am told what to expect for going to Scotland, I shall be reddy to obey my Lord Treasurer's commands. Till then I hope my friends will think it fitt I stay here unless I have sumbody putt over my head, and in that case I shall lett my Lord Marlboro' give my post to sumbody who chances to be more to his mind, which will be a very noble reward for my service, and I'll goe and play Camilla in her own country.

While Argyll was writing this letter, the Union Talks were near an honourable conclusion. A few days hence (22 July), Chancellor Seafield and Lord Keeper Cowper would lead their respective Commissions in procession through Westminster Hall to present Her Majesty with a document that represented the constitutional triumph of her reign.

Meanwhile, in Flanders the next stage of siege warfare was being set by bringing up military forces and cannon in vessels to Courtray. On accomplishment of this operation, Marlborough extended the left wing of his camp towards Menin where six thousand French troops composed the garrison, and sent a detachment there under the Duke of Argyll's command. As one of the leaders of the storming-party responsible for the capture of a key counter-scarp, the warrior Duke showed himself 'more like a young subaltern than a great statesman on whom so largely rested the burden of guiding the Union Treaty through two Parliaments.'[11]

Menin capitulated towards the end of August. Soon afterwards Lord Stair, writing to the Earl of Mar, stated: 'The Duke of Marlborough seems resolved to do everything to gratify the Duke of Argyle who has indeed acquired a great deal of honour in the campaign. He seems resolved to gratify him in his pretensions of being Major-General and having the first English regiment.'

In sequel to this report, the Lord Treasurer Godolphin wrote on 17 September to Robert Harley: 'I hear the Duke of Argyle will be here [London] to-morrow, I find by the Duke of Marlborough's to me he will expect the commission of Major-General should be ready for him, and perhaps other things which will not be ready for him. The Duke of Marlborough writes also that these new commissions must all bear date from the day of the battle of Ramillies.'[12]

On that same day, Sir David Nairn informed the Earl of Mar: 'His Lordship [Treasurer] also told me that the Duke of Argyle was made Major-General and was to come over and goe to Scotland presently, and since my comeing to town, I hear his Grace came hither last night.'

To this letter the Earl of Mar replied:

I'm very glad the Court has done these things for the Duke of Argyle which he desired and I hope he'll come down here in good humor. It falls well out that he's to come for some of his people were beginning to talk pretty oddly of our affairs and we were afraid of some difficulty in getting them manadged, so we were thinking of writing to you to speak to friends to get them wrote to. Since the Duke is now comeing himself there will, I hope, be no need of it.

If the Duke of Argyle be yet with you, pray give him my most humble service.[13]

To Argyll has been attributed an ambition so boundless as to over-rule his greater qualities. Is it not natural, however, for a man, young, of splendid appearance, noble birth, and gifted with brilliant abilities, ever to desire foremost place in the race for power? That Argyll was ambitious for his own advancement could not be denied. At the same time, he had a loyalty which outweighed personal sentiments. The Monarch always claimed his actions and thoughts.

'I shall make my own inclinations give way to the duty I owe and ever shall pay Her Majesty in whatever conditions I am and though I give Her Majesty no assurances of success shall do what I can towards obtaining it.'

In that spirit he returned to stand beside the men who could not do without his leadership in the final phase of the march to Union.

Chapter II

'TO PLAY CAMILLA IN HER OWN COUNTRY'

REPORT that he had been killed at the siege of Menin, coupled with account of his exploits, caused Argyll to be acclaimed with much honour on his appearance at St James's towards the middle of September. Yet the prospect of 'playing Camilla' did not give him enthusiasm. On this occasion, he would not be Commissioner. The Duke of Queensberry now held that office.

After ten days in London he was ready to depart for the north. As a kinsman – David Campbell – stated in a letter written on 28 September to the Earl of Mar: 'The Duke of Argyle has desired me to write to say that he leaves for Scotland on Monday, and will be with you in a fortnight. If the Parliament could be put off by adjournments till his arrival to shaw [show] his inclinations and us his interest for so good a cause under the caire of his best friends, it will be most acceptable.'

While the Duke travelled the Great North Road, the Earl of Mar was engaged in correspondence of a speculative character. To the Lord-Treasurer he wrote on 8 October: 'When my Lord Argyle comes here I hope He'll join cordially with us and then we are sure of succeeding, but his brother is just now in such a humor that if he shou'd influence the Duke it may give us trouble. But I hope the Duke is wiser, tho' if it shou'd happen otherways I hope we shall carry the grand affair notwithstanding.'

That same day the Earl also sent word to Sir David Nairn in London: 'If the Duke of Argyle and his people be right we have nothing to fear, and I hope they will be so upon their own account, the grand affair, and our own. But if unluckily they shou'd chance to be otherwise I do not . . . our succeeding.'

Five days later – 13 October – the Earl of Mar informed Sir David Nairn:

The Duke of Argyle came here on Thursday. His brother had made him angry with us all, but when we mett him and reason'd what he had to say, it was quickly over and now he is in very good temper and he and all his people will concur heartily. He is very desireous to have his brother made a peer of Scotland and made us all promise to write to the Treasurer of it which I have done. We represented to him that the Queen wou'd have difficulty of doing it at this time, betwixt the Treaty's being concluded and the Union not yet perfected by us and that she had refused severalls on that account. But he insisted and I must acknowledge not without reason, for his being a peer of England himself, he will not have a vote in choosing his peers for Scotland who are to sit in the Parliament of Britain, and it's fit for him to have one of his family to take [care] of his interests here in that case. Besides if it be done it will put him in good humor, and satisfy him at least until Parliament is over, so consequently strengthen our hands, whereas if it be refused it will have quite other effects.[1]

The Duke found the citizens of Edinburgh charged with an animosity ready to declare itself in revolt. On the eve of a Parliament likely to ratify the Treaty, rumour circulated that its terms, hitherto unpublished, favoured an 'incorporating' Union and not a Federation as had been commonly believed.[2] If this proved correct, then the Scots Commissioners had made only a pretence of patriotism and were to be branded, together with everyone else who went by the title of 'Unionist', as traitors. That ugly word arose from the populace as Argyll's equipage passed on its way. There was no sign of the welcome due to him as a hero of the war.

Parliament opened in its traditional manner with a message from the Queen and a speech by the Commissioner – the Duke of Queensberry. On this occasion, the slogan was Union's value and an urge to uphold the Treaty. Then, after the Articles of Union had been read, order was given for records relating to past treaties to be laid open for inspection. This served a useful purpose by reminding members of the truth that Scotland's existing structure did not provide the system of internal liberty vital to a nation's security. Except for the fact of her own Parliament and Privy Council, she was bound to the English ministry.[3] Nor could she enjoy full benefits of the commerce which went England's way, and in an era beginning to witness the birth of international trade, and that was a serious handicap to her economic growth. Thus, the latest Treaty demanded support. The day had arrived when, for the future interests of Scotland, her fate must be finally sealed, either to advance in absolute unity with England or be totally free. There could be no 'half-way house'.

Despite their hostility to Queensberry's regime, they had at last become awake to Scotland's position were Union to be rejected. She must become an open door for enemies to enter and threaten her most precious heritage – the Presbyterian establishment. England's intervention would inevitably follow, and then the Scotsman could not hope for a voice in Government. Therefore it was best to vote for the cause of a Scotland and England joined as Great Britain, to defy all trespassers upon traditions of religion and custom. Their points of view were expressed in pamphlet form[4] with great effect to the Presbyterian clergy who kept silent while the rest of Scotland clashed in argument.

From the moment that the Estates settled to discuss the Treaty, clause by clause, there was evidence of the ultimate end. Queensberry's skilled diplomacy, Argyll's energy working in alliance with the shrewd counsel of his brother,[5] and the Squadrone's resolve to support the Union cause, were assets too powerful for resistance by an Opposition whose leaders – Hamilton and Atholl – did not enter whole-heartedly into the fight. Nevertheless, heated disputes would result in Sessions lasting many hours.

The first of a series of lengthy debates came on Wednesday, 23 October, when the Duke of Hamilton urged the printing of an English book of rules and English acts relating to the regulations of trade. After prolonged discussion, it was resolved to nominate a Committee to examine calculation of the equivalent[6] and the Duke of Argyll was appointed a member.[7]

Meanwhile, in the streets of Edinburgh, the clamour against Union and all its promoters grew more intense and mob hostility increased to violence.

'If one stone had been thrown at us there had been five hundred and some of the mob were heard to say after we had passed the Cross that they were to blame for letting Argyle and Loudoun pass unpunished.' Thus wrote the Earl of Mar to Sir David Nairn on 26 October.

During that last week of October, the situation became serious. Revolt too turbulent for the City Guard to restrain broke in earnest. The rioters surrounded Parliament House and stormed its bolted doors. It was an hour that demanded drastic action on the part of the Government. They had their man for the purpose. 'His Grace the Duke of Argyle, mounted at the head of the Horse Guards, and the Troops, occupied the High Street and Parliament Close in military form.'

The action brought protest from the Opposition. 'To impose a show of force so that the Debates might not be hindered marked the Government as tyrants ready for any measures, however arbitrary, in order to carry the "grand affair".'[8]

There was no need to make an issue of the challenge. The rebellious attitude of the crowd who continued to throng Parliament's neighbourhood and would have got completely beyond control but for military presence convinced every sane-minded person that extreme security precautions were justified.

During those days of tense national feelings only one man could enter or leave Parliament without fear of molestation. Indeed the cheers of the mob rang loud whenever he appeared. The Duke of Hamilton emerged as the possible champion of Scotland restored to full sovereign rights.[9]

His role before the Estates had always been that of the 'patriot Duke' who upheld the cause of Scotland's crown on the head of her own monarch.[10] At a recent debate on the resolve that 'The House proceed to take the first article of the Treaty into consideration' he had spoken with such pathos as to bring tears to the eyes of many of his audience.

What – shall we in half-an-hour give up what our forefathers maintained with their lives and fortunes for many ages? Are there none of the descendants of those worthy patriots who defended the liberty of their council against all invaders, who assisted the great king Robert Bruce to restore the Constitution and revenge the falsehood of England and the usurpation of Balliol? Where are the Douglasses and Campbells? Where are the peers, where are the barons, once the bulwark of the Nation?

Surely this speech indicated that he would take the initiative of rescuing Scotland from the frontier she was about to cross?

Thus citizens questioned and waited upon his action. It did not come. Perhaps out of interest for himself, or lack of enthusiasm for the Pretender's claim, or even foresight that Union might, after all, be the wisest course, he remained silent.

The state of revolt was not confined to Edinburgh. Glasgow witnessed riots between the rabble of the community and the merchants who were enthusiastic for Union because of its value to their growing commerce. In Covenanting districts anti-Unionists collided over the two questions which inevitably made fanatics of men; the Kirk and the Jacobite cause. Elsewhere, groups of people met to compose addresses either for or against Union, and send these to Parliament where argument also prevailed.

On the day of 5 November, when the Treaty articles were being considered, Andrew Fletcher arose and vehemently declared that the 'Commissioners had betrayed their trust'. According to a parliamentary report on this occasion: 'Hamilton, Atholl and Belhaven endeavoured to justify or extenuate him. Argyle, having said much to advantage of the Treaters and much against Mr. Fletcher's expressions, owned he had a relation to him and an old friendship for him and wished the House would accept of his submission and that he would not trouble the House as he had too often done before, and the House agreed to it.'

At that time, Argyll's office might be aptly termed one of 'Chief Whip'. The role admirably suited the Duke's capacity for drive and firmness. The proof that he was playing it well came in a letter dated 1 November and addressed by Sir David Nairn to the Earl of Mar. 'George Dalrymple gives me account of proceedings some time. In his last he says: "I hope the Union will doe and if it shou'd it will be chiefly owing to the Duke of Argyle".'

Although Union's supporters encountered strong opposition, there was confidence among them. As Lord Islay wrote in a letter to his uncle, Lord Dysart:

> . . . there appears to be so great a majority who think it the only interest of this nation, that I think in all human probability it cannot fail to pass tho' not without severall alterations in the Articles . . . The only handle the opposing party has left to defeat the Union by, is to endeavour to crowd into the Articles some unreasonable amendments which may throw out the Union to the Parliament of England.

As the debates drew to a climax, it became clear that the Government would triumph. Apart from the Squadrone who abided by their decision to support Union, each party counted a small majority in the Treaty's favour.

The final votes were cast in January and by the end of that month Scotland's destiny was decreed.

At about this time, Argyll addressed a letter to the Duke of Marlborough.

Edinburgh – 7th January, 1707
From the Duke of Argyle to the Duke of Marlborough.
My Lord Duke,

I beg leave to joyn with my Lord Commissioner and the two Secretarys in recommending Brigadier George Hamilton to your Grace's favour. We think it would be recommendation to the States if Her Majesty would be pleased to give him a Major-General's Commission which we humbly think can no ways interfere with the Generall Officers of Her Majesty's forces, he being settled in another service. I can't tell if the Brigadier has the happiness to be well known to Your Grace but if he were I dare say he would need no recommendation. I assure Your Grace he has been very serviceable to Her Majesty here in the great affair of the Union by using his interest with some relations of his in Parliament who always oppos'd the Queen's measures till he came hither.

I beg pardon for giving Your Grace this trouble and am
With great Respect My Lord
Your Grace's Most obedient and most humble servant

Argyle

During the last days of the Session 'The Duke of Argyle gott in an Act for the expenses of the 1,000 pounds paid to each nobleman, 500 to each . . . [illegible] . . . and their Clerks and accomptants, amounting to about 3,000 p.s. payable with the Equivalent . . . will be first of the English publick debt.'

To complete the business of what was destined to be Scotland's last Parliament, the question of electing a representative body of peers to sit in the English House of Lords was discussed.

The moment did not find Argyll in the best of humours. Things had occurred to annoy him. He could not long tolerate the argument and intrigue always so rife among his fellow-politicians. Accordingly, on 1 February he left Edinburgh for London.

That same day, the Earl of Mar informed Sir David Nairn:

The Duke of Argyle went away to-day & I'm afraid he's not in good humour with any of us as you'll soon see when he comes to London. He has put himself so much in his mother's and brother's hands that they turn him against us when they will upon their own views. Tho' he seems not pleased with us he is with nobody else, which is a great comfort.

When he comes to London, he'll take the wholle praise of the carrying the Union to himself. He did his part very well indeed but that he was the only doer of it nobody can aver for 'tis known that our business was all lay'd and well begun before he came. He now pretends that tho' as one English peer he has priviledge to sit in the House of Lords, yet after the Union he can elect the sixteen peers from Scotland and grants that any Scots peers who, after the Union, are made peers of Britain, cannot.

This to me, I confess, looks pretty odd for since he cannot be elected I know not how he can elect.

However, he takes this very high and told the Commissioner last night that if it went against him in the House he would either be an English Duke before Union or quit the Queen's services; and by this he would after the Union have the place of Commissioner or the Duke of Hamilton tho' the Queen were pleased to give her priviledge of sitting always in the House of Lords. This would be very hard on them, and I'm sure not for the Duke of Argyle's interest to bring such an odium upon himself and family since they have the place of him now. What would this signify to the Duke for after Union he's a Duke of Britain however. I fear this part will go against him in the House. If so he'll certainly be at the Queen to be made an English Duke before Union.

One reason for the Duke's anger is that the Commissioner and some of us would not concent a list of the sixteen peers to be chosen for the first Parliament of Britain and go soon into the election, and there seclude the Squadrone or a part of them. That we could by no means agree to for it would certainly break us all entirely either with the Squadrone or the Duke of Argyle or perhaps with them both or others of our friends . . .

Some days later, the Earl had more to tell Sir David: 'I received the order you sent me under the Queen's hand for delivering to Argyle that gun which belonged to his family and is in Edinburgh Castle. I told my Lord Hay of it, the Duke being gone. He said he would write to his brother of it but he believed he would not take that order until he saw how the Queen determined his other pretension. I'll long to hear from you what humour Argyle is in when he comes to London, and what accompt he gives of our affairs here.'

In reference to the election of the sixteen peers, he had this to say: 'The Duke of Argyle asks to have in the sixteen, three which with the other five of the Squadrone, makes eight. He told us that if we nam'd Marchmont he would take it very ill and neither he nor his friends could join with us.'

On 13 February, Mar sent a further letter to Sir David Nairn:
'The day appointed for Parliament to make elections of those to
serve in the Parliament of Great Britain. The Duke of Argyle is
earnest to have Lord Lothian and the Earl Hay so these two there
was a necessity of naming. He was desireous of Sutherland too . . .'

What of Argyll? While these communications were being written
he was enduring the rigours of winter on the Great North Road.
Conditions made it impossible for him to continue by coach. He was
forced to take to horseback, strap his travelling cloak around him
and ride headling into the biting wind which drove the snow full
into his face.

PARLIAMENT OF GREAT BRITAIN – 1707

The Duke of Argyll met the London world as Baron Chatham and
Earl of Greenwich and a Major-General in the British army. Then
in the month of March came a further reward.

> The Parliament of Great Britain ratified in favour of John, Duke
> of Argyle, a gift approving his rights of Office as Great Master of
> the Household within this Kingdom.

On the threshold of a new political era, Scotland's representative
peers manifested the desire to apply themselves zealously to the task
of consolidating the Union's structures so that mutual benefits might
emerge. Argyll gave his blessing to this sentiment. It was precisely
the doctrine which he had preached with such heat throughout the
Union struggle.

Consequently, when the first Parliament of Great Britain
assembled in autumn they lost no time in giving effect to their
resolution for future relations along sound constitutional lines. The
first step should be the abolition of Scotland's most unpopular
institution – the Edinburgh Privy Council.[11] It had never been a
source of national pride as sessions were held in secret and often
produced decisions of a despotic character.[12] For all save Godolphin
and his ministry to whom it might serve as an instrument of power
outside the sphere of Parliament, its disappearance would be
welcome.

The Squadrone, backed by Argyll, took the initiative, through
persuading the English Whigs and Tories to support their resolution
for an Act to abolish the Scottish Privy Council.

Despite the distance between the capitals and the rigours of travel in the winter season, report of this event travelled fast over the border and evoked a reaction of gossip. As illustration, there is a letter dated 23 November, written by Lord Grange in Edinburgh to the Earl of Mar.[13] Referring to the talk of the people, he states: '. . . they talk a while that the Dukes of Argyle, Montrose and Roxburgh are forming a sort of triumvirate to head the Squadrone, and of great alterations to be made in our Session, particular[ly] that we are to be divided and such a number of us sent to Aberdeen, as many to Glasgow.'

From that hour, the couriers of noblemen were employed carrying accounts of the progress at Westminster to their masters in the north. In evidence, a letter with Edinburgh as the address went to the Duke of Atholl on 5 December. Its author was a kinsman – Sir James Murray. After alluding to the 'Debate in continuance of the abolition of the Scots Privy Council, opened in the House of Commons by Jerviswood and backed by the Squadrone' Sir James continued: 'Both the English and Scots Courtiers[14] opposed the takeing away the Scots Privy Council with all their might. The Scots' members kept up the debate pro and con for three hours, and there was fourteen that spoke and after they gave it over, the English continued the debate for two hours longer before they went to the House. It was not known what party would carry, however the Squadrone carried six to one which occasioned a great buzz. Argyle, Montrose and Roxburgh, who are of a side, were watching that event from the gallery.'

Later in December, the Duke of Atholl received a further report on developments. The writer of this letter was John Flemyng: 'Since my last I am told that after the Squadrone had made use of my Lord Argyle, and Montrose who is for taking away the Council, settling the Militia and Justices of Peace, they proposed the takeing away the Superiorities, this did very much supprize them and 'tis now said that Argyle and all his friends in the House of Commons are gone over to the Court Party . . .'

The report was correct. The Duke of Argyll, who had so firmly advocated abrogation of the Scots Privy Council, suddenly took an opposite direction. According to a historian of the period[15]: 'The Duke of Argyle, for the sake of an office of jurisdiction, and fear of losing somewhat of his right, drew back from the concerted enterprise and went over to the Court Party.'

Although he had a reputation for unpredictable moods, this action gave rise to surprise as well as criticism. To quote the same

S'Madam — London: 21th Feb': 17[...]

Upon the first day of Apriell ni[...]
pay to John Campbell or order fiv[...]
hundered pounds sterling with int[...]
est for scid soum from the thirtin[...]
day of febuary [...] valuo reuved
and place the same to my
accourent. J am

To her Grace
The Dutches
of Argyll

Your Graces Duttyfull
and most obediant
sorin.

accept to pay
acct of my hand
Argyll
Argyll

Facsimile of letter written by John, 2nd Duke of Argyll, to his mother, the
Dowager-Duchess

historian: 'Though the Duke of Argyle well knew the unjustifiable proceedings of the Privy Council of Scotland, and how many times their hands had been stained with the blood of his ancestors, yet lest the abrogation thereto should prejudice his own offices and nor that any man should give up his own rights for nothing; he showed also, with great learning, that their jurisdictions were secured both by old and new laws, and weighed firmly against justices of the peace. The Earl of Islay agreed in opinion with the Duke'.

Whether these are accurate reasons for his withdrawal, or merely based upon supposition, must be left open to question. Or could he have been influenced by his brother's political craft?

The change of side did not affect the final issue. Victory went to the Squadrone and their partisans. The Act for Abrogation became law.

In this day of new-conceived relations, Argyll, as Captain of the Horse Guards in Scotland, arranged that the troops who had preserved order during the critical days of Scotland's last Parliament should receive a recognition. He procured orders for bringing them to London to attend, in their turn, at court. The fact that their uniforms had silver trimming, whereas those of the English Guards were trimmed with gold, immediately sparked malicious comment.[16]

The forces of jealousy were always at Argyll's back, using every opportunity to belittle him. The truth was that he had a passion for independence of action and the tradition of his native land, even when it affected clothing. The silver lace of Scotland's Horse Guards was a pride to them and also to him as their Commander.

Chapter III

CAMPAIGN: OUDENARDE, LILLE, GHENT — 1708

As Colonel of the 3rd Foot – 'Buffs'[1] – the Duke of Argyll found himself with Marlborough's forces in the midsummer of 1708.

For the Captain-General this was one of the most critical periods in his career. The failure to continue his victorious march of the Ramillies year had made a disappointing impression upon the leaders of the Alliance. At home, the breach in his relations with the court was widening, and an element of indifference in the Whig tone towards the war disturbed him. On the Continent the mainspring of his trouble lay in Belgium, exposed to dangers both political and military. His only hope to outride these adverse weathers was to gain a brilliant success which would renew confidence among the Allies and restore him to the height of honour in Great Britain.

There were two bright lights on his horizon: the presence of Prince Eugene[2] and signs of discord between the two French Commanders – Vendôme and the Duke of Burgundy. The former afforded an extra strength to his forces; the latter predicted a weakness that might be turned to good account. The vital issue was how to contrive an action which would be of advantage to himself and satisfy the Dutch generals[3]. He realized that the enemy's morale had received stimulus through the recent capture of the fortresses of Ghent and Bruges. Vendôme and Burgundy marched as victors; but personal animosities produced argument and caused them to fall into the abyss of indecision. Burgundy desired the investment of another strategically-placed fortress and chose Menin. Vendôme was emphatic for a move on Oudenarde with its fort and bridges which were held by the Allies. Because he was the more experienced Commander, his advice ruled. It would be Oudenarde, and this time France must triumph. In this elated mood they took the direction most favourable to Marlborough's tactics.

During the late afternoon of 11 July, the armies of France and

Great Britain encountered in a region of varied character and offering scope for a widely extended front.

As with Ramillies, the only part of the battle relevant to these pages is that in which the Duke of Argyll figures.

The 'Buffs' under Eugene's command[4] had their position in the right-wing sector where, over ground enclosed by small plantations and woodlands,[5] the most violent shock of the fighting was to fall. The Duke 'commanded twenty battalions of infantry which were the first foot regiments to engage the enemy'. According to report, his display of bravery excited a 'spirit of emulation among the troops under his orders and paved the way to victory'.

During those moments when the French assault was at its zenith, the body of the Prussians became disordered. In sequel, for some considerable time a mere handful of men long maintained their ground against a great number of the enemy.

While they were thus unequally engaged, the Duke of Argyle came up very seasonably to their rescue with twenty battalions. The Duke, relieving those tired soldiers with fresh recruits, renewed the fight and repulsed the foremost of the Enemy with prodigious slaughter. The Enemy, being yet much superior in number, thought to fall upon the Confederates on the open flank and at the same time to surround them behind, and returned again to the fight. Argyle received them with firmness and drove them back again into the neighbouring hedges. The small number of his own Forces and the apprehension of an ambuscade hindered him for pursuing them further, or forcing his way through the inclosures. Here the Duke maintained a long and bloody fight both in front and flank till Count Lottum – the Prussian General – arrived and posted his fresh troops on a vaccent [vacant] space on the left of Argyle.

Marlborough observed this and foreseeing that the fight could be hard on the right wing, ordered a reinforcement of twenty battalions to be sent from the left wing to support the men on the right. On this, Argyle and Count Lottum fell furiously upon the enemy with all their forces on the right and the left wing, having passed the river [Scheldt] began now, about seven o'clock, to joint themselves in order of battle.[6]

The conflict became more intense as the evening light faded. It was a last stupendous effort with both sides to attain a supreme climax. They might have succeeded had nightfall not put an end to

H

hostilities. By that time, however, there could be no doubt of the result. Vendôme's forces were in confusion.

Oudenarde was a battle which belonged pre-eminently to the Infantry. It must have been a great pride to Argyll and the captains of the other Foot regiments to know that they were largely responsible for the victory that enabled Marlborough to announce: 'We are now masters of marching where we please, but can make no siege till we are masters of Ghent.'

The arrival of Eugene's army reinforced the Allies and increased the sense of exultation which Oudenarde had inspired. The hope was for an onward march, although they knew that an army equally strong in numbers yet not so well ordered would be at their back. The way which most appealed to Marlborough was an advance on Paris, taking control of the sea-ports as they went so that supply communications with England might lie open. Eugene opposed this plan as being far too bold an enterprise, and Marlborough allowed himself to be dissuaded. Consequently, the objective became Lille, one of France's principal cities with a fortress regarded as the finest example of Vauban's fortification skill. The garrison counted a strength of sixteen thousand men under the command of that superb engineer and valiant soldier – Marshal Boufflers. He had an additional advantage of being supported from outside by the forces of Vendôme and Marshal Berwick. To besiege so formidable a citadel not merely presented a colossal task, but demanded intrepid commanders. Indeed, it would be the greatest and undoubtedly the most severe undertaking that the war had yet produced.

While Marlborough took charge of the enormous covering operations Eugene commanded the siege. The 'Buffs' and five other British regiments played a conspicuous part against the odds of heavy casualties. Argyll, always to the fore with heroic exploits, was slightly wounded.

> My Lord,
> I hope this will find Your Grace well after your glorious siege, the success of which we long to hear of . . .

wrote the Earl of Mar in the middle of September. Then, however, grave crisis threatened the siege's success,[8] and it was not until the beginning of December that the tide turned in favour of the Allies.

On 9 December, Boufflers surrendered the city of Lille and retired to the citadel which he defended for six weeks, by which time starvation conditions and exhausted man-power compelled him to capitulate.

In sequel to Lille was the siege of Ghent, and there again Argyll won distinction. To quote a contemporary historian: 'After the Count de la Motte, with thirty battalions and fifteen squadrons, had marched out of Ghent towards Tournai, Argyle, with a garrison of six squadrons, took possession of both the city and citadel.'

It was 9 January, and Ghent's capture brought the campaign to an end for the remainder of the winter. It would renew in early spring.

Meanwhile, political business recalled Argyll to Westminster. Anglo-Scottish relations were seriously jeopardized by the Government's introduction of a bill for an Act of Treason to apply to Great Britain and be subject to English Law. To him, as to other patriot Scotsmen, this constituted a trespass upon the judicial independence granted under the terms of the Treaty. Therefore it must be denounced.

The Duke joined the Scottish representative peers in denunciation of so provocative a measure which could only injure the efforts to improve the Union. Their protest did not prevent the passage of the bill; but it brought amendments which temporarily appeased the deterioration of relations between the Scots people towards their English neighbours. Nevertheless, the bad feelings remained, and six years later[9] would be revived.

For Argyll the direction was back to the Continent and the spring campaign.

TOURNAI AND MALPLAQUET

With the rank of Lieutenant-General, the Duke of Argyll rejoined the 'Buffs' in time to lead them to the attack on Tournai. Although wounded during the early stage of the siege, he refused to yield to suffering and commanded the regiment in the final assault of the citadel.

By Tournai's fall, all the chief fortresses were back in Allied hands and the war on the Flanders front virtually won. Surely now the issue must be peace? That had become the universal thought both at home and in Europe. In France especially the desire for a 'cease-fire' was urgently felt. The defeats of the past year had enhanced the distress of a population gravely diminished through the severity of an exceptional winter. They could no longer endure a scene of famine in their country and immense toll of life outside. Of his own accord, Louis appointed himself their spokesman and begged the Allies for peace. The French Foreign Minister – Torcy – proceeded to the Hague for talks with leaders of the Alliance.

The trend of the conference pointed to success. Forty preliminary articles presented by the ambassadors of Great Britain, Austria and the States-General, appeared to be acceptable to Louis who gave his assent to all save the 'Thirty-Seventh': SPAIN; there lay the obstacle. He could not agree to a clause[10] compelling the deposition of his grandson – Philip – who was acknowledged king by the majority of the Spanish population[11]. Thus, his answer took the form of a positive 'no'. From the Allies came the retort that they would not contemplate peace until the question of the Spanish Monarch had been resolved after their own pattern.

So the hopes that had been aroused throughout the international world were dashed, and another round of war became the order of the day. The bloodiest battle yet to be witnessed was the result.

Malplaquet, fought in the month of September 1709, might be termed a battle of destiny for the Dukes of Argyll and Marlborough. It also gave the former opportunity for conspicuous acts of valour.

> The Duke of Argyle first led up the British Force through the woods against the enemy on the right of the main canal. After he had received the enemy's fire, he fell upon their entrenchments and cut through and overthrew them and their works together. Then, pursuing those who fled to their second entrenchment, he vanquished and drove them out of that also, and after that, pushing through the midst of the enemy and trampling down all before him, he stopped not till he came to their third entrench-ment, where he cut through them again, and bravely maintained his ground . . .[12]

Another eye-witness wrote :

> The Duke of Argyle exposed his person in such manner that he had several musket shots through his wig and clothes. It was not from an over-heated valour which runs into all places of danger merely to show a contempt of it, but that might animate the troops to imitate his example and to perform those miracles which, from their being put upon such an attack, seems to have been expected from them.

As it was, his regiment suffered the heaviest casualties.[13]

The carnage that followed the attack launched by the Allies evoked passions. These were especially strong among those officers who had disapproved of an action at Malplaquet. The Duke of

Argyll was one of them. In his view, the Captain-General, with lives of men to consider, should not have pressed an offensive. This judgement which would later become censure before Parliament marked a decisive point in their personal relations. Despite the discord[14] between them, their profession had formed its own ties, with mutual regard for one another's abilities of command. A departure from the loyalty that Argyll had always observed towards his senior contemporary widened the breach.

Meanwhile, there was the immediate aftermath of Malplaquet. The 'Buffs' proceeded to the fortress zone of Flanders for garrison duty,[15] and remained there until winter set in when they moved either to Brussels or Ghent. Then, certain officers crossed the Channel on a mission to recruit man-power and supplies for the regiment most sorely hit.[16]

The direction of their Colonel, the Duke of Argyll, was Westminster and a prominent role in the upheaval which followed the last of Marlborough's battles.

Chapter IV

REVOLT FOR PEACE

WHEN London awoke one morning to learn that the Allies had struck the first blow at Malplaquet, applause as for a victory prevailed. Throughout the day church bells pealed, guns fired salvoes of salute, and at nightfall bonfires blazed around the city. Citizens emerged from the dejection which had claimed them since collapse of the peace negotiations in spring. Once more they became patriots extolling Marlborough and looking forward to further news. According to their estimation of the Captain-General, he would not take the initiative unless confident of a decisive result. Perhaps, after all, the end of the war was in sight : the sequel to an Allied triumph must be advance on Paris.

A week or so passed with that atmosphere of jubilation predominant. Then, as September drew to a close, came reports which changed the temperature of thought. The battle, although to the advantage of the Allies, could not be termed a total success. In fighting of awful savagery their forces had suffered far heavier losses than the enemy.[1]

Faced by that truth, besides realization of the encouragement to Louis and his captains to know that a proportion of their army had survived, patriotic sentiments died. Another disappointment; the sap of discontent began to stir.

It was a moment for the Tories. An action which had caused such sacrifice of lives merely to prolong hostilities and the Captain-General's fame might be used as a weapon against the promoters of the war machine.

Meanwhile, the Whig Chiefs proclaimed a thanksgiving. To St Paul's, the Queen and her ministers went in state. 'We thank Thee all our God, With hearts and minds and voices . . .' Yet even while singing the 'Old Hundredth', they must have known that the praise was not shared in the world outside.

These autumn weeks were to prove fatal to Marlborough and

propitious to his adversaries. When he sought the Queen's prerogative to be appointed 'Captain-General for Life', public resentment against him augmented. Particularly in the army, where the anti-war faction had been gaining ground, strong exception was taken to a request which marked the Captain-General as aiming to bask permanently in his own glory. 'Perpetual Dictator!' declared the Duke of Argyll, who was supported in this opinion by many officers and all the Tory leaders.

During the closing days of 1709, two dramas were being enacted on the political stage. The first, in full view of the nation, presented a spectacle neither encouraging for peace nor the promotion of sound international relations. Marlborough and Godolphin were in collision with their colleagues to such extent that the former deemed it more prudent to leave the conduct of affairs entirely to the Lord-Treasurer. Thus Godolphin was alone to lead a ministry resolved, at all costs, to secure the Spanish Crown for the candidate of the Alliance – Austria's Imperial Prince Charles. Their policy directed them to Holland. In order to secure her support for negotiations to be re-opened with France, they offered a Treaty which, by virtue of its terms, amounted to coercion.[2]

The second, and perhaps the more thrilling drama, was being played in stealth behind the Westminster scene. The actors were few; but their plot carried a great ideal.

The Duke of Shrewsbury, an independent Whig of broad vision, had the ear of another idealist – Robert Harley. Both were patriotic enough to appreciate the accent which must be placed upon peace. In talks that led him up the back stairs of St James's Palace to the Queen's apartment, Harley engaged Her Majesty's sympathy and the aid of her new favourite – Abigail Masham. Through correspondence with the Duke of Shrewsbury, plans were laid. A third person joined them.

The Duke of Argyll decided to lend his energies to the design for a 'Middle Party' whose policies would be peace and consolidation of the Hanoverian Succession.

In this manner, Argyll entered the orbit of the Queen's favour. The fact did not escape Marlborough's vigilance.[3]

The turn of the year found national opinion strengthened in Tory favour. When the last Parliament to be held under Whig administration assembled in February, the burden of war made itself more sharply felt through increased taxation to subsist the armed forces greatly in arrears of pay and a Government heavily in debt. It would not take much to arouse a revolt for change.

As events proved, Dr Sacheverell became that agent. His impeachment by the Whigs for a sermon[4] which, they were persuaded, constituted defamation of the Revolution aims,[5] afforded an opportunity for men to raise their voices. While London crowds cheered Sacheverell and displayed vigorous animosity against his prosecutors, Parliament heard speeches of a national, rather than an individual, character.[6] In the debates, the 'rebel' noblemen who had hitherto maintained secrecy in the creation of a 'Middle Party' emerged into the open. Reflecting, as they did, the popular mood to dismiss the ministry and introduce one whose road was peace, their challenge commanded attention. Shrewsbury evoked surprise by his vote of 'Not Guilty' in the final hours of Sacheverell's trial. The Earl of Greenwich (to give Argyll the title he used in the House of Lords) caused a stir. At one point of the proceedings, he felt unable :

> To bring himself entirely to vote for an acquittal because he has very freely and openly given his opinion that the Sermon deserved censure. He thinks too that an absolute acquittal would rather tend to promote a High Tory scheme than to ruin the interest of the Junto ; besides he's afraid he should prejudice his interest in Scotland by it. However, he thinks he may fairly oppose any excessive punishment that shall be proposed and he believes the Duke of Somerset may be brought to concur with him.[7]

Then, some days afterwards, it was made known to Harley that Argyll 'had now come to a resolution to oppose all sorts of punishment that shall be proposed by the Junta'.

By this statement, the Chief of Scotland's most Whiggish clan established himself a Tory partisan.

Although the outcome of the trial[8] proved beyond doubt that the Whigs had lost the nation's support, they were still adequately strong in Parliament. Therefore, the next step of their way led to Gertruydenberg and negotiations with France.[9] Through the Dutch as intermediaries, Louis was presented with terms that rendered peace impossible and brought the Alliance into the eighth year of war.[10]

Again the troops came out from winter quarters for another campaign.

At about this time, an incident occurred to deepen Argyll's hostility to the Captain-General. He had entertained hopes of being appointed General of the Foot; but 'there were other Generals senior to him and Marlborough had all military appointments'. The Earl of Orkney was nominated.[11] So Argyll, still as Major-General, rejoined the 'Buffs'[12] to take part in the covering operations for the sieges of the fortress towns of Douai and Béthune.

Since the Sacheverell affair, rumour had been busy in Scotland with the names of Argyll and his brother as acting against the interests of their church's revolution establishment. At the beginning of July, the Earl of Islay found it necessary to write to Mr Carstares on the subject:

London, July 5th, 1710
Sir,

I have heard lately from Scotland that there are some very busy in insinuating that my brother and I are taking measures against the interest of our Church's revolution establishment.

I was always of the opinion it was very obviously our interest not to mingle ourselves too much with the factions here, I mean as Scotchmen, for it being very plain that no party here has our country much at heart, the exasperating any side here might at some conjuncture or other draw both upon us, and crush us at once.

The Queen has been pleased to remove the Earl of Sunderland and t'is said for behaving himself disrespectfully towards her, and some are so bold as to presume to censure even Her Majesty's making that step. I, for my part, think it my duty to approve of it, as I shall of any other alteration she may happen to make, and think our interest, both of Church and State, as secure under those she may employ as it has been hitherto. I write thus freely to you, that you may judge better of the matter. I flatter myself that my brother and I have not been the least zealous for the maintaining the rights of our Church, where they have been conceived, and we dare never (though there were no other reason) enter upon any other schemes; because, to speak plainly, we know very well, and and I am sur [sure] our forefathers felt it, the mercy of our enemies.

Sir, I hope, as you have occasion, you will be so kind to take our part if any of those malicious reports should reach your ears. I am glad this affair of the chaplain [Sacheverell] is so well settled to your mind, as I take a little pride to myself in having assisted in it.

I am, Sir,

Your faithful, humble servant,

Islay

First, the Earl of Sunderland dismissed by the Queen; then the Lord-Treasurer Godolphin; and the Whigs moved nearer to their downfall. In September, the climax arrived with a General Election which proved a Tory triumph. In sequel, the Duke of Shrewsbury communicated with Robert Harley (20 October): 'If you resolve to go into the country there are very many things to be settled first; the state of the House of Lords is bad and a great prospect that Argyle, Rivers, Peterborough, Jersey, and Haversham will be dissatisfied, and Nottingham and Guernsey cool, unless Her Majesty use some means to please them, which nobody can so much contribute to persuade as yourself . . .'

Soon afterwards, Her Majesty summoned the Duke of Argyll to St James's. As testimony of her appreciation for his swing to the Tory cause and enmity towards Marlborough, she intended to reward him with the Order of the Garter.

It was on the eve of Christmas that he received the Order and so become the first (ordinary) Knight of the Thistle to be thus honoured.[13] Sir James Dunbar reported to Lord Grange in a letter dated 21 December: 'To-morrow the Duke of Hanover, Duke of Devonshire, and Duke of Argyle, are to be installed Knights of the Garter at Windsor, and many of our Scots members go there (hearing it is to be the finest show that can be seen in London).'

A few days before that event, Argyll had occasion to communicate with his friend Blairhall on a subject which gave him much pleasure. His sister – Anne – was to marry the Marquis of Bute.

I received my dear Dugal's letter. I am well satisfied my sister can not dispose of herself into a family upon whose friendship I can more depend than I do upon your's, and I do assure you my Lord Bute is a young man in Scotland who I think the best turned to make a figure in the world, compliments I do not make well, for which reason I shall plainly tell you that if you please to move this matter to my mother with whose advice both my sister and myself do by inclination as we are bound in duty act if you persuade her I assure you it will be a great pleasure to me to have my Lord Bute for a brother-in-law and if it so falls out I don't question I shall have a great deal of honour by him. Pray dear Dugal believe that I am

Your most faithful humble servant

Argyle

1710

I receiv'd my Dear Dugald letter, I am
well sattyfied my Sister Can Not dispose of her
selfe into a Famely upon who's friendship I
can more depend then I doe upon yours, &
I doe assure you My Lord Bute is y⁰ young
man in Scottland who I think y⁰ Best turn'd
to make a figure in y⁰ world, Complimenty
I doe not make well, for which reason I
shall plainly tell you y⁰ if you please to
move this matter to my Mother, with whos
advice both my Sister & my Selfe doe by
inclynation, as we are bound in duty, Act,
if you perswade her, I assure you it will be
a great pleasure to me to have my Lord Bute
for a Brother in Law, & if it so falls out I don
question I shall have a great deal of Honour

London, Dec. 17th
Forgive me that you have not heard sooner from me. I could not see to write.

In sequel to his installation, the Duke was close to the Queen on 25 December: 'The Queen spent Xmas Day at St James's . . . It being a "caller day", the Queen, having recently installed the celebrated John, Duke of Argyle, at Windsor as a Knight of the Garter, he attended her in the costume of the Order.'[14]

Parliament under Tory administration had opened towards the end of November. January 1710/11 witnessed the first 'fireworks' of the Session. The scene was the House of Lords. The Duke of Argyll and the Earl of Peterborough[15] decided to launch an investigation into the disastrous trend of the war in Spain. In order to give it the flavour of a party issue, Marlborough as director of military affairs, Sunderland – the late minister – and their generals in the Peninsular – Stanhope and Galway[16] – must all receive a measure of censure.

On the 11th of January, the Peers being set, three letters from the Earl of Sunderland were delivered in, viz., one to General Stanhope of the 23rd December, 1706; another to the Earl of Galway of the same date; and the third to the said Earl, of the 27th of the same month. The order of the day being read, an officer was sent to know whether the Earl of Galway attended, and the House being informed he did not, the Earl of Poulett made a long speech wherein he represented: 'That the nation having, for many years, been engaged in an expensive war, it was necessary to give the people the satisfaction to let them know how their money had been spent, and who deserved thanks, and who to be blamed; that it appeared, the service of Spain had been very much neglected, that many officers upon that establishment looked on their employments as sinecures, being favourites of the party; and that the council held in Valencia, being the spring to all our misfortunes, the Lords ought to censure those that influenced it: . . .

Thus the second debate on the war in Spain opened.

After petitions from the Earl of Galway and Lord Tyrawley[17] had been read and discussed by the Dukes of Bedford, Buckingham and Devonshire, the Lords North and Grey, and the Earl of Rochester, the Lord Somers stated: '. . . The Lords Galway and Tyrawley had a right to be heard, and clear the matters of facts as subjects of Great Britain; that the Lords ought besides to be cautious how they proceeded in enquiries of things done before the Act of Oblivion and Indemnity; concluding it was but a natural justice, that men in danger of being censured should have time to justify themselves.'

The Duke of Argyll replied: 'He did not know what services it would do the petitioning lords to have time, and to tell the House that they differed from the House; that it had already been put to them whether they had any thing to say to that point, and that two days had been allowed them to answer the Earl of Peterborough's recapitulation; that as to the Act of Indemnity, he did not care how little use was made of it; that the said Indemnity hinders not enquiries; that the people of Great Britain ought to know to whom their misfortunes are owing; but that, however, he desired nobody should be punished.'

At a later stage of the Debate, Argyll 'desired that he might offer a question', which was readily agreed to; put by the Earl of Abingdon it took the following form: 'That it appears by the Earl of Sunderland's Letter that the carrying on the war offensively in

Spain was approved and directed by the Ministers, notwithstanding the design of attempting Toulon, which the Ministers knew at that time was concerted with the Duke of Savoy, and therefore are justly to be blamed for contributing to all our misfortunes in Spain, and to the disappointment of the Expedition against Toulon.'

At this point came a division and the Earls of Portland and Islay were appointed tellers. 'It appeared that there were 68 Lords content and 48 not content.'

After a vote of thanks to the Earl of Peterborough[18] the Duke of Argyll made a speech, importing in substance :

That he was informed that the Earl of Peterborough had the Queen's commands to negotiate matters of great importance, and was to set out the next day. That he hoped every member of that House was convinced that he had performed great and eminent services to his country, notwithstanding the difficulties and discouragements he laboured under; and how, with a handful of men – His Grace thought he might call them a handful, since they never amounted to 10,000 men – he took the important city of Barcelona, and reduced to many provinces of Spain. That he needed not tell their Lordships how he had been rewarded for those great services; but that it was his opinion they ought to pass a compliment upon him, which was all the reward they could, at that time, bestow; and therefore it was His Grace's Motion that this question be put : That the Earl of Peterborough, during the time he had the honour of commanding the Army in Spain, did perform many great and eminent services; and if the opinion he gave in the Council of War at Valencia had been followed, it might, very probably, have prevented the misfortunes that have happened in Spain.

The resolution was carried and Peterborough acknowledged as the hero of Barcelona, a marked rebuff to Marlborough and the late ministers who had been responsible for his recall. Thus both Argyll and the Earl scored victory over their principal adversaries – Marlborough and the late ministers.[19]

It did not, however, suit the reigning ministry that these two men who had brought things so boldly into the open should remain near at hand. They feared Argyll because of his persuasive speech and Whiggish principles. He refused to serve again under Marlborough. The alternative was a separate command. To Spain he would go as chief of the remaining British forces in that tragic theatre of war.

In the last days of January, a certain Thomas Bruce reported from London to Mr Justice Clerk in Scotland :

Within these two days our affairs here seem to have taken an unprecedented turn . . . The first symptom was that the Committee of the whole House was turned into a select Committee which was plainly to lessen the authority of the matter. Hitherto it has been uncertain whether the Duke of Marlborough was to go over or not, and when people observed the indignities put upon him by taking away his dutchess's key and places, it was reasonable to think he was not to go. But this day it is as good as certain that he commands for the ensuing year. And with the same breath, the Duke of Argyle goes away Ambassador and General for Spain. This, to be sure, seems ground for speculation . . .

I do not hear that the Duke of Argyle seemes anyway dissatisfied with his Command, but I find our other countrymen are somewhat uneasy.

Everything was done to encourage Argyll away from Britain's shores, as he could be a volcanic element in the politics of the hour. On 22 January, the Queen granted him a pension 'Out of the Post Office revenue for a term of ninety-nine years if Her Majesty so long live'. Parliament voted a supply of £1,500,000 for the Spanish service with £1,000 to the Duke for 'equipage expenses'. As Ambassador he would receive the remuneration of £50 weekly, and also pay as Commander-in-Chief of the British forces. Finally, he was permitted to sell his Colonelcy of the 'Buffs' who were to remain in Flanders. He disposed of it to Colonel John Selwyn for £7,000.

So there was no reason then for him to be dissatisfied with his appointment, although an independent command[20] would have been of greater value. However, the nation's service came first; in that spirit he viewed his mission to the Peninsula.

Some weeks remained before departure, and during that time destiny had a part to play in the Duke's life.

Chapter V

THE MAID OF HONOUR

AT Kensington Palace on the evening of 6 February 1711, the Duke of Shrewsbury – as Lord Chamberlain of the Household – entertained the maids of honour to dinner. Such was the custom on the Queen's birthday. One subject governed the conversation.

'They say he is very handsome and has a wit that charms.'

'I have heard on good authority that to hear him speak is like listening to rich music – such a melodious voice – and so eloquent.'

'According to Bishop Burnet he has seen most countries of Europe.'

'Yet he is a soldier more than a courtier. Some declare him to be scarcely inferior to my Lord Marlborough.'

'And now 'tis said that the cockpit of Westminster will feel his power.'

'Is it true what report says about his averseness to our sex?'

So the talk continued – always on the same theme. There was only one who did not take part in it. She listened with an attention which brought to a rather plain countenance an expression of animation.

Dinner came to an end. Then the host arose to propose 'Her Majesty the Queen' – and when the toast had been drunk he called for the 'Ladies' Toasts'. Names of bishops and generals passed around the table until it came to the turn of the young lady who had kept silence. In striking contrast to the dignity with which the others had toasted the person of their choice, she literally 'bounced up' and in a shrill voice uttered the name 'John Campbell – Duke of Argyll' – spontaneously adding – 'God bless him'.

A shout of laughter which had the ring of scorn in it greeted this breach in the traditional etiquette of toasting only a personage elderly enough to be a grandfather.

It was so typical of Jenny Warburton to make these indiscretions; thus the reaction in the minds of her colleagues, and always enjoying a jest at her expense they began a bombardment of caustic remarks.

'Oh ho – so the handsome Duke is Mistress Jane Warburton's favourite, is he?'

'Truly – you have taken care not to choose too humbly.'

'It is to be hoped that he does not know of his valuable conquest . . .' and so forth in the same manner as only a short while before they had discussed him. At length their remarks became so harshly satirical that Jane – or Jenny as she was generally known – burst into tears. Then, the Duke of Shrewsbury interposed to establish peace.

Later that evening there was a reception in the new apartment and a play with music and dancing in the ball-chamber. Among the distinguished company was one whose presence always commanded attention; but even more so this evening because he wore the Garter ribbon.

'His Grace the Duke of Argyll' –

The announcement of that name caused a stir. Everyone strained to catch a glimpse of his entry into the thronged room and during these moments the buzz of conversation was subdued. When it resumed, more animated than ever, there could be little doubt of the subject. Constant glances were cast in the direction of the man who, in general opinion, stood next to Marlborough. His exploits as a soldier had for some time been common talk in London's drawing rooms and coffee-houses. Besides, there was that remarkable personal charm which made so strong an impact upon people – even those who knew him only through hearsay. Perhaps the essence of his magnetic influence emanated from the fact that he was something of an enigma. He seldom attended society's functions. On the rare occasions, like tonight, when he appeared, it was not to mix with the company, but rather to remain aloof. Gossip asked questions. 'Why this reserve from one possessing such brilliant qualities?' 'Could there be a secret which he wished to keep hidden from the world?' Some attributed the reason to his unhappy marriage. Others were of the notion that his thoughts were dedicated to a campaigning life and elegance held no attraction. Or might it be due to his preoccupation in political affairs? Rumours were then beginning to circulate that of all Scotland's statesmen Argyll was alone endowed with the capacity of oratory. None, however, had an opportunity of penetrating the armour which he had placed between himself and them.

I

This evening was no exception. Apart from acknowledging the salutations of acquaintances, he did not join any particular group. Those who tried to draw him into conversation were unsuccessful except for a few polite words. Then he moved, always contriving to keep on the fringe of the crowd. The expression on his fair-complexioned countenance, reflecting charm as well as force, conformed to that attitude of aloofness which he had adopted since entering the palace. It could have repelled. Instead, it won him many admirers – especially among the women who discerned something intensely masculine and challenging in the tall splendid figure that maintained so remote an air. From behind fans, every movement of his was watched with an eager anticipation – surely before evening was over he must unbend to one of the young beauties present.

The Duke of Shrewsbury found his way to Argyll's side : 'My Lord, you little think what mischief you have occasioned today. A poor young lady has been shedding bitter tears on your account.' 'Upon my account? How so?' His haughty expression vanished. In its place came a lively interest. The sudden change was not missed by vigilant eyes.

Shrewsbury related the incident of the dinner table.

'Oh! poor thing!' exclaimed Argyll. 'It was very hard upon her. Indeed I have a great mind to go and talk to her by way of avenging her cause. Which is she? Introduce me.'

Feminine curiosity now received a stimulus. Shrewsbury had taken Argyll's arm and was piloting the way through the throng to a corner at the far end of the room where the maids of honour and their friends were gathered. Only one had no share in the gay chatter and stood forlornly apart. Before her the two Dukes stopped.

'Mistress Jane Warburton – His Grace the Duke of Argyll desires your acquaintance.'

For Jenny that moment when Shrewsbury addressed her with the accompanying words would ever be the most memorable in her life. It was the fulfilment of a much-dreamed dream. A few minutes earlier she had been feeling piqued and so out of tune with the gaiety around her. Now, curtseying to the hero of her heart, exaltation replaced ennui. She smiled with eyes radiant with an absolutely sincere candour. To Argyll, it was a revelation. He had never seen honesty so vividly portrayed in a woman's face. It quite fascinated him. With the most charming courtesy he offered her his arm and escorted her to a settee in one of those alcoves where flambeaux set in sconces shed a rich glow.

The music of the fiddles effectively concealed the buzz of excited comment. The fact that the magnificent Argyll had 'singled out' 'the plain Mistress Warburton' and evidently intended to converse with her was certainly remarkable.

This astonishment increased when nearly an hour later it was observed that he continued to devote himself to her company. The other maids of honour were particularly intrigued by the sight of His Grace bestowing such favour upon the one member of Her Majesty's Household who was always the scapegoat.[1]

'What can he see in her?' 'She has none of the coquette's arts or graces.' 'Yet no man can help being flattered when a woman boldly displays her preference for him – and Mistress Warburton has surely done so . . . See how she cajoles him . . .' So ran the remarks. Meanwhile the Duke and Jenny were engaged in animated conversation. Listening to that melodious voice perfectly modulated and very sympathetic, inspiration of the highest order possessed her. Nothing of what had gone before counted. Challenge and triumph were at her command.

Hitherto, Jane Warburton had often found herself the target at court either of scorn or jest – caused by manners and speech both reflecting her lack of education. Her father — Squire Thomas Warburton of Winnington – belonged to Cheshire's oldest landed gentry. Her mother was daughter of a Welsh baronet, Sir Robert Penryhyn. In the same way that urban and rural England was divided through lack of communications, so the Maid of Honour from distant Cheshire was separated from her contemporaries. Whereas they had received the advantages of training in the habits of fashionable society, she had only known a rustic environment. This evening, for the Duke, Jenny relived her life before coming to Kensington. In the most sparkling manner and naive language she played the role of dairymaid. The dairy was her favourite province, but the seasons brought other activities. Autumn took her to the harvest-field. Winter found her following the hounds or – at times of hard frosts – joining the skaters. There were also visits to estate tenants and all of them had a definite place in her perspective. Indeed, whatever the occupation, she entered into it with zest and the description harmonized.

Argyll was so captivated that he felt himself actually sharing that even course of routine and could readily understand what the change to London meant. It must have come as a sudden squall of wind disturbing the placid flow of a stream.

'You should consider yourself very fortunate, Mistress Warburton', her parents had remarked when news of her appointment as a maid of honour arrived. So too she had thought in the first glow of excitement. Besides the privilege of being one of the Queen's attendants, there would be the pageantry; thus her girlish fancy imagined court life.

Then came departure in the dawn of a mid-summer day. As she entered the family coach to be jolted over hills and moors, down into valleys and along highways to London, a wave of sadness drowned enthusiasm. The reality of the wide gulf lying between the Cheshire countryside and England's capital loomed large. How would she, neither blessed with good looks nor intellectual blandishments, mix with ladies of quality? The question accompanied her throughout the journey. Very soon after arrival at Kensington she knew the answer.

The Duke heard all this – told so frankly, without frills – and besides fascination he felt a strong sympathy. His love of an outdoor life made it easy for him to appreciate the existence of this country girl – buxom of figure, plain featured except for a natural rose-tinted complexion and awkward in deportment, among these women with their rouge, smart clothes and dignified bearing. Yet something far more attractive distinguished Jenny in his opinion. This was her straightforward gaze through vivaciously sincere brown eyes.

A few days later Argyll called at Kensington Palace to 'wait upon' Mistress Warburton. Their second conversation was even more pleasing to him than the first, because in speaking of himself and the unhappiness of his married life he found Jenny a sympathetic listener. She seemed to be quite free of either jealousy or egoism, and this feature counted highly in his estimation. He could do what he had never yet done with a woman; release all his thoughts knowing that they would be understood. The friendship ripened. From then until his departure for Spain, a carriage drawn by four horses and showing on its panels the Argyll crest was regularly seen driving up the avenue to Kensington Palace. It always stopped before the entrance reserved to officials of the household.

'The Duke must be making headway with Mistress Jenny . . . what attraction can she, of all persons, hold for him?' Thus the talk spread to the outside world. It soon became known that the Duke of Argyll was devoting far more time to Jane Warburton than to the politics of the hour.

'Is it a case of genuine attachment on his part, and what then of the wife in the background? More likely 'tis a passing fancy – but even so most add . . .' 'We have heard such extraordinary tales about the girl from Cheshire.' 'Yet perhaps she has more in her than accounts of her crude manners would lead one to believe . . .'

The talk in circles where actions of celebrities were invariably the popular theme followed such lines. It was a situation which caught the imagination because of its romantic and incongruous character. It also appealed to those who delighted in scandalmongering and they were numerous in that age of intrigue.

Meanwhile Argyll and Jenny had no thought for what others might be saying about them. Her open language and vivacity stirred and released the passionate elements which were so strong a part of his being. The pleasure which she manifested when he gave expression to these feelings and the recollection of admiration that she had so boldly revealed at their first meeting made him toy with the prospect of an easy conquest. The maid of honour would be no different to other women whom he had known. None had ever resisted his advances, but readily yielded, proud, as he supposed, to be honoured by a span in his company. He was convinced that no woman could bear claim to the title 'Virtuous'. 'Ay – they are papists and they are all whores.' The words of Captain Winterbottom in *The Mirror* matched his opinion. So with Jenny there seemed to be no reason for an exception.

Accordingly, as sentiments mutually deepened, he approached her with a certain question, not for one moment doubting its answer in the affirmative. To his amazement Jenny replied that 'she would not positively be his mistress'.

Under the impression that she raised this armour merely to lead him on, he took the line of passionate pleading, interspersed with promises that everything within his power to confer would be hers if only she would give herself to him. These moments when he poured out his infatuation in that same voice which would 'forcibly ravish' must have been an ordeal to Jenny. She was truly in love with him and doubtless had to wrestle with that human part of her being which urged acceptance and the real self that counselled constancy. As strongly as he protested and strove to persuade, so she remained adamant in refusal. Yet, with good-natured tact, she intimated that his proposal did not cause offence. There would be no withdrawal of her friendship.

The manner in which she stood her ground – fearlessly and with such an indomitable firmness – brought an awakening which John, a cynic in regard to womanhood, had never contemplated. Beyond that outward facade of resistance lived a love born of the ideal and nurtured by sincerity. A profound regard began to temper the heat of passion. At last he had met a woman who was not afraid to defy him.

Henceforth their bond became a companionship woven of loyalty and respect. During those hours together in the apartment where maids of honour were allowed to entertain their friends, he did most of the talking and all the while felt conscious of a complete understanding. In that manner, time would pass without taint of scandal touching them. Both had their integrities and these triumphed.

Chapter VI

HER MAJESTY'S AMBASSADOR AND COMMANDER-IN-CHIEF, BRITISH FORCES IN SPAIN 1711

S P A I N – chess-board of Europe with two kings, both of them pawns in this particular game; on the one side stood Charles set there by the Alliance upon whom he depended for every move. He had his small kingdom in the part known as Catalonia with Barcelona the capital. On the other was Philip V holding the rest of Spain. After five years of conflict his position had become secure. The majority of the Spanish people acknowledged him as their monarch and no influence, however strong, would deflect them from that allegiance.[1]

Nevertheless, England and her Allies persisted in their struggle to impose their pawn upon an unwilling nation. Even in 1711, when the war had already been decided through the disastrous Battle of Brihuega, they seemed to be blind to the fact that there was nothing to be gained and everything to be lost. Its duration could be interminable for Louis pronounced an adamant 'No' to any form of negotiation which repudiated his grandson. The expenditures to maintain forces there proved an economic catastrophe. Finally, there was the enormous toll of life and anguish; apart from the warfare between the Allied forces and the Spaniards, the Catalonian partisans of Charles were at strife with the rest of the country. It was indeed an ugly scene and the role to which the Duke of Argyll was committed was the most unenvied one in Europe. While fully aware of the difficulties to be encountered, he did not know that his colleagues at home had no intention of honouring their financial agreements.

On 24 February his appointment was gazetted and three days later James Taylor, at the Horse Guards, informed Horace Walpole[2]: 'The Duke of Argyle will be setting out for Spain in about eight or ten days'.

As a right hand on his military staff he would have the Earl of Barrymore. Mr Granville, Secretary-at-War, writing on 13 March to the Earl of Portmore, stated '. . . At the same time I am to let

Your Lordship understand that Her Majesty has approved the Earl of Barrymore a Lieutenant-General to serve with the Duke of Argyle in Spain.'[3]

From the hour of Argyll's departure in the early days of March, he ceased to exist for the politicians. Only the tragic letters that Robert Harley, Henry St John, and others were to receive would remind them of a man whom they had treated as a 'monkey'. They would also be reminded that he was dauntless in his dealings with them and unflinching in loyalty to the Queen's service.

Travelling by way of the Hague, Argyll stayed there some days for talks with the British Ambassador, Lord Strafford. Then he proceeded to Frankfurt for the purpose of fulfilling the Queen's commands to negotiate an exchange of prisoners captured at the disastrous Battle of Brihuega. To Lord Dartmouth,[4] from whom the orders had come, he replied : '. . . if this step, My Lord, succeeds, it will provide us with men and I don't at all doubt but the like care is taken to supply us with money which I hope I shall finde when I come to Genoa'.

In Genoa, fourteen days later, he faced circumstances which compelled a truth tragic for him – a soldier and man of high integrity – to admit : 'It is very hard that the Army in Spain of all others should be so unhappy as to be forgot.'[5]

The opening lines of a poignant letter to his friend, the Duke of Shrewsbury, set the scene : 'I am sorry, my Lord, to tell you that after all the assurances I had of support in this difficult service, I find myself here without one penny of money or Credit ; notwithstanding the sums due to the Troops on account of former years and that there is four months unpaid of this, by which means they are now starving, and ready to mutiny every day.'

Argyll's heart bled. To face those destitute men who had so anxiously awaited his arrival as their Commander-in-Chief bringing salvation was a humiliation beyond the limits of endurance.

'I am farr from being so fond of serving as to ruin my reputation for the sake of it . . .' Thus he wrote when communicating the situation to Mr Henry St John, Chief Minister,[6] and then continued : 'I shall only beg the favour, Mr St John, as being an old servant of your's that you will prevail with Her Majesty to dispose of my Posts in Spain to somebody who may be able to do her service, for my part I protest on the foot affairs are at present unhappily reduced, I am altogether incapable of the employment.'

In even stronger terms, he described his position to Lord Dartmouth: 'I have neither address enough to persuade the King of Spain to think himself supported when the Troops are ready to mutiny for want of pay, nor have I skill sufficient to make an army starve and serve . . .'

Meanwhile, he had to reconcile himself to going forward. The encounter which he most dreaded was the one which awaited him in Barcelona: people who were depending upon his arrival with a considerable sum of money. Thought of arriving penniless among them determined him to delay his departure in the hope that word of credit might still arrive.

Out in Genoa's harbour a man-of-war rode at anchor; she was the *Dartmouth*, new, cleaned and ready for Argyll's passage to Barcelona. Away at Vado, the fleet, with the troops on board, lay under orders from the Admiral, Sir John Norris,[7] to sail whenever the wind permitted.

Thus the scene when, on 11 May, Argyll found himself forced to report to Lord Dartmouth: '. . . Badness of weather still detains the Fleet and which is worse we have no news of money. I shall stay here no longer than the wind obliges me, tho' when I am in Spain I can only serve as a Witness of our Army's starving in Garrison at a time when they might be doing good service in the field if they had been so fortunate to have met with the same treatment Her Majesty's Armys do meet with in other parts of the world.'

With that letter, he enclosed one for the Queen.

It would not be too great a stretch of the imagination to visualize him, after the despatch of those communications, waiting in agonies of suspense for change to come in weather and finance. In the last days of May, a favourable wind blew and the fleet put to sea. He boarded the *Dartmouth*; though without satisfaction of credit.

Argyll arrived in Barcelona to witness a state of affairs which predicted catastrophe for the forthcoming campaign. The sums of money due to the forces were enormous, and the credit was sunk so low that unless aid came very soon there could be no hope of subsisting the troops.

'We are in the most miserable condition that it is possible to imagine . . .' after writing those words to Mr Henry St John he turned to his first official duty as Her Majesty's Ambassador. This took the form of a note to King Charles of Spain:

I, undersigned Ambassador Extraordinary of Her Majesty the Queen of Great Britain, am obliged to represent to Your Majesty on behalf of the Queen – my Majesty – how much it matters to the maintenance of the Alliance and particularly to the interests of Your Majesty in regard to the war of Spain, to propose to the enemy, & try by all means possible, to reduce them to an exchange of the prisoners captured by them during the last campaign; I am ordered above all to solicit quickly the exchange of those troops who were at Brihuega under the command of General Stanhope . . . Not only can they be useful to Your Majesty in the present situation, but they are a charge upon your Allies who find themselves obliged to make a great expense in enemy country to subsist so great a number of prisoners when they have need of money to act quickly against the enemy . . .

Argyll then gave all his attention to the plight of soldiers on the point of starvation. While he wrestled with the problem, merchants pressed with demands for settlement of long-standing debts. To aggravate a terrible position, he had to justify matters with the King who 'desired that the furnishing of the troops be made in his name'.

A lengthy correspondence ensued with the King's Chief Minister, Marquis de Rialp. On his part, Argyll expressed hope that the people employed by the King to undertake the contract would be capable and offer terms 'so as best to ensure the accomplishment of so important an affair'.

As the end of June approached, threat of an offensive from the enemy gained strength and increased the stresses which Argyll was undergoing due to silence on the subject most vital to success. Only with great difficulty had he found credit to keep them from starving in their quarters. The English merchants regretfully refused aid. 'Having already lent more than ten thousand pistoles for the sub-sistance of the troops, it is impossible for them to do more'; he was forced to inform the Marquis de Rialp. At the same time he had this to say to Henry St John in a letter dated 26 June:

. . . the not paying the Bills that were drawn from hence the last year, has entirely destroyed Her Majesties' Credit in this place . . . The Enemy is already in motion and will be a few days in a body, so that if we remain in quarters we shall be destroyed in detaile; and to get together is not in nature till we have money for the whole body of troops that were here last year are without all manner of necessary; both officers and soldiers having lost all their tents, baggage, and equipages at the battle of Villaviciosa, besides that the Contractors for the mules to draw the Artillery

and ammunition will by no means be permitted to serve any more
till we have money to pay them.

He went on to describe the state of the towns:

in every way unprovided, their fortifications which are by farr
the worst that can be imagined, quite out of repair, but seventeen
hundred spare arms in both, which are old, and most of them
unserviceable, nor the third part of the powder that is sufficient
for their defence; a great part of their Cannon unfit for service,
ball and bombs such as will not fit their guns and mortars . . . I
say, Sir, this altogether I believe will satisfie you that nothing but
a miracle can save us.

Beyond that 'shadow of an Army' were the forces at work in
diverse quarters to explode the jealousies and corruption which
existed. In that part of the Peninsula known as Catalonia, the
situation was particularly critical on account of the corrupt elements
rife among the Catalans who had plainly intimated that 'they would
have the Queen of Brittain have no other share in affairs here, than
the providing of great sums of money for them to imbezle'.[8]

When Argyll moved among the leaders in order to discuss and
plan operations, he was thwarted by the discord which prevailed
among them.

Mareschall Stahremberg, in command of the army, was dissatisfied
that he did not have entire control in the war's management; the
ministry, composed of Germans, Spaniards and Italians, were in
perpetual dispute and agreed only upon one point – how to make
their private profits out of the war; the King considered it the
business of England to make him a gift of the Spanish Monarchy,
and so gave little care to the scene around him.

In view of all these circumstances, Argyll could not hope for
Spain's rescue from the House of Bourbon unless drastic measures
of reform were immediately adopted.

I know but two shapes that the management of this War can be
put in; the one is to place the whole authority and Direction of
every thing whatsoever in the hands of the Mareschall in which
case I believe he would be glad to have the British troops changed,
and indeed they would be no less fond of parting with him; the
other is to have a Generall in chief a subject of Her Majesty's,
invested with the same power before mentioned and this, I think,
considering that Her Majesty is at the whole expense of this war,

appears to be the most naturall of the two, and I am confident
will be most agreeable to the people of this country. Above all,
the King's Ministry ought to be excluded from any manner or
share of management in anything whatsoever.[9]

During the early days of July, the Fleet's arrival from Lisbon
raised expectations. Argyll, Mareschall Stahremberg, and others of
the King's court, eagerly awaited the ships coming into Barcelona's
harbour. Their hopes – high as those billowing sails – were once
more frustrated. As Argyll's despatch of 13 July to Lord Dartmouth
stated:

> The Fleet is arrived from Lisbon with *Only* three of the four
> Battalions on board which we expected . . . the Paymaster in
> Portugall has sent with this Fleet Twenty Thousand Noidres,
> which amounts to about Thirty Thousand Pistoles, so that our
> Paymaster since 24 December last had seventy-one thousand
> pounds a month to defray the charges of this war, which, if
> regularly supported, would amount to about Eighty thousand
> pounds a month . . . everybody's patience is near wore out, this
> Fleet's arriving with so very inconsiderable a sum of money having
> put an end to the poor remains of hope that subsisted till that
> time.

There was no doubt that the Duke of Argyll's circumstances
were the worst in which a Commander-in-Chief could be found.

> John, Duke of Argyle, Earle of Greenwich, Captain of her
> Majesties Fourth Troops of Horse Guards, One of Her Majesties
> most Hon[ble]. Privy Councill, Ambassador Extraordinary and
> General commanding in chief Her Majesties Forces in Spain,
> and Knight of the most noble Order of the Garter.
> I do hereby order and Direct you out of such money as may
> come to your hands for the use of Her Majesties Service in Spain,
> to pay to Brigadier-Generall Breton the Sum of Two Hundred
> Pistoles, and place it to accompt of his pay as Brigadier Generall
> on this Establishment, taking his receipt for the same, which with
> this shall be you sufficient warrant. Given at Barcelona, the 28th
> July 1711.
>
> Argyll

To John Meas
En[gr]. Deputy Pay Master
Gen[ll]. of Her Majesties Forces for Spain

When Argyll issued this order, how was he to know whether it could be fulfilled? Yet under his full titles, he had to take the risk for the sake of upholding the Queen's honour before fellow-officers. This was only one of his trials; there were others even greater.

People came to him with complaints. There was a general suspicion and uneasiness as to his inability to remedy a state of affairs which was so catastrophic; while he, himself, was wracked with the pain of witnessing the ruin of Great Britain in Spain intensify as each night passed to another day. He feared that the whole blame would attach to him and prepared to make good the old proverb: 'the weakest must go to the wall'. All that he could do in an attempt to rescue the men doomed to sink with him in the morass of failure, was to address letters to Lord Dartmouth, the Earl of Oxford,[10] Mr St John and Mr Granville, imploring release from the 'Galley to which I am chained!'

During the first days of August there were signs of enemy activity. On the 3rd, Mareschall Stahremberg informed the Duke that: 'the enemy were still close to our frontier, employing many troops from Cote d'Arens and Benasque.'

From then onwards the Mareschall maintained an almost daily correspondence with Argyll who based his movements upon the advice received.[11] Accordingly, the middle of the month found him establishing quarters at the Camp of Moublanc.

Meanwhile, Stahremberg summoned chiefs of the various corps and in cohesion with them assembled the forces in three groups, the two main ones being the English, Dutch and Palatines under Argyll's command; and the Imperialists, Portuguese, and part of the Spaniards were delegated to Lieutenant-General Pattée who also kept Argyll posted with intelligence reports.

The only action which occurred at this time came as a result of information that an enemy convoy was daily passing between Lerida and Tarragona.

Accordingly, Argyll detached two hundred horse under one Grand 'Jean of the Dutch Troops' to attack it; this he successfully did 'and captured two hundred and seventy mules'.

In the middle of August, Argyll received orders to make a march towards the Mareschall who was then in camp at Tavus. The Post of St Colomba was suggested. He therefore marched to Rocafort where half of the artillery from Tarragona had joined him; on the 19th they arrived at the Camp of St Colomba.

Argyll was somewhat baffled by the Mareschall's designs, for according to his assessment the enemy strength showed superiority.

However, he could only await developments and struggle with the perpetual problem of subsisting the troops.

He was still in the camp of St Colomba when, on 31 August, Mareschall Stahremberg 'Ordered the Chiefs of the Corps to attend him, the King having desired to have an opinion whether or not he should leave the Queen to govern this Country in his absence. We are unanimously of opinion that Her Majesty's presence was absolutely necessary . . .'

At this meeting, the Mareschall announced that 'The Duke of Savoy had no more hopes of wintering this side of the mountains, so that about the beginning of October the Enemy would have it in their power to make what Detachments they pleased from their Army in Dauphine to reinforce Monsieur de Vendôme . . . We did agree that it was necessary to advertise Her Majesty our Queen and her Allies of the dangerous effects such a junction of the Enemies might produce in this Country, if not prevented by our Receiving timely reinforcements in proportion to those of the Enemy . . .'[12]

Fortunately for the Allies, no major action happened and activities were merely those of reconnaissance and holding ground. By mid-September, Argyll was able to inform the Queen in a letter that he addressed to her:

> It is no small pleasure to me that notwithstanding the unhappy State of affairs here, I can have the honour to acquaint Your Majesty that as yet we have lost no ground, and that the Duke of Vendôme can have very little hopes of doing any thing this year if not assisted either by a reinforcement from France, or by the King of Spain's Ministers letting our Army want bread, which tho' it must seem strange to Your Majesty, yet I do assure you they are very Capable of doing, having nothing less at heart, than Your Majesties and the Kings Service, and nothing so much as inriching themselves at Your Majesties cost, which as I think it my Duty to do all I can to prevent, I can not hope for the honour of their good Graces, tho' I humbly hope I may for that inestimable satisfaction of Your Majesties approbation of my Conduct who am . . . etc.

Argyll and the troops under his comand continued to 'play a very bad game to the best advantage', holding their own against shortage of food, want of money, and the proper equipment. The end of September found him in the Camp at Prato del Rey, and writing to

Iohn Duke of Argyll &
Greenwich,

Portrait of the Duke at the period of Ramillies

John, 2nd Duke of Argyll

Mr Granville on the subject of officers and men on his establishment. Recruits were urgently needed. 'It will require the matter of three thousand men to recruit Her Majesty's Infantry here for next year's service, and if any action happens we shall want still more, so that there is but one way under heaven of recruiting these troops which is by Draughts [drafts] out of the Troops in Britain and Ireland . . .'

The stress and tension which Argyll had been experiencing these past months began to have effect upon his health, and in the middle of October he fell 'violently ill with a very dangerous feavour [fever]'. For four or five days he lay in a tent in the Camp, but becoming worse it was decided to remove him to Iqualada where, for two or three days, his state improved. Then came a relapse and he grew 'infinitely worse than ever, in consequence of which they brought him to Barcelona'. His recuperation was slow; indeed, it was only a few days before 20 November when he informed Henry St John and Lord Dartmouth of his illness, that the fever passed. To the former he wrote:

> I thank God my feavour is off, but my strength and flesh return but very slowly, it is the opinion of my Phisitians [Physicians] that it is necessary for my thorough Recovery that I should be some time in my native air, and indeed I am myself so thoroughly persuaded of the great advantage I should reap by being tho' it were never so little time at the Bath, that I must beg the favour of you, if you have any regard left for an old friend, that you would obtain me Her Majesties leave to go to England, if it were for never so short a time and I cannot but hope Her Majesties great goodness will prevent her refusing me this favour when asked for so strong a reason. I am sorry my weakness will not allow of my writting to you with my own hand.

There is a post-script to this letter:

> My dear Harry,
> I must put you in mind of the assistance you promised me in procuring me my allowance as Ambassador, punctually paid, and must beg you'll put my Lord Treasurer in mind of it, in case what is allready due is not remitted, since it is all I have to live upon, and this place being so very dear . . .

The year closed on a note more hopeful to the trend of the war.

From Barcelona – on 26 December – Argyll was able, for the first time, to send Lord Dartmouth a hopeful report:

> My Lord,
>
> My Lord Forbes is going Express with an account of what has hapned [happened]. I only make use of this occasion, which is a very uncertain one, to tell Your Lordship that there hapned an action the 22nd inst. between a Detachment of our Troops commanded by Lieut.Generall Pattée and the Enemy who were besieging Cardona, who were beat with Considerable loss having left their Tents and Baggage, Eighteen pieces of Cannon, four Mortars, with 600 sick and wounded in their Hospitall besides other prisoners, among which is a Genll. Officer; The Duke of Vendôme the 25th removed from before our Army and encamped about four miles from us, no doubt with a Design to retire into Quarters, so that I think we may count this Campaign at an end, and I hope infinitely a better one than could possibly have been expected which, no doubt, must do our Mareschall great honour . . .[13]

Argyll could now express the opinion that as the result of the success at Cardona affairs had so greatly changed that if troops and money were sent in time 'much may be hoped from next year'. A letter, written on 30 December, assured Lord Dartmouth of that fact and, at the same time, commended to him the 'bearer of the good news – Lord Forbes'. 'I beg leave to recommend him to your Lordship's protection as one I profess the greatest friendship for, but who is even worthy of Your Lordship's patronage, I find he enclines to come into the Land Service, so if Her Majesty is pleased to let me name a Colonell to the Detachment of Dragoons which I long since humbly proposed to be made a Regiment, I design him to be it . . .'

The last day of a year which had caused him both mental and physical suffering found Argyll still a soldier on active service for his country. In the final hours of 1711, he was writing to Lord Dartmouth to refer him to past talks when Port Mahon and its importance to the trade of Her Majesty's Kingdoms was the subject: 'Before I left England I had the honour to receive from Your Lordship two letters, in one of which you were pleased to acquaint me that Her Majesty approved of my going to Port Mahon when I shall judge it fit for the Service, and in the other that I am permitted to change Governour'.

The moment had arrived when he 'judged it fit for Her Majesty's Service' that his presence at Mahon was imperative, and gave the reasons :

> Mr. Petyt who commands in Mahon has accepted of a Commission as Lieut. Governr. from the King of Spain and made use of the Spanish Colours, there is also a Governour with Commission from the King of Spain residing in the Island; the Inhabitants have been armed since Her Majesty has been in possession, who openly declare against the Brittish, and a Spanish Garrison in Fort of Fourniers, on the opposite side of the Island of Port Mahon, where there is a harbour of Equall goodness, these things appear to me so very much Contrary to Her Majesties Interest, that if it is my fate to serve Her Majesty here next year I hope she will allow me to alter them.

In order to prevent any jealousies that his resolve might have stirred among ministers, he kept secret from them the reasons for the coming voyage. Yet 'They are entirely convinced of the consequence that Mahon is to the Trade of Brittain, and whatever face they put upon the matter have not the least hopes of ever seeing it without an English Garrison.'

There was one great sorrow which remained to disturb Argyll as the bells of Barcelona's churches sounded midnight and the turn of the year :

ALL THE MONEY WE HAVE LEFT NOW WILL BUT JUST KEEP THE TROOPS FROM STARVING TILL THE END OF FEBRUARY . . .

THE ROAD TO GOVERNOR — MINORCA, 1712

MAHON   LONDON – 1712

In the night of 1 January 1712, Colonel Killigrew arrived from England with the Queen's Orders for the Duke of Argyll. He was to proceed to Mahon, inspect the fortifications, review the situation, and then embark for England.

It so happened that the Duke had to write to Lord Strafford and, after reference to the 'happier turn of affairs', announced his own feelings: 'For my own part I am perfectly satisfied since Her Majesty has been pleased to give me leave to goe home, for I count by it either to settle matters so as to be able to serve agreeable for the future or else I have leave to be my own master which does not want its charms . . .'

K

The Duke's first inspection of Mahon confirmed the opinion which he had earlier communicated to Lord Dartmouth. Conditions were 'contrary to Her Majesty's interests' and demanded reform.

A fortnight later, while at Leghorn on the first stage of his homeward voyage, Argyll sent plans of Mahon's fortifications and estimate of what it would cost to complete them, to Lord Dartmouth :

> As to my opinion of the plan I think it will very well answer the design, the works are well wrought so far as they are carried on, and indeed there is a good deall of work done for the money, but I must say it has been an unpardonable fault to open so much ground at a time, for by that means too much is begun so little is finished that the place is not in a much better posture of Defence than when it was taken, for which reason I am humbly of the opinion there ought by no means any time to be lost in furnishing the works.

It was apparently by way of Belgium that he crossed from the Continent to England during the month of April.

> With much adoe [he wrote to Lord Strafford] I have persuaded the Bruges pacquet boat to sail with me upon assurance that your Lordsp. will approve of his so doing; and since there is another here I hope you will not think that I have done amiss. You know, my dear Lord, 'tis both for Her Majesty's Service and for my poor interest to be there as soon as possible which makes me take this upon me. I beg pardon and am my dear Lord –
> Most faithful and most obedient humble servant
>
> Argyll

Soon after his arrival in London, Argyll was 'under very great concerne' on account of a misunderstanding that had arisen between him and a senior military colleague – Lord Barrymore. He hastened to rectify it by means of a letter written on 29 April :

> I am persuaded you think it very strange that you have not heard from me since I came to this place, 'tis true you have all the reason in the world so to do, but the matter is in a word that I have had nothing to say, for tho' I have represented over and over again the State of affairs in Spain, I have never as yet been able to persuade those entrusted with Her Majesties affairs to determine any thing in relation to them, in short I have not

failled in my duty, I have done all that man can do to get matters set right, so what ever happens I shall be able to justify myself.

I have this moment received an order to attand the Councill to-morrow . . .

On that day of 29 April, he also wrote to his friend − Colonel Farmer − at Mahon:

My dear John,

I have received yours and am in as much pain as 'tis possible for man to be for you and the rest of my friends at Mahone, you may assure your self, and I desire you will let my friends know it, that I have not been wanting to represent the condition of the Spanish affairs, and particularly the State of Mahone, but for what reason I know not the consideration of them has been put off from day to day. I am told it will be now so no longer, but that every thing relating to Mahone will be entirely settled, and that my poor advice is to be taken in the matter, that moment that any step is made you shall hear from me fully, till then I beg you will have patience, I assure you 'tis what I am forced to, notwithstanding all I have done to serve my friends in power, so that you see delays are much in favour here, pray give my Service to all our friends and believe I neither forget you nor them for I am . . . etc.

Argyll

Towards the end of May a question important to Argyll as a soldier demanded his presence in Parliament.

The Lords met in a full House on 28 May to debate the 'Restraining Orders' issued to the Duke of Ormonde[14] during the 1712 Campaign.

In his speech, which followed one by Marlborough[15], the Duke of Argyll 'Excused the Orders given to the Duke of Ormonde'. In his opinion, 'Since the time of Julius Caesar, there had not been a greater captain than Prince Eugene of Savoy; but that, nevertheless, considering the different interests of the House of Austria and of Great Britain, it might not consist with prudence to trust him with the management of the War, because a battle, won or lost, might intirely break off a negociation of Peace which, in all probability, was near being concluded.' According to his knowledge, 'Nothing was more uncertain than the issue of a battle where victory was still wavering, and so often changed sides, that they who, after five or six successful charges, thought themselves sure of gaining the day had at last been routed and put to flight.' The Duke added: 'That two years before, the Confederates might have taken Arras or Cambrai instead of amusing themselves with the insignificant conquests of Aire, Béthune, and St Venant'.

During the month of June, Argyll received two appointments. The one – as Governor of Edinburgh Castle – carried the element of irony! There his grandfather had been imprisoned. The other brought to an end the anxious period of waiting for things to be settled. The Queen appointed him to be Governor of Minorca.

At the time of receiving the news, he had occasion again to write to Lord Barrymore:

> Colonell Ligonier informs me that your Lordship intends to fetch the two best Regiments out of Mahon to serve the Campaign in Catalonia. I am indeed hopeful the War is pretty near at end, but should it continue I beg of you never to think of having less than the four best of Her Majestie's Regiments in Minorca. I can assure you the Queen has this Island much at heart and all manner of care must be taken for its preservation. She has been pleased to make me Governor of it, but that I would have kept to your Self till you hear it from the Office . . .

The next weeks were passed in forming plans, and these must have become generally known by the end of July. On the 22nd of that month, the Earl of Mar informed his brother – the Justice-Clerk – 'The Duke of Argyle goes one of these days for his government of Minorca; he goes throw [through] France and I believe is to take our troops to Catalonia along with him. And the Duke of Hamilton goes very soon into France, of which he makes no secret, else I should be shy of telling it. They seem both to be mightily pleased with themselves . . .'

In the middle of September, Argyll visited Windsor for an audience with the Queen. She honoured him with a letter addressed to the King of France (Louis XIV):[16]

Monsieur mon Frère,
   Ayant trouvé à propos d'envoyer le *Duc d'Argyle* à Minorque pour y regler plusieurs affaires et entre autres celles qui regardent les Troupes Impériales et les miennes en Catalogne, je luy ay donné ordre de salüer votre Majesté avant de s'y rendre, Je vous prie donc de le vouloir recevoir favorablement et d'ajouter foy à

ce qu'il vous dire de ma part, principalement lorsqu'il vous
assurera de la veritable amitié avec laquelle je suis
    Monsieur mon Frère
      Votre bonne Soeur
        signé: Anne
Au Chateau de Windsor
le 15e Sepre. 1712

Official business in preparation for Minorca had prevented Argyll
from visiting Scotland that summer. At Canterbury on the eve of
his departure he wrote to his brother-in-law, the Marquess of Bute:

29th September –
    I was once this summer in hopes of having seen you, but the
Queen's service calling me elsewhere, I must now delay that
pleasure till next, when I hope I shall have time to be among my
friends in the north. I am got thus far on my way to Minorca
where I hope I shall be able to comply with the Queen's Commands by the end of November so that towards the beginning of
January at furthest I hope to be in England.

In early October, the Duke was set on his way.
'I have had letters from my brother out of France' Lord Islay
told a friend on or about 7 October. 'He is very well and by this
time I believe he will be a good way in his journey, having intended
to stay only one day at the Court of France.'
However, Argyll was destined to incur misfortunes which im-
peded his progress and only brought him to his port of embarkation
(Toulon) at the end of the month.
'The ill fortune I have had in the roads and weather with the
badness and scarcity of post horses, are the reason of my coming to
this place no sooner than last night, from whence I propose to set
out the moment wind and weather will permit me.' Thus he wrote
to the Earl of Oxford. In this same letter, he expressed his sorrow
at having to report that:

Our troops in Catalonia and Minorca are in the same scarcity of
money as when I left them. I can hear nothing of the sums you
told me you had lately remitted for that Service, nor was there
any news of them when these ships that are here came from
Spain, and to make this misfortune yet greater, it seems Mr.
Hammond has in obedience to a Minute which he pretends to

have received from the Treasury without either the order, approbation or so much as the knowledge of the Commander-in-Chief, paid about twenty-thousand pounds to the Portuguese so that the Queen's troops are reduced to the greatest misery imaginable . . .

Once more the Duke of Argyll looked at a scene of trouble. It was only compassion for 'these poor officers and soldiers entrusted to my command' that fortified his zeal for Her Majesty's service.

GOVERNOR – MINORCA

MINORCA – WINTER, 1712

On 5 November, the Duke of Argyll sailed from Toulon, and four days later arrived at Port Mahon. The following day he despatched a letter to Mareschall Stahremberg. The subject was distasteful for him as the Queen's envoy to communicate. It treated of 'Her Imperial Majesty's difficulty to continue the Spanish struggle'. 'It appears that the Catalonian War is insurmountable, even not having the Fleet to evacuate the Troops whose retreat can therefore be opposed by the Enemy; . . . Measures are being taken in a manner that the Enemy Powers will consent to a Truce for a reasonable time, so it is advisable to withdraw the Emperor's Troops from Catalonia, and give them the utmost aid and assistance in their retreat . . . The Queen's Fleet is in the Mediteranean to serve as escort.'

With headquarters established at St Philip's of Mahon, Argyll attended first to the business of re-ordering the forces in Catalonia. To one of his brigadiers – Brigadier Price – he issued orders to 'disband Brigadier Leppell's Regiment of Dragoons' and 'with all convenient speed to embark the Six Battalions of Foot under your Command to this place and put them under the command of Colonel Kane – Her Majesty's Lieutenant-Governor of Minorca.' To another officer – Colonel Davis – went a despatch ordering the embarkation of 'Men under your command, with the Cannon, Ammunition, and other Stores belonging to the British traine of Artillery on board such Shipps as shall be appointed for that purpose, in order to be transported to this Island at the same time with Her Majesty's Forces.'

His next step was to inform the General Magistrates that the island had become the possession of the Queen and they should

My dear Lord

I doe most heartily aske your pardon that I have ... power acknowledg'd the favour of your letter, & I am sure you will grant it me when you consider how little esteem ... to be measur'd by my writing. I doe assure you were ... a mark of my valueing people, you had had ... letters then you could have red, but on the contrary ... those with words, who I desire, my ... should convince of my inclinations to serve them ... I was one this summer in hopes of haveing seen you, ... the queens service calling me elswhere, I must ... delay that pleasure till next, when I hope I ... all have time to be among my friends in ... ... I am gott thus fare on my way to Minorka

Letter from Argyll to Lord Bute, 29 September 1712

where I hope I shall be able to comp[ly]
with y[ou]r Queens Commands by y[e] en[d]
of November so that towards y[e] beg[inning]
of January at farthest I hope to be in y[our]
[...] the favour [...] to give [...]
[...] to my Sister & believe that I a[m]
[...] you can desire
your Affection[ate]
Brother & faithfu[ll]
servant
[signature]

Canterbury Sep[t]: y[e] 2[9]
1712

acknowledge only her authority. He invited them to a meeting to receive from him the Queen's assurances of 'preserving to them their Liberties and Religion.'

One person did not take easily to the change.

While Argyll was busy with the issuing of orders and preparation of reports, the Emperor's[17] Governor called. His attitude predicted challenge. 'He had not received any instructions from the Court at Barcelona to relinquish the Government; but would send for them. Meanwhile, in consort with some others in the Emperor's service, he desired to deliver a protest.'[18]

Argyll, in firm though eloquent tone, replied that 'He was at liberty to doe what he thought fit.' 'Whoever belongs to the Emperor shall be sure to meet with all the respect and civility that is in my power to pay them, till such time as His Majesty will be pleased to send for them.'

To such speech there could be but one answer. The ex-Governor retired with assurances that he would not meddle in the Government's affairs.

So all was set upon the right foot to advance towards a new order of affairs.

The meeting of the magistrates was held, and in sequel Argyll addressed them a letter:

St Philip's – November the 17th
1712.

Gentlemen,
Having by our Queen's Commands and in her name assured you of the continuance of all your rights and privileges both ecclesiastical and Civill; and with her intentions to doe every thing that may tend to the making you a happy and flourishing people, I think it will be for Her Majesty's Service, as well as to the satisfaction of the inhabitants of this Island, that you should acquaint them with Her Majesty's Gracious intentions towards them. I leave it to you to take the proper methods of doing it and am . . . etc.

To the Bailie General; and the Jurats of Ciuadella, Mahon, Alayor, and Mercandall.

By the end of November, Argyll was able to send an official communication to the Baille-General of the island; 'Her Majesty

had been pleased to enter into a Cessation of Arms with France
and Spain until the 22nd December.'

> I am likewise to acquaint you in regard that the reason for which
> it has hitherto been found necessary to have the Commonality of
> this Island armed such as the War and the smallness of the
> Garrison now ceasing, and it being observable that it has had the
> ill effect of making the people neglect the labouring of the ground
> and other business in hopes to get a livelihood by hunting – a
> practice greatly tending to the detriment of the Island : It is Her
> Majesty's pleasure that for the future none should be allowed to
> have fire-arms in their possession but the Gentry and Magistrates
> and that all other persons should deliver their arms to be carefully
> laid up in the town houses of the severall districts where they
> may be ready to be returned to the people when the defence of
> the Island shall so require.[19]

Although Minorca's affairs were his prior claim, Argyll still had
responsibilities on the Spanish side. Therefore, when ships arrived
from Barcelona without an expected document, he felt compelled to
action of a strong character. It was a note of protest to the Chief
Minister – the Marquis de Rialp.

> Sir,
>   To spare you a long letter I send you Memorandums which will
> explain outrages committed against Subjects of the Queen my
> Mistress. I would have written to you on my arrival if I had
> not been informed that you had already received complaints.
> That is why I did not doubt that by the last ships from Barcelona,
> you would have sent not only orders for an entire satisfaction but
> also for the punishment of the Authors of these acts of brigandage.
> Observing, however, that nothing has been done, I find myself
> obliged to demand an ample and immediate satisfaction for the
> interested persons . . . The Queen my Mistress must be extremely
> surprised to learn of such great violence done to her Subjects and
> even more that they have remained unpunished. So I do not
> doubt that you will instantly give the necessary satisfaction to
> the outraged persons . . .

It was Argyll's intention to leave for home before the year
closed. Problems, however, still loomed on his horizon. Of these the
most urgent was the dire want of corn. To deal with this circumstance he addressed a request to the

Patroons of the Sageas Loaden
with Corne at Port Fornelles.

The Magistrates of Ciudadella having complained to me that they are in very great want of corne, and I being informed that you have considerable quantities on board your vessels, I do for Her Majesty's Service require of you that you sell to the said Magistrates at the market price such quantities as they shall inform you they absolutely stand in need of and you shall be sure upon all occasions in return to receive what service shall be convenient for you.

Argyll's mission was not complete until he had positively established the rights and privileges of the people, as well as the benefits which would be conferred in order to bring production to the island. This he did through his reply to a Memoriall from the Jurato of Ciudadella.

The review of Argyll's work as pioneer Governor of Britain's new island outpost belongs to the last official communication from Minorca. It is to the Earl of Dartmouth :

My Lord,

The Shipps with the troops from Catalonia arrived in this road the 10th, but the wind not serving to brng them into the Harbour that Night and it hapening to blow hard, six of the transports were forced to see not getting all in till the 15th, which gave me a good deal of trouble in obeying Her Majesty's Commands, but I have at last regulated everything to the best of my Judgment : Leppells Dragoons are disbanded and will in a few dayes be sent from hence together with the recruit Dragoons and such other useless people as the Shipps ordered for their transportation can contain; there are likewise disbanded five Battalions of Foot out of which I have Compleated the five remaining, upon the High establishment after which there remaines about seven hundred Supernumerarys Sergeants and Soldiers, which I have divided into five bodyes each Commanded by a reformed Captain, Lieutenant and Ensigns of the Regiment they belong to, and have order'd them to be paid as I am Commanded upon a Contingent List; and the Standing regiments to be Compleated out of them as Vacancies shall happen; these Supernumerarys together with one Battalion I have quarter'd in St Phillips, two at Ciudadella, one at Alayor, out of which there is a detachment of 50 men at Fornelle, and one at Mahon.

As to Civil affairs I have Continued all the Magistrates and other officers of the Island in their employments except one who would not continue and they have taken of their owne accord the oaths to Her Majesty which they have been used to take to the Kings of Spaine, most of the Inhabitants seeming well satisfyd with the Change.

The Cessation of arms has been published in the usuall form and I have given orders that all the Inhabitants excepting Gentlemen and Magistrates should deliver up their fire arms to be kept in the towne houses of the different districts which will be obeyd in two or three days and I have reason to believe without much discontent.

As to my Commission to the Princes of Barbary I have wrote to them to acquaint them with Her Majesty's accession to the Sovereignty of this Island and desired that they would give orders to their Officers to treat the People of it as Subjects of Her Majesty and would encourage their Subjects to furnish this Garrison, by way of trafick with such parts of the product of their Country as wee should stand in need of, promising all Civility and Service to such of their embarkations as shall at any time come into these harbours. I have likewise as I am empower'd by Her Majestys Deputed Colonel Kane to treat with these Princes and have ordered him to obey the instructions given me by Her Majesty of which I have delivered him a coppy.

I received, my Lord, with the Shipps from Barcelona, an answer from the Marshall of the Letter I wrote him upon the subject of the Germans returning out of Spaine and have writ him a reply, both which will be delivered to your Lordship.

In short, my Lord, I have to the best of my poore understanding obey'd Her Majestys instructions, and I hope as well as the miserable Circumstance of affairs here would admit of indeed as to clearing the Regiments that either stand or are disbanded that instruction is in no measure complyd with for Mr. Hammond brought with him to this place but 19600 Dollers, and how far that will goe in clearing these ten Battaillons of Foot and a Regiment of Dragoons and subsist five Compleat Battaillons with the Supernumerarys till the 24th of December, Sr. John Lamberts bills for November being protested and that of December not payable till the last day of the month it 'twere come, a Short View of the Establishment and accounts of the troops will suffice to explaine. I have indeed with great difficulty today prevailed with Mr. Gascoigne who serves Her Mahesty here as Agent victualer, of the Fleet to lend Mr. Hammond 20000 dollers for the subsistance of the troops taking his bills on Mr. Bridges but I am forced to endorse them myself; I must therefore beg that they may be accepted the moment they are produced, that I may not suffer for doing a Service which I hope I may think 'tis a little hard I should be put to; and I believe it will be for Her Majestys Service that they should be very punctually payd.

I am to set out from hence tomorrow to visit the different Garrisons which I count will take up about eight days so that in a day or two after my returne I shall embark for Thoulon [Toulon] in my way home; the Shipps order'd to attend me thither not being able to stay longer than Sunday come Sevennight for want of Provisions; the Admiral being obliged to saile for Italy with the Fleet next Sunday for the same reason.

The Consequences, My Lord, that will in all human probability attend the matters of fact which I have mentioned, are but too easily discovered; I shall not offend by naming them, but I hope there are of Her Majtys. Ministers who will do me the Justice to say that I foresaw plainly the main of what has happened and begged that measures might be put upon a clear foot before I left England, but my Zeal was unfortunately misinterpreted, which I should the less regret notwithstanding all I undergoe if Her Majestys Service and these poor miserable officers and Soldiers under my Command did not suffer with me I take the Liberty my Lord, not to be so particular as I otherways would be, to attend you in about a fortnight after this Comes to your hands; I have the honour to be with the Greatest Respect etc.

Argyll.

Soldiers and officers of the garrison, citizens of the island, and magistrates of the various districts, were assembled on the quay-side at St Phillips to watch the passage out from harbour of a man-of-war.

As the sails of the stately vessel unfurled to billow forth in the evening breeze, guns fired salute and then, after a moment's hush, there arose a cheer so loud that the echo reached the man who stood alone on port-side of the ship.

Thus, Minorca's tribute to the Scots Ambassador who had fulfilled a delicate mission in such manner that Great Britain was a name to be honoured.

Chapter VII

I STAND BY SCOTLAND

An evening in December, 1712, found Elizabeth, Dowager Duchess of Argyll, writing anxiously from her home in Kintyre to the Marquis of Bute.

> I received yours with the copy of the letter you received. I understood it writ promptly to inform you how he [the Duke of Argyle] and his brother is situate and what he requires of you. 'Tis on information what your opinion is of the several designs of their enemies which is very sure to destroy their intirest with Court and Country, and to prevent it you may very freely advise their joyning with men of honour and such as can make no intirest by any other way, and recommend any you think they may depend upon, for as to the publick, except the signatorie, I think there's more but may be friends or enemies as their intirest leads them, for there's a general fear has seized all persons. One apprehends a disappointment.
>
> I truly regret poor Duke Hamilton's unhappy end, the more that's like to be made of the business, for that may involve the nation in blood. Alas his temper was not so meek as to sett with an affront, and I cant think Mr. McCartnee such a villain to murder him. Let it be as it will, his friends makes a loss which my sons will find, who was very intyre, and the person in opposition to their intirest will set up to lead the Law's intirest which he owned he would never be succeeded in.
>
> I long to know who succeeds him a peer among the sixteen . . .

The mother had reason for her anxieties, especially on account of her elder son. He was on an 'Opposition foot' to the Tories and not yet restored to the Whigs. In these circumstances, he lay open to the designs of foes ever alert to undermine his power and the Earl of Islay's dangerous sublety. As the discerning mind of the Dowager-Duchess recognized the situation, unless high-principled guidance intervened the brothers must fall from Royal favour.

Argyll, however, was not in a mood to obey any advice save his own bold intuition. Scottish affairs were the cause.

Five years after the Queen, in her message to the first Parliament of Great Britain, had exhorted 'every good man to improve the Union between the two Kingdoms', Scotland's temper was such that to certain of her leaders the Treaty's dissolution seemed the wisest course. Hitherto, it had only brought 'fatal consequences' to their people. They pointed an accusing finger at England for injustices upon national as well as individual rights.

In the first instance, the economic benefits promised by the Treaty were still unrealized. With the exception of Glasgow where merchants had established a profitable overseas trade, the commercial state of the country was almost worse than in the days before Union. Then, the linen manufacturers were at least able to find outlet for this staple product. Yet by 1712 it appeared that Scotland had become a victim of exploitation by English traders whose merchandise was permitted to invade the north at cheap prices to the prejudice of the Scottish market.

The second charge raised against the English politicians touched that most delicate of subjects – religion. The Toleration Act passed in March 1712, and a law reviving the system of patronage which followed a few months later, inflamed Scotsmen with the apprehension that the Jacobite-minded ministry intended to impose a policy of an Episcopalian character upon the ecclesiastical affairs of Scotland. In view of so grave a threat to their traditional establishment, Argyll and other staunch Presbyterians felt more than ever convinced that the word 'Independence' should be written in place of Union.

The third count of injustice laid at Westminster's door cited the Lords' refusal to permit the Duke of Hamilton to sit in his own right as Duke of Brandon. The fact that the same Whigs who had been so adamant for the Treaty as an instrument of concord were responsible for this example of 'Man's inhumanity to fellow-man' aroused the contempt and indignation of their Scots' contemporaries. For Argyll, with his experience in Spain, it was a further proof that the majority of England's statesmen were without regard for the rugged land beyond the Tweed. The only man in the English ministry who took an independent stand in relation to Scotland was Lord Oxford (Robert Harley).

'My soul has been among lions, even the sons of men whose teeth are spears and arrows and their tongues sharp swords', he wrote to Carstares, and thus allied himself with the thoughts prevailing with a people whose statutes were founded upon liberty and not thraldom.

It only required one other action on the part of the British Parliament to bring Scotland's statesmen forward in a united front of challenge. That hour arrived in the spring of 1713.

A tax of sixpence a bushel was imposed upon all British Malt. Yet on account of the supposed inferior quality of Scottish malt, a clause in the Union Treaty stated that – "Malt to be made and consumed in that part of the United Kingdom now called Scotland shall not be charged with any imposition during this present war.'

Scots members of the Lords lost no time in taking action against this blatant repudiation of words that formed part of a document sealed with the seal of Great Britain. The Duke of Argyll led the debate for measures to dissolve the 'Union of Unions'.

'I am by some reflected on as if I were disgusted and had changed sides, but I despise their persons as much as I undervalue their judgement.' Thus opened his speech. He continued by 'Urging that the malt-tax in Scotland was like taxing land by the acre throughout England because land was worth five pounds more in the neighbourhood of London and would not fetch as many shillings in the remote counties. In the summer, the English malt was valued at four times the price of that which was made in Scotland; therefore the tax in this country must be levied by a squadron of dragoons.'

Pronounced in that forcible tone which he used on those occasions when his temper was aroused, the Duke owned: 'I had a great share in making the Union with a view to secure the Protestant Succession; but I am now satisfied that this end might be severed as effectually as if the Union was dissolved, and if this step should not be taken I do not expect long to have either property left in Scotland or liberty in England."[1]

In sequel to this declaration which had the support of all his fellow Scots in the House, the Duke carried a petition for Union's repeal to the Queen. He was accompanied by two Jacobites – the son of Sir George Lockhart of Carnwath and the Earl of Mar, and the Whig Cockburne of Ormiston.

A contemporary historian gives an account of the visit, beginning with Lockhart's own words:

We set out [he says], to Kensington where the Queen then was, and though we made what haste we could the Earl of

aroline House, Edinburgh *see page* 227

Ham House *see page* 17

Sudbrook House *see page* 203

The coat-of-arms above the fireplace at Sudbrook

Oxford, having been made acquainted with our design, was set before us with the Queen. Coming out of the presence as we were admitted, he told us he understood our errand and the Queen was prepared to agree to the answer.

On being introduced to the Queen, the Duke of Aryle laid open to Her Majesty the 'many fatal consequences' of the Union and the bad treatment the Scots had received in the matter of the malt-tax.

When the Queen had listened, or seemed to listen, to the speech of the Whig Duke, the Earl of Mar addressed her with an harangue on the same subject. The reply of Her Majesty was hostile to the repeal of the Union.

'I am sorry', said Her Majesty, 'that the Scots believe they have reason to complain; but I am of opinion that they drive their resentment too far. I wish they may not repent it.'

The deputation – Whig, Tory and Jacobite, withdrew in silence.

While the Scots members of Westminster had the support of English Junto Whigs, and a motion to proceed to the Treaty's abrogation was carried by four votes, the further step of introducing a bill did not materialize.

On giving the matter deeper reflection, a question emerged to prominence and because of its gravity influenced a halt with the Whig statesmen of both nations. 'In the event of Union being dissolved, what would happen to the Succession? Security of the Crown to the House of Hanover must take precedence.'

It was then midsummer. The remaining months of the year at home witnessed a general election which brought the Tories back to power; an interesting move on the part of the Earl of Oxford in relation to Scotland; and finally the Queen's serious illness.

Since the death, in 1711, of the Duke of Queensberry, his office as 'Third' or Scottish Secretary of State had been vacant and Scotland's affairs were principally directed by Lord Bolingbroke who termed himself 'Northern Secretary of State'. In September, however, Oxford, ever wary of his powerful rival, decided to embarrass him. He revived the Third Secretaryship and conferred it upon the Earl of Mar. To Argyll and his circle, the appointment could have important consequences, for Mar's unpredictable qualities were well-known.

It was just before Christmas that Her Majesty fell gravely ill. The event brought the Succession forward and renewed the controversies

L

bound with an issue so vital to Great Britain's fortunes. As the situation existed, the Act of Settlement was still law. In the event of the Queen's death, the House of Hanover would preside over the United Kingdom. For Tory ministers averse to that course, action must be taken before it was too late. Thus the energies of intrigue were set in motion.

Savoy or Stuart? Victor Amadeus, the young great-grandson of Charles I, or James, brother of the Queen? The question engaged the principal schemers, Bolingbroke and Oxford. In both quarters stood the barrier of religion. Otherwise, the two Princes were eligible, although the stronger claim belonged to James. So to him they turned with a demand that he should join the Church of England. His reply to the ultimatum was an emphatic refusal.

Confronted by this deadlock, and unable to find any solution to the problem, the rival chiefs embarked on a way as fatal to themselves as it was disloyal to their colleagues. They settled down to resume a personal conflict, regardless of the fact that a lead positively given to unite Parties in the best national interest would have averted disorders of rumour and division.

At that hour there began a rising tide of reaction towards Hanover as the safest direction for the British constitution. Tories of the Cavalier order recognizing the danger to which their nation would be exposed if the Protestant rule was broken, veered to the Hanoverian faction. Of even greater significance came the move of certain prominent figures in the High Church circle. They formed a nation-wide crusade and entered into conference with the Dukes of Shrewsbury, Somerset and Argyll.

Amidst this crisis which embraced every section of the population, the Duke of Argyll emerged in open conflict with the ministers whom he had supported in the autumn of 1710. Their conduct towards him when Commander in Spain had already earned his contempt, which he only needed the right moment to express. This came in spring 1714. At a debate in the Lords on the state of the nation, the Protestant Succession was 'voted out of danger'. Then he spoke his mind:

> I have lately crossed the kingdom of France both in going to and returning from Minorca. It is indeed one of the finest countries in the universe; but there were marks of a general desolation in all the places through which I passed. I rid forty miles together without meeting a man fit to carry arms. The rest of the people were in the utmost misery and want. Therefore I

do not apprehend what necessity there is to conclude a Peace so precipitately with a Prince whose dominions are so exhausted of men, money, and provisions. As to the question now under Debate :

I firmly believe the Succession in the Electoral House of Hanover to be in danger from the present Ministers whom I durst charge with maladministration within these walls and without. I know and offer to prove that the Lord Treasurer has yearly remitted 1,000 pounds to the Highland Clans of Scotland, who are known to be intirely devoted to the Pretender, in order to keep them under discipline and ready for an attempt; on the other hand, the new modelling of the Army by disbanding some regiments out of their turn, and by removing from their employments a vast number of officers merely upon account of their known affections to the House of Hanover, are clear indications of the designs in hand.

It is a disgrace to the nation to see men who have never looked an enemy in the face, advanced to the posts of several brave officers who, after they had often exposed their lives for their country, are now starving in prison for want of pay.

The Ministers retaliated by removing the Duke of Argyll from his military and state offices. One appointment, however, could not be removed : that of Privy Councillor.

The Queen recovered; but it was apparent to all who knew her that her recovery would not last long. During those evening days of her life, the Succession storm raged in Parliament and outside. At the Court of Hanover agitation was as strong as at home. Anne's contemporary and rival – the Electress Sophia – ambitious, even at eighty years of age, to have a hand on Britain's crown, negotiated with her agent – Schutz – to demand 'a Writ of Summons' for her son as Duke of Cambridge and Peer of the British realm to visit London.

His method of action produced repercussions which fanned Jacobite hopes. Reports swiftly circulated that the Queen declined further relations with the prospective heir and intended to restore her brother's rights. 'Perhaps the Act of Settlement might be repealed' was the whisper that travelled on the Home and Continental winds. To strengthen the confidence of James's partisans, Lord Oxford paid four thousand pounds to 'certain Highland Clans – mostly Jacobite'. Once more, Argyll thundered denunciation : 'It was money given to arm for the Pretender . . .'

Thus the summer moved on and brought strange acts of fate. The Electress Sophia died – possibly disappointed by failure of a coup which might have proved her triumph. Marlborough, in exile, allied himself with Prince George of Hanover. Oxford passed from power. Bolingbroke stepped in (though only for 'a little hour').

Despite all these agitations, the Queen's health was ever pre-eminent with her subjects in every part of the British island.

'. . . 'Tis not known how things will goe. The Queen is certainly better in her health than she has been several years. She has put off her journey to Windsor for a week . . .' the Dowager Duchess of Argyll, away in Kintyre, was writing to Lord Bute on 31 July. Yet even as her pen formed these words, Anne, who had become ill the previous day, approached the end.

"Tis not known how things will goe . . .'

All England watched and wondered.

In that hour of grave national anxiety and climax to a great woman's life, the Privy Council took command: and a Privy Councillor, the Duke of Argyll, came into his own.

Chapter VIII

GOD BLESS THE QUEEN, LONG LIVE THE KING

IN the early hours of Friday morning, 30 July, a carriage stopped before the London residence of Bothmar – Envoy of Hanover to the Court of St James.[1] Two men alighted, mounted the steps, and knocked in peremptory fashion upon the front door. On its being opened, they announced themselves and demanded audience with the Ambassador; the business was urgent. A few minutes later, the Dukes of Argyll and Somerset entered Bothmar's presence to inform him of the Queen's condition and that, although unsummoned, they proposed to attend the Privy Council for the purpose of establishing the Elector's rights. They would notify him immediately the Queen died, and secure the necessary measures for the proclamation of Prince George as King of the British Realm.

After the interview, their direction was Kensington Palace where certain members of the Privy Council had just assembled for one of the gravest emergency sessions yet known to history.

Around the table in the Council Chamber next to the death chamber sat the councillors who had been called: the Duke of Shrewsbury, Robinson – Bishop of London, Lord Dartmouth – each of them ardent Hanover supporters; Bolingbroke, Wyndham,[2] Ormonde, Buckingham, Lord Lansdowne (formerly Mr Granville) – all Tories with Jacobite principles. Their expressions, as they followed the usual courtesies of acknowledgement, denoted the tension which dominated them. Bolingbroke and his colleagues had no fixed plan. The three Hanoverians, and especially Shrewsbury, were anxious because they waited. Yet he was the least moved when suddenly a door opened and the names of two un-invited members were announced:

His Grace the Duke of Argyll; His Grace the Duke of Somerset. For the others it must have been like that moment in the fairy-tale when the feared Hathor appears. No one could deny them entrance for they had their privilege as Privy Councillors and were able to use it if occasion demanded.

The conspicuous feature of the proceedings which ensued both that day and the next was the lack of initiative either from the Tories – in the majority on the Council – or the Whig Junto Lords[3] who attended on the 31st. The onus of direction fell upon the three members of the Middle Party,[4] as holders of the balance-scales in the crisis.

Reconciliation of parties present at the Council table was the first purpose. In order to attain it, the conduct of affairs must go to one who would be generally acceptable. The Duke of Shrewsbury, whose views embraced so wide a horizon, was the choice as agreeable to everyone.[5] Accordingly, the Queen, dying but sufficiently conscious to understand the formality required of her, was exhorted to 'constitute Shrewsbury Lord Treasurer'. Then, at last united in accord for the interests of their nation and crown, they settled to the task of preparation which began with a 'Letter signed by the Council, sent Express by James Craggs Esq., Jnr., to desire his Electoral Highness of Brunswick to be pleased to hasten over hither.' Likewise, Bothmar was summoned and told of all that had passed.

The issue of various commands followed these initial formalities.

Orders were sent to all the Officers of the Militia of Great Britain to repair to their respective Posts, to take care that no disturbance be offered to the Public Tranquility.

Order was also sent to the Earl of Strafford to desire the States-General to get ready to perform the Treatty of Guaranty of the Protestant Succession if need shall require.

Orders were also sent for some Battalions to come over immediately from Flanders.

Throughout that fateful Saturday, a constant stream of couriers passed between the Council Chamber and all parts of Britain.

'On Sunday morning, a little after seven o'clock, Her Majesty died in the 51st year of her age.'

No time was lost in leading the British people forward to a new decade. Even while the blinds were being drawn over the windows of Kensington Palace, and the gates closed to all save those with duties to perform, doors of St James's Palace opened to a great throng of distinguished personages.[6]

The following Lords and others, Her Late Majesty's most Honourable Privy Council, Assembled at St. James's soon after Her Majesty's death . . .

Immediately, the List of the Lords whom His Electoral Highness of Brunswick had chosen to be added to the Seven General Officers of the Kingdom was produced by the Lord Archbishop of Canterbury [who, on this extraordinary occasion, notwithstanding his ill state of health, came over to St James's], the Lord Chancellor, and Mr. Kreienberg – Resident of Brunswick – and was found to be written with His Sacred Majesty's own Hand, as follows:

Archbishop of York; Dukes Shrewsbury, Somerset, Argyll, Bolton, Devonshire, Kent, Montrose, Roxburgh; Earls Pembroke, Anglesea, Carlisle, Nottingham, Abingdon, Scarborrow, Orford; Viscount Townshend; Barons Halifax, Cowper.

There followed the proclamation of the 'High and Mighty Prince George, Elector of Brunswick-Lunenberg, Duke and Prince of Hanover and Zel, and High Treasurer of the Sacred Empire, to be King of Great Britain, France, and Ireland.'

It was on 5 August that Scotland received news of these events.

Edinburgh – 5th August.

By an Express arrived last Night, about 12, Directed to the Right Honourable the Earl of Islay – Lord Justice General – wee had the Melancholy Account of the Demise of Her Majesty Queen Anne of Blessed Memory, which happened upon Sabbath the 1st instant, in the Morning. On its arrival His Lordship advertised such of Her Late Majesty's other Servants as were in the Town to be with him at Eight this morning . . .

At the Town House, the new Sovereign was proclaimed, and nobles who, not so long ago, had been divided over the policy of his Succession, responded loudly to the call that went forth over the City of Edinburgh to the accompaniment of guns fired from the Castle: 'God save the king'

At this time the Dowager Duchess of Argyll was on a visit to Edinburgh and the day of 9 August found her engaged in a favourite pursuit – that of letter-writing. To Lord Bute – away at Mount Stuart – she wrote in racy style of events and her impressions:

My dear Lord,

Your Lordship will wonder you heard not from me of the Queen's death, but our people, though I offered to send an Express, thought fit to send on their letters their own way the . . . of Roseneath and then leave it to me to be at the expense of forwarding them to Inveraray . . . Everything appears very quietly both here and at London, and I hope people will be so wise for their own saftee to continue so, for the king will not govern in fact as the queen did.

I have not spock [spoke] some words to my Lord Islay since I came for he stayed in town till the Season was up and the Monday after he gott the news, and will come out to take in some papers and till last night he came not out except for a moment this day . . . when I delivered your letter to remember to writ, he was so sleepie he could not hold open his eyes and this morning by seven o'clock there was companie with him.

What the Parliament has done is not known as yet, but the Regent has ordered the Secretaries letters to be brought to them unopened. Glendaruel is suspended from his new post, I suppose the Earl with his 100 knights in arms will not believe the news of the queen's death till Glendaruel advises them, though they hear King George proclaimed the day come one, so feel that my son could not goe; . . .

There's a report the King of France is dead; though generally believed I dont because it comes not from very good hands. There would be an Express sent with the account of it, it being next to the queen's death the greatest strength to the Pretender and his friends . . .

I suppose when my sons come, Wee must recourse to the Abie [Abbey] for 'tis thought certainly upon the King's arrival the Parliament be dissolved and a new one called.

My blessings to my dear Lord,

Adieu

In writing those concluding words, the Dowager-Duchess was probably reminded of a task which required speedy attention; to unearth her state robes – not worn for so long – and have them in readiness for the hour when she would accompany her brilliant sons to the celebrations of King George's coronation.

NOTES

Chapter I

1 On 12 April, Lockhart refers first to a threatened attack by the 'Table' on Chancellor Seafield and then to an interview which he had with him. 'The Chancellor told me they had not concluded which measures to take. I told him I supposed before the Duke of Argyle accepted his office that the Queen and he had concluded upon the conditions that were to be required of him, so that they could not but know and everyone pretended to know what it was they had engadged to do to the Queen and the English Ministry.'

   Another example of the intrigue surrounding Argyll's name may be cited in a memoir given to Monsieur de Torcy and dated 27 April 1706: 'The Duke of Argyle, the Duke of Atholl, and all the Chiefs of the ancient and powerful Houses are extremely irritated, and will do all that they can to prevent the Union from succeeding, but there is no great evidence that they are in a state to raise an obstacle in Parliament if England distributes a certain amount of money among the Deputies of the Burghs.'

2 With equivalent rank in the Dutch army.

3 The plateau, as source of the Rivers Mehaigne and Geet formed the highest ground in that region of Flanders. The battle area was over a ground varied by slight undulations and dotted with coppices.

4 It secured Belgian's sovereignty, for three generations, to the House of Austria; set Marlborough on the road of conquest; and halted France's bid for supremacy.

5 The area was flanked by the villages of Ramillies and Taviers.

6 This document, bound up with the *London Gazette* for 1706, is found in the British Museum.

7 'The greatest fire was at the village of Ramillies of which the enemy had possessed themselves. General Churchill's, the Duke of Argyll's and Lord Mordaunt's Regiments which attacked with the Foreigners, suffered most.' (Extract from a regimental history of the period.)

8 The Treaty talks had opened in mid-April, and on the twenty-second of that month the English Commissioners led by Lord Somers, proposed to the Scots Commissioners: 'That the two Kingdoms of Scotland and England be for ever united into one Kingdom by the name of Great Britain. That the United Kingdom of Great Britain be represented by one and the same Parliament, and that the Succession to the Monarchy of Great Britain, in case of failure of heirs of Her Majesty's body, be governed by the terms of the English Act of Settlement in favour of the House of Hanover.' (See Trevelyan, *England under Queen Anne* (Vol. 2) London).

9 These sieges opened in the latter part of June and ended at the beginning of October with victorious results for the Allies.

10 Among his correspondence was a letter addressed 'To My Managers' and written to Mr Ronald Campbell – Writer to the Signet.

   I have writt to my mother to desire she would lett that matter lye over till I goe to England, I must take notis to you that I did intreat you to have my Peaper put in Order but I have had no account of what progress you have made with it, I assure you I know nothing in my affairs of more consequence than that I should know what peapers I have and that they should be disposed in such manner that their [there] may be no difficulty in finding them. I am very glad to hear there is plenty of everything in the Country except mony [money] for if there be plenty of everything else it will be sumthing difficult to persuade me that mony can be extreamly scarce but indeed one thing I shall easely believe that I shall always be told it is scarce. I disire I may be always pay'd the small portion of the Esteat I take to myselfe out of the first and reddis of the whole and then I think thier [there] be a little roome for excuse for not being puntuall in paying me, in short I am made so uneasy by the trouble I am put to to gett that little shair [share] I ristricted myselfe to that I see I shall in spite of my heart be oblig'd to take sum measures that will not be agreeable to those who I know no otherways to be my friends.

. . . their [there] will not be the least hope put to the payment of that mony for if their [there] be upon my honour I dont known where to turne me to gett so much mony as will buy meat and drink.

I am, Gentlemen,

Yours . . .

11 There are interesting anecdotes in the memoirs of the Marquis de Torcy about incidents at the time of the capitulation.
   a) 'Milord Dalrymple and Mr Cadogan – the two favourites of the Duke of Marlborough, assured me of his good intentions, and the Duke of Argyle who had come to take possession of town showed me much friendship. The Duke, my Lord Orkney, and Lord Dalrymple, lent me horses to take me to Douay.' (The Marquis was on his way to Armand and Lille.)
   b) 'Having come out from Menin with the Marquis de Gondrin, on the 23rd August, to make the capitulation, I met before the gates my Lord Orkney, father of the Duke of Hamilton and Lieutenant-General, who told me that he was going to ask to see me . . . with the Duke of Argyle. The next day Lord Orkney came to the quarters of M. de Salisch to bring M. de Gondrin and me to dinner . . . On the way the Duke of Argyle, whom I had known particularly in Holland, made me a thousand offers of service and pointed out all the troops on that side. This action left me no longer in doubt that my journey to Scotland was discovered, as he had been Commissioner at that time . . .' (French texts in Appendix at end of book).
12 Bath MSS (Historical Manuscripts Commission).
13 Mar papers (Historical Manuscripts Commission).

Chapter II

1 The Secretary of State in Scotland (Hugh Campbell, 3rd Earl of Loudon) wrote to Lord Godolphin to recommend a peerage for Lord Archibald Campbell:

> My Lord,
>   My Lord Commissioner sends by this paquet a patent in favour Lord Archibald Campbell who served Her Majesty as Lord Treasurer the last Session of Parliament, and was one of the Commissioners in the Treatie. The Duke of Argyle desires to have one of his familie amongst our peers. I hope it will be the advantage to the Queen's Service which makes me take the libertie to recommend his affair to your Lordship's favour . . .

2 Throughout the negotiations, secrecy and subterfuge had governed the work of the Scots Commissioners. Aware of the close watch kept upon them by spies carrying reports calculated to sharpen the suspicions of the Scottish population, they had adopted measures of finesse. Besides maintaining a rigid aloofness from their English contemporaries both within and without the Whitehall Cockpit, they had countered England with the proposal of Federation under a single monarch though with separate Parliaments. The scheme, as they knew, would be impossible to implement and must be rejected. Yet it provided a shield behind which their work could proceed without inflaming a dangerous situation in Scotland. By this method of manoeuvre they had arrived at the goal.

3 Godolphin – as Chief Minister – had the final word in all appointments to Office.

4 The 'news-letters' of that age.

5 On 19 October, the Earl of Mar, writing to Sir David Nairn, stated: 'The Earl of Islay takes his seat in Parliament.'

6 The financial clauses of the Treaty were lenient to Scotland. To offset the fact that the Scottish taxpayer would be called upon to bear part of England's national debt, contracted before Union, a generous equivalent was offered. It amounted, in figures worked out by Sir John Clerk (the financial expert of that day), to £398,085/10 shillings.

7 Extract from *Parliamentary Debates* – 1706.

8 The ironical term for Union.

9 On 4 July 1706, Lord Godolphin wrote from Windsor to Robert Harley: '. . . I received yesterday a letter from the Duke of Argyle which though it takes no notice of the particular mentioned in Grey's letter, yet all he says there is I doubt but too great a confirmation of the Duke of Hamilton's superiority. I enclose the letter.'

10 It was often rumoured that he contemplated the Crown for himself.

11 Cunningham's *History of Great Britain.*

12 During the reigns of Charles II, James II, and at the time of the Captain Green affair, its measures were almost tyrannical and caused human suffering.

13 Mar and Kellie Papers.
14 Members of the Court Party.
15 Agnes Strickland – author of *A Life of Queen Anne*.
16 Report of a contemporary historian, Agnes Strickland, in her *Life of Queen Anne* also recounts the incident. According to her version: 'Since the Union with Scotland, the Duke of Argyle had prevailed on Queen Anne to add to the companies of the English Guards the Scottish Royal Guard; they had new uniforms and appointments; but to distinguish them from the English Guards their uniforms were trimmed with silver lace. Her Majesty was displeased with this Company and exclaimed – "I do not know my own Guards". She evidently preferred them according to their former picturesque appointments. So recently as the year of her succession, these Guards, commanded by the Earl of Orkney, had not adopted the use of fire-arms, for the Scots Royals wore heavy steel caps and used bows and arrows with broad-swords and targets. Thus Anne had known them in her youth when she lived in Edinburgh with her father. It is not certain that they had ever guarded the royal person in England until after the Union.'

Chapter III

1 Gazetted 24 February 1707. 'During the winter of 1707, a change in the colonelcy of the "Buffs" had occurred. General Charles Churchill who, for nineteen years, had been Colonel was appointed Colonel of the 2nd or Coldstream Regiment of Foot Guards. Major-General the Duke of Argyle was selected to succeed him as Colonel of Prince George of Denmark's Regiment.' (Regimental History of the 'Buffs' (East Kent Regiment, 3rd Foot), by C. R. B. Knight.)
2 Marlborough had arranged for Eugene to move from his place on the Moselle and combine with him in the new campaign.
3 On account of the failures that their interference with Marlborough had caused during the 1707 campaign, the Dutch General had adopted a neutral attitude, leaving the Captain-General at liberty to make his own plans.
4 As compliment to Eugene whose army had not yet arrived, Marlborough confided the crack British Infantry regiments to his command.
5 This enclosed area was in the neighbourhood of villages along the Marollebeck and Diepenbeck Rivers.
6 Regimental History of the 'Buffs'.
7 These were rendered particularly difficult through the fact that the siege train and cannon from Holland could not be brought directly by waterway, due to the French occupation of Ghent. So indirect methods of transport had to be devised.
8 Besides the losses sustained (1,600 men according to Trevelyan), Eugene had fallen ill as the result of wounds, so that the entire direction of operations fell upon Marlborough. The supply route from Holland had been closed by the French and all depended on the passage of the convoy from Ostend. This was under the command of General Webb who, by his action at Wynaendel, saved the situation.

9   When the 1715 Rebellion occurred.
10 This clause stipulated that war in Spain could only end if the Throne was forfeited by Charles III – Imperial Prince of Austria – within two months. Otherwise it would mean the renewal of hostilities against France in the region of the fortresses.
11 The province of Catalonia supported Charles.
12 Contemporary historian's account. There has been, however, certain controversy as to the actual position of regiments. According to evidence, the precise order was not followed, and the 'Buffs' were attached to Lottum. To quote the Earl of Orkney: 'Lottum's, Argyle's and Webb's Foot marched and fronted to the wood to attack. I fronted quite another way to the high ground where the mouth of the defile was.' (*English Historical Review*, April 1904.)
13 *Officers killed*
Captain Byron
Captain Smith
Captain Scott
Captain Melor
Captain Pine
Captain Leadman
Officers wounded
Captain Talbot
Captain Selwin
Captain Greaison
Captain Blessington
Lieut. Wilson
Lieut. Montgomery
Lieut. Horwood
Ensign Barnes
Ensign Nairne
14 There has been speculation as to the causes of the discord. It may have emanated from a similarity in temperaments – both so ambitious for power.
15 In consort with some other regiments that had suffered severe casualties. According to a despatch from the Duke of Marlborough on 7 October 1709: 'We have already received twenty-four fresh Battalions since the Battle, from Garrisons four whereof are English, and the rest Dutch, and fourteen of our weakest Battalions are sent away to supply their Places.'
      The *London Gazette* of 27 or 29 October 1709 states that 'five British Battalions were stationed in Brussels, and sixteen battalions and nine squadrons in Ghent.'
16 From Whitehall a spate of letters and orders went out relating to the Duke of Argyll's regiment.

Chapter IV

1   No quarter was given.
      The accusation against Marlborough seeking to dominate the Army

in Cromwell fashion did not stop there. Parliament would hear Argyll
in speech which caused Marlborough's remark that 'he had not
deserved it from that Gentleman'.

According to a contemporary historian (Agnes Strickland):

> The Duke of Argyll and several lords in whom she thought she
> could confide were secretly brought to confer with Her Majesty on
> this subject. They were consulted as to what course should be taken
> by the Queen, if on her refusal of the Duke of Marlborough's demand
> to be made Generalissimo for life, any design should be apprehended
> from him. The Duke of Argyll suddenly answered – 'Her Majesty
> need not be in pain, for he would undertake, if ever she commanded,
> to seize the Duke of Marlborough at the head of his troops and
> bring him before her dead or alive'.

2 The Barrier Treaty. By its terms, the Dutch were granted permission
   to garrison cities and fortresses not only near the French frontier, but
   in the Spanish Netherlands.
3 Marlborough wrote to Godolphin:

> By the different accounts I have from England it will be a great
> ease to me to know from you how far you and I may safely depend
> upon the sincerity of Shrewsbury. The encouragement Argyle has
> received by the favour the Queen has shown him makes it absolutely
> necessary for me to countenance Lord Orkney in opposition to
> Argyle, which makes me beg of you that you will use your intirest
> with the Queen that they will be pleased to allow me to give assurance
> to Orkney that when any of his Countrymen (the Scotts) are made
> Pears [Peers] that he shall be made an English Baron . . .

(Extract from a letter quoted by Trevelyan in *The Peace*, Vol. 3 in
series *England in the Reign of Queen Anne*.)
4 Preached in St Paul's Cathedral on 5 November 1709. Its principal
   theme, based on the text 'In perils among false brethren', was a
   denunciation of Whigs and Dissenters.
5 The Act of Settlement and the Hanoverian Succession.
6 At the trial, argument of the Whig and Tory views regarding the
   constitution's laws as founded by the Revolution predominated.
7 The Duke of Somerset had allied himself with the Middle Party's aims.
8 A light sentence on Dr Sacheverell who received a hero's reception from
   Tories throughout the country.
9 Marlborough and his Generals assembled at The Hague.
10 The principal clause was to the effect that King Louis should, with his
   own forces, compel his grandson – Philip – to abdicate the Spanish
   Throne. If he refused, the Allies were at liberty to continue the war
   in France.
11 The Earl of Sunderland remarked that he 'wished Orkney was made
   General of the Foot as he believed it would make Argyle shoot himself
   through the head'.

12 At the siege of the former, the 'Buffs' had their position at Bouchain; at the latter, in the vicinity of Villers Brulin.

13 Reference – the *Complete Peerage* (1910 Ed.). John, Duke of Argyll resigned the Thistle on 22 March 1709/10. Incidentally, the 8th and 9th Dukes were ordered by Queen Victoria and King Edward VII to wear both the Garter and the Thistle.

14 *Lives of the Queens of England* Vol. XII – *Queen Anne*, by Agnes Strickland.

15 Who had been Commander in Spain until recalled by Marlborough and the Junto chiefs.

16 Stanhope was cited as responsible for the disaster at the Battle of Brihuega in December; but as he had suffered through being taken prisoner, escaped the heavy censure imposed upon Galway who, in fighting an offensive at Alemanza (1706) had incurred a defeat which resulted in the recall of Peterborough – then in Command in Spain.

17 A fellow officer with Galway.

18 Throughout the debates, Lord Peterborough received a hero's tribute.

19 Marlborough had been responsible for Peterborough's recall.

20 The Commander-in-Chief of King Charles's forces was the Austrian General Stahremberg.

Chapter V

1 As illustration is an incident which occurred during one of the frequent removals of the Court from palace to palace. On these occasions, a state officer, known as the Harbinger, superintended the packing. As the ladies consulted together about their packages, when once a rumour of the Queen's sudden departure to Windsor spread, Jenny announced: 'Well, for my part, I shan't trouble myself. Must not the *Scavenger* take us Maids of Honour.' (*Memoirs of Lady Mary Wortley Montague*).

Chapter VI

1 Nine years previously, Louis XIV could have influenced Philip's abdication.

2 Horace Walpole (4th Earl of Orford) – author, wit and letter writer.

3 State Papers, Domestic – Public Record Office.

4 Lord Dartmouth was Secretary of State.

5 John, Duke of Argyll, in his letter to the Duke of Shrewsbury.

6 Mr Henry St John had been Chief Minister since the Tories came into power. On 8 May, Mr St John had communicated with Lord Dartmouth regarding the mission of Mr Murray, Aide-de-Camp to the Duke of Argyll, with new directions to the Duke, 'If he does not make haste he will scarce find King Charles at Barcelona', he wrote.

7 Sir John Norris was then Admiral in the States.

8 John, Duke of Argyll.

9 Letter from the Duke of Argyll to Lord Dartmouth.

10 The Earl of Oxford was formerly Robert Harley.

11 *Suivant tous les avis que je reçois, il semble que les Ennemis formeront un Camp a la Collorada entre Tarraga et Cervera, et l'on ne veut assurer les qu'ils ye seront tous qu'ils ne seront pas 13m hommes . . . J'apprens que les Equipages du Duc de Vendôme sont effectivement parti de Saragosse, et pour ce qui est du chateau d'Arens, il n'est que trôp vray qu'il se soit rendu à discretion, et les Ennemis après y avoir laissé seulement 250 hommes sont marché vers un autre chateau dont le nom ne me revient pas.*

(Extract from a letter addressed by General Pattée to the Duke of Argyll, 7 August, 1711.)

12 Argyll counted the numbers as follows:
Allies: 36 Battalions (330 men), 44 Squadrons (between 90 and 100 men); Artillery – 16 pieces of 3-pounders and two Hobits.
Enemy: 49 Battalions, 72 Squadrons.

13 Mareschall Stahremberg, at the Camp de Prato del Rey, addressed a letter to the Duke of Argyll:

Milord Duc,
J'ai l'honneur de donner part à V^{re}. Ex^{ce}. par ces lignes de grand avantage, que nos venons de remporter sur les ennemis – Notre dettachement n'aiant pas seulement trouvé le moien de secourur apres deux actions très vigoureuses, qui se sont passées hier et avanthier, le Chateau de Cardonne, mais aiant aussi obligé par la, les ennemis a lever le siège avec beaucoup de confusion et précipitations, et a laisser leur artilleries et malades derrière eux.
J'espère que ce même coup obligera les ennemis a se retirer par tout et qu'ainsi dans peu de jours j'aurai le plaisir d'assurer v^{re}. Ex^{ce}. de bouche de la sincerité de . . . etc.

P.S. Les troupes anglaises y ont fait tout ce que l'on peut humainement souhaiter, mais la perte que nos avons fait due Colonell Stanhope nous doit affliger particulierement; c'etoit l'Officier qui faisoit honneur a ce Nation et qui c'quroit fait un des meilleurs Capitaines.

(Note: Colonel Stanhope was killed in this action.)

14 The Duke of Ormonde was Commander of the British Troops in the Netherlands, besides certain foreign regiments in the pay of England and Holland. He obeyed the 'Restraining Orders' which later constituted the principal charge against Bolingbroke, and involved the Earl of Oxford.

15 Marlborough said that 'he did not know how to reconcile orders not to hazard a battle and to join in a siege, to the rules of war'.

16 French Foreign Office Archives.
English translation from Her Majesty Queen Anne to her brother, the exiled James, known as the 'Pretender'.

Sir my Brother,
Having found it necessary to send the Duke of Argyle to Minorca to regulate several affairs and among them those which concern the

Imperial Troops and mine in Catalonia, I have given him orders to salute Your Majesty before proceeding there. I pray you then to receive him favourably and place faith on what he tells you on my part, principally when he will assure you of the true friendship with which I am

Sir my Brother,

      Your good Sister

                                  signed – Anne

At Windsor Castle
15th September, 1712.

17   Emperor Leopold of Austria.
18   John, Duke of Argyll – report.
19   An order interesting because it indicates that the law governing fire arms was the same as that in force today on certain occasions.

Chapter VII

1   According to Woodrow in his *Analecta* – 'At a meeting of Scots Peers – 'Argyle put his hand to his sword and swore that with that he would fight against Episcopacy in Scotland as well as against the Duke of Marlburrou in England.'

Chapter VIII

1   Bothmar had lately been appointed by the Elector in place of Schutz.
2   Sir William Wyndham had succeeded George Granville as Secretary at War in June 1712.
3   The Earl of Sunderland, Lord Somers, Lord Cowper, Lord Wharton.
4   The Dukes of Argyll, Shrewsbury, and Somerset. They acted as on the eve of the 1710 election.
5   Even to Bolingbroke, despite the fact that he had only held power for a few days, and not as Lord Treasurer.
6   Thomas Lord Archbishop of Canterbury, Simon Lord Harcourt – Chancellor, Charles Duke of Shrewsbury – High Treasurer, John Duke of Buckingham, William Earl of Dartmouth, Charles Duke of Somerset, James Duke of Ormonde, George Duke of Northumberland, John Duke of Argyll, John Duke of Roxburgh, Henry Duke of Kent, John Earl of Poulet, George Earl of Nottingham, Charles Earl of Sunderland, Charles Bodvile Earl of Radnor, Henry Earl of Rochester, Edward Earl of Orford, John Earl of Mar, Hugh Earl of Loudoun, Robert Earl of Oxford, David Earl of Portmore, Henry Viscount Bolingbroke, John Lord Bishop of London, Robert Lord Lexington, William Lord Berkley of Stratton, Francis Lord Guildford, John Lord Somers, Henage Lord Guernsey, William Lord Cowper, Thomas Lord Mansel, George Lord Landsdowne, Robert Lord Bingley, William Broomley Esq., Henry Boyl Esq., Thomas Coke Esq., Sir William Wyndham, Sir John Trevor, Sir John Holland, John Hill Esq., Sir Richard Onslow, John Smith Esq.

M

PART THREE

Statesman

Chapter *I*

A NEW ERA

KENSINGTON Palace closed; the curtains drawn over the windows of rooms which, not so long ago, had witnessed the animation of Court life. In contrast to its forlorn aspect was St James's Palace, thronged, in these opening days of the Hanoverian decade, with statesmen, diplomats, and the monarch's entourage from Hanover. The Duke of Argyll – as one of King George's most favoured men – was constantly present. On 13 June 1715 he had been appointed Colonel of the Royal Horse Guards (the 'Blues') in place of Charles Mordaunt[1] – 3rd Earl of Peterborough – who went as Ambassador to the Hatian States.

A new appointment and reinstatement to a former one were both gazetted during the month of September.

By an authority issued from St James's on 25 September: 'John Duke of Argyle to be Generall of our Foot in Scotland'; and a few days later (the 29th): 'John, Duke of Argyle, to be Governor of Minorca and Port Mahon.'

At Court, too, he received the honour of office. It came from George Augustus – Prince of Wales. On their first meeting a friendship, destined for endurance despite the stresses to which they would both be subject, was born. The young heir discerned in Argyll one who could prove a trusted counsellor. Therefore, he invited the Duke to enter his Household as 'Groom of the Stole' and 'Lord of the Bedchamber'.

The reign had certainly opened auspiciously for Argyll and he should have been in the best of humours. Yet a care prevailed. Soon he would be bidding farewell to Jenny Warburton who was preparing for departure to her Cheshire home. His sentiments for her had deepened during the past ten years. Indeed, she was the only woman who could rule his heart. The fact that many times she had refused advances passionately pleaded merely served to enhance the regard which he felt for her. The brightest moments of his life in London had been those passed in her company either strolling in the gardens of Kensington Palace or sitting by the fireside in the apartment reserved to the Maids of Honour. Now these 'summer days' were over; at least so he believed, and the thought gave him a moodiness which did not escape observation by certain persons acutely anxious as to his future political plans. They guessed the reason.

In an age given to intrigue of such order that even the private lives of people were exploited if occasion warranted, the name of Jenny Warburton was whispered among Whig chiefs. With their Party restored to power, they desired Argyll's whole-hearted allegiance. How might it best be won? The question, debated in their astute minds, brought the answer: 'We must provide for Mrs Warburton that we may secure the Duke of Argyle'.

Accordingly, Jenny's name was foremost on the list of ladies appointed Maids of Honour to Caroline Anspach-Brandenburg, Princess of Wales.[2]

On arrival in London, the Princess made it her first duty to become acquainted with the personal backgrounds of ladies designed for Court appointments and how they stood in relation to the world about them. So when the names of the chosen Maids of Honour were submitted for review, that of Jane Warburton predominated in her interest. Although evidently on such strong terms of friendship with the Duke of Argyll, there was nothing to her discredit. This fact, and the more important one of the Duke's power in the State, evoked a resolve: 'I shall take good care to treat the object of His Grace the Duke of Argyle's regard with particular attention.'[3]

When told of her good fortune, it probably did not occur to Jenny's naive mind how the change had happened. In down-to-earth fashion she accepted thankfully and took her place amidst the Leicester House[4] circle. The Princess's keen solicitude for her welfare might have caused some wonderment; most likely she regarded it as a matter of course.

Argyll's reaction was one of pleasure. The shadow which had been over him passed and the personality that charmed became apparent. To the Chiefs who had contrived this ingenious 'plot' he turned an agreeable countenance. There seemed every prospect of their designs being fulfilled. Certainly, at the moment, Argyll applauded ministerial policy; but events were to prove that he was pre-eminently a 'King's man' and would only lend himself to Party if it matched the Sovereign's interests. In this hour of spring 1715, he gave allegiance, though *not* whole-hearted.

Restoration of Whig supremacy by will of the King and accord of the nation; such was the political scene.[5] The reins of Government were in the hands of statesmen[6] chosen by King George for their ability to redeem Britain from the international isolation into which she had collapsed during the last days of Queen Anne's reign. One of the first measures taken was to form a secret committee for the purpose of investigating the documents of certain men who had been suspected of subversive activities in the Jacobite cause. As a result of the committee's findings, Bolingbroke (Henry St John) fled the country to join the Pretender. Ormonde, Oxford and Strafford were impeached.

In the light of reason it seemed that their removal must be a warning signal to Jacobites both in Britain and on the Continent. Besides, France had given diplomatic blessing to the House of Hanover.

Yet there existed two threats to the security of the realm.

The first was a military weakness. The total establishment, including Colonial Garrisons, counted less than 30,000 men. The decline in the state of the armed forces owed its origin to the departure of Marlborough's influence towards the close of the late reign. In the eyes of the British nation, the censure brought to bear upon Marlborough by Parliament cast a reflection on the entire army.[7] Swift to take advantage of this deplorable condition among the defenders of Britain, whether at home or abroad, were the adherents of the exiled James – Chevalier St George.[8] Through their partisans at Westminster, they kept alive the animosity against Marlborough's army. By fanning popular feeling into a clamour, the forces could be degraded and their power broken.

The other threat emanated from the Chevalier's Court at St Germains. Plot and intrigue quickened. James still maintained his hereditary claim to Britain's Crown and urged by others who styled themselves 'advisers' resolved to make a bid for this right. To encourage him further in the decision was the fact of new and strong supporters in the persons of Oxford, Ormonde and Strafford. On the political side stood the brilliant Bolingbroke; on the military one was the Earl of Mar who would soon be granted the title of 'Duke' with command of the Chevalier's forces in Scotland.

As reports[9] from agents at Versailles reachd England, war-like preparations were set on foot, though the reason was not disclosed. Yet citizens observed the Foot Guards encamped in Hyde Park. The Horse Guards were also called out; several regiments received orders to march nearer London and five or six regiments, among them the 'Buffs', were recalled from Ireland.

During those midsummer days, the west of Scotland claimed Argyll's attention. His own clansmen were divided to 'the extent of one half in favour of a Scottish rising against Union'. Campbell of Glendaruel, Campbell of Glenlyon and Lord Breadalbane declared their allegiance to the Chevalier. On the other hand, those who, by tradition as well as conviction, were staunch Whigs gathered at Inveraray on 11 August and signed a bond pledging their loyalty. To this the Duke sent the following reply:

Gentlemen,

I think myself obliged to return you my thanks for the zeal you have showed in your late victory for the peace of the country and for the defence of His Majesties Government. I shall not fail to do you the Justice to acquaint the King of the alacrity and duty you have expressed upon this occasion against the intended rebellious attempts to destroy our Religion and Liberties. I do not doubt but it will appear at this time how false these suggestions have been which have been made of late years that the Pretender to the Crown of these Kingdoms and the Usurper of His Majesties royal titles had encreased in his interest in the shire of Argyle so famed in the worst of times for the supporting the Protestant Religion and the resisting of Tyranny. My Family and consequently you have formerly suffered for their sake. I glory in it, and I hope you do so too, but I can with great satisfaction acquaint you the King has taken such precautions and is so much resolved to protect his fathful subjects that we cannot run any hazzard but from too great security. Our old and new Enemies will soon see their errors and those who have always been ready in the worst of times to affront the right cause will now with the greater pleasure follow to support their principles in the best.

I shall immediately as your heritable Lieutenant appoint Deputy Lieutenants and other Officers to command our fensible men and I shall neglect nothing which may tend to your safety and prosperity.

I am, Gentlemen,

Your most obedient and most humble servant

Argyle

London,
Aug: 29 1715

On the part of the Chevalier and his captains there was to be no withdrawal from their bid for the Crown. In the first week of

September 1715 the glow of rebellion illumined Britain. At Braemar, the Earl of Mar raised the standard of the exiled Prince who counselled him as follows:

> In case Argyle, upon the reinforcements he gets from Ireland, should think fitt to move towards Perth before Seaforth and General Gordon come up, those at Perth have nothing to do but defend the town the best way they can, and retire to the north side of the Tay; when they can defend it no longer, in which case the enemy being in possession of Perth, it could be almost impossible for the King's army to repass Tay again that season without assistance of the Forces in the South, so that the King's friends there upon this supposed motion of Argyle's should certainly march after him by the heads of Forth to harass him; prevent all they can his returning to Stirling and to follow such other directions as should be sent them when they come betwixt Stirling and Perth . . .

This letter was dated on the same day as Mar raised the standard. The next weeks would prove how far the Chevalier's speculations were correct.

On the eve of setting out to take up his command, Argyll found urgent need to communicate with Lord Townshend – Secretary of State: 'I was this moment at the Treasury where I was told that the ten thousand pound credit is not yet gone to Scotland and the thousand pound I was to receive is not to be had to-day; by this Your Lordship will see that I may be detained here and I not be in fault.'

It was an old experience – this unnecessary delay on the part of Whitehall officials.

Meanwhile, he offered advice based upon his knowledge of Scotland. Stirling – key-point between the Highlands and Low-lands – should be secured by the assembly there of troops. At the same time, adequate man-power and armaments were essential. Unless there was military strength the revolt could prove difficult to suppress speedily; and prolonged into the rigours of a Scottish winter the scene would be one of suffering for the innocent as well as the guilty. It distressed him to contemplate a high toll of life; after all, the rebels were members of Great Britain, and his own fellow-countrymen. In strongest terms he urged that reinforcements be despatched so as to avert hindrance at the outset of the campaign.

Unhappily neither argument nor entreaty prevailed with the

politicians at Westminster. Argyll, Commander-in-Chief of the Royal Army in Scotland, had His Majesty's order to proceed forthwith and take command of the troops that would be awaiting him at the borders. Meanwhile, couriers were busy on the road between Edinburgh and London, with news for Monsieur d'Iberville – France's Agent in London. This he forwarded to Louis XIV and his Ministers at Versailles:

POSTSCRIPT TO THE ST. JAMES'S POST N° 100

London, Sept. 14. This Day we had the following Advices from Scotland.

Edinburgh, Sept. the 10th.

We have an Account, That the Earl of Mar, and several others that seem desperate, are resolv'd to push their Way with Fire and Sword; but great Numbers have deserted them, by which it's thought Matters will soon come to an Issue. However, we are assur'd, That the Bulk of the Nation, both Gentry and Commonalty, are in the Interest of King George, and will stand by him as one Man: They may give some disturbance to the Government and honest People; but it must at last end in the total Subversion of Jacobitism in this Part of the Kingdom. The Malcontents flatter themselves with mighty Success if the Pretender should land in Scotland, only from the foolish Imaginations of the Duke of Berwick's Interest in England, and James Butler's (late Duke of Ormonde) in Ireland.

Just now we have an Account, That the Rebels design'd to surprize the Castle of Edinburgh (towards the West Side) with Scaling-Ladders; Five of the Men got in, and were seized, the rest Escap'd.[10]

Argyll, travelling north, was at Burrowbridge when report of the attempts upon Edinburgh Castle reached him. Immediately, by letter to Lord Townshend, he repeated his entreaty for reinforcement. Then he resumed his journey and on 13 September arrived at the borders near Berwick. There he received his troops. The sight appalled him. 'They are quite insufficient to prevent the rebels from reaching England.'[11]

Chapter II

'WORSE THAN TURKISH GENERALS'

ON 14 September, the Duke of Argyll entered Edinburgh to find 'all the friends of the Government in the last consternation and all its enemies in the greatest hopes'.[1] 'Nobody in arms for King George; yet throughout Scotland the Rebels were either armed or ready to rise.'[2] He promptly acted. Before nightfall five hundred arms, together with ammunition, had gone to the 'Fencible' men of Fife.

The following day he gave directions for Edinburgh's defence and wrote a full account of affairs to Lord Townshend.[3] Next morning, he was on horseback, ready to start for Stirling, when a courier arrived with news that Mar's rebels had secured Perth. The move endangered the west, so he ordered the dispatch of one thousand arms to Argyllshire.

Soon after arrival at Stirling, Argyll held a review of the fourteen hundred regular troops who had been stationed there on his advice. Their presence as guardians of that highly strategical pass 'saved at least Scotland'[4] in those early hours of the Rebellion. On the other hand, they were inadequate for movement on a large scale. This circumstance compelled pressure for reinforcement. A letter to Lord Townshend concluded: '. . . I must end with insisting on considerable reinforcement for without it or a miracle not only this country will be utterly destroyed but the rest of His Majesty's dominions put in the extremest danger'.

His plight was closely watched by France's agents. A report from Monsieur d'Iberville to the French court stated: 'I have already had the honour to inform Your Majesty that at Edinburgh the Duke of Argyle had written that he was unable to despatch the few Regular Troops – the number of 1400 men – whom he had at Stirling, to march against the enemy and that he had instantly asked a reinforcement with money. He added that he was not determined on which of the two steps to take, either to dispute the way of Stirling or to retire to Berwick in endeavour to oppose their entry into England.'[5]

Argyll decided to 'dispute the way of Stirling' and secure its river. Although two Dragoon regiments joined him and raised his strength by two hundred, he was still without the force necessary for defence measures against an enemy strong in numbers. Besides, each day brought calls for help from royalist supporters threatened by rebel detachments on the march. Only one course remained: he summoned the militia.[6]

The first days of October found him busy with the issue of Orders[7]; and as the month passed there occurred incidents which proved what little reliance could be placed upon those who had charge of seeing that his commands were fulfilled. The most serious one was the threat to Edinburgh through the passage of fifteen hundred rebels across the Forth into Lothian by North Berwick. Argyll's prompt action of marching at the head of a hundred Dragoons and two hundred Foot mounted on country horses saved the panic-striken capital from falling to the enemy when they had gained access to its citadel.[8]

On receiving news that the Earl of Mar, with baggage and cannon, had marched past Auchterarder southward, Argyll speeded his return to Stirling. He arrived to learn of the rebel force at Dunblane, and immediately made preparations. However, a few hours later came information which demonstrated his rival's reluctance for a clash. They had quickly taken the road home to Perth.

Back in camp and facing the facts of winter at hand and an enemy causing alarms but not venturing to the field, Argyll felt in the 'state of the damned'. To accentuate this sentiment, he was aware that certain actions had been censured by ministers who sought to damage his prestige with the King.

'I find we are in so much on a worse foot even than Turkish Generals that we are only to serve without being gott the better of by the enemy . . .' Thus the opening lines of a letter which he wrote during one of his darkest hours to a friend, William Stuart, Member of Parliament for Inverness.

He had indeed cause for anxiety. In the first place, his reinforcement amounted to a mere three thousand horse and foot. The season made it impossible to keep to the open. Even at Stirling, where his army were encamped on the dryest ground in that region, men began to fall sick.

'We are at present under as miserable a dilemma as can possibly be imagined', he wrote to Lord Townshend. 'If the enemy advances we have but one of two pairts to take – to fight or to retire. In the

first case, I think that the country and this Corps of troops will be lost. In the latter, the country is lost and which adds to our difficulties our Foot do not at all think they can beat more than their own numbers.'

Towards the second week of November, Argyll received reports which had the element of surprise. The Earl of Mar's forces were moving south[9]. By the 12th, they had reached Ardoch in Perthshire. Leaving the Glasgow regiment of militia to guard Stirling, he immediately marched at the head of 2,500 Foot and 1,000 Horse; his objective was to intercept the enemy in the vicinity of Dunblane.

Nightfall found Argyll's army beneath the slopes of Sheriffmuir. Here he ordered them to bivouack in the formation planned for the forthcoming engagement. Despite the icy weather, he forbade either the pitching of tents or lighting of fires. He also issued orders that the men should not stir from their arms : this command was observed so stringently that even at the hour – next day – while the drums were beating 'the General' (signal to prepare to march) there was no immediate move to assemble.[10]

In the morning of Sunday 13 November, the two armies started to advance at the same time, evidently unnoticed by the one another until they were well up the slopes of the plateau. They encountered in a manner which might have proved disastrous for Argyll when his left flank – under General Witham – was caught in a broadsword charge by Mar's Highlanders and put to confusion. His right flank, however, not only sustained the initial charge, but repulsed the enemy who were then scattered by cavalry.

Two circumstances favoured Argyll in a battle which evolved without advantage to either side.

A delay by Rob Roy (commanding Macphersons and Macgregors) enabled him to lead into action the 'Buffs' (commanded by Lord Forfar)[11] together with Wightman's and Shannon's regiments.

Secondly, Mar's neglect to follow the opportunity gained at the outset by the successful attack on the royalist left gave these troops time to reform.

By the end of that day, Argyll had the satisfaction of returning to the camp at Stirling with nearly all the enemy's transport captured, besides a number of prisoners. His losses, too, were less than those of the Highlanders.[12]

Three days later he issued the following order :
John, Duke of Argyle, General and Commander-in-Chief of His Majesties Forces in North Britain.

You are hereby ordered and required to take proper measures for bringing in alle the hay, corn, and fodder remaining in the barn-yards belonging to the rebels in your Shire or in the hands of any person or persons for their behoof yta [that] lay up of the Same in Magazines at such places and under the care of such persons as the Lords Lieutenants shall think fit. To be disposed of for the use of His Majesties Forces, ande for your so doing this shall be your Warrant.

Given at the Camp at Stirling this 16th November 1715.

Argyle

To the Rt. Honble. The Lords
Polwarth, Lords Lieutenants &
Deputy Lieutenants & Justices
of the Peace of the Shire of Berwick

Although Sheriffmuir might be termed a drawn battle, Argyll felt a measure of pride at the way in which it had gone for him.

'Some of our Troops behaved as ill as ever any did in this world which makes it the more wonderful that the day should have ended as it did', he wrote, some days afterwards, to Lord Townshend, and went on to repeat the need for greater strength: '. . . I have had further accounts of the preparations of the Rebels whose vigilance and furious zeal is inexpressible. They are ten times more formidable than our friends in England ever believed tho' your Lordship will do me the justice that from the beginning very long before I left I had the fortune to guess pretty tightly of what has happened since, and if I am not more mistaken than ever I was in my life, His Majesty will need to employ a considerable army in this country . . .'

As December advanced, rumour persisted that the Chevalier had landed in Scotland. Aware that were this to prove true many High-landers would rally to Mar's side, Argyll set measures afoot to fore-stall such occurrence. From one of his Captains – Sir Archibald Grant – went a communication to Lord Lovat:

Stirling – Dec. 22
. . . The Duke of Argyle earnestly desires you and everybody with you convene as many together as you possibly can which will keep your neighbours from joining Earl Mar; lest you should fall into their countries or if they should endeavour to march South that by all means in the world you have a strike at them . . .

The end of the year was at hand. From the military aspect,

John Duke of Argyll
Earle of Greenewich &c Captain
of Her Majesties Fourth Troop
of Horse Guards. One of Her
Majesties most Hon.ble Privy
Cuncil, Ambassa. Extry
& General comanding in chief
her Majesties forces in Spain
& Knight of the most noble
order of the Garter.

I do hereby order & Direct you out of such
money as may come to your hands for the
use of her Majesties service in Spain, to
pay to Brigadeer Generall Bret___ the
Sum of Two Hundred Pistoles, and place it
to account of his pay as Brigadeer Genll
on this Establishment, taking his receipt
for the same, which with this shall be
your sufficient Warrant. Given at
Barcelona the 20th July 1711. J. R

To John Mead Esq.r Deputy
Master Genll of her Majesties
forces In Spa.

By his graces comand
James Cockburn

Orders issued by Argyll during the 1715 Rebellion

John Duke of Argyll General &
Commander in chief of his Majesties forces in North Brit[ain]

You are hereby ordered & required to take proper measures for bring[ing]
in all the hay corn & fodder remaining in the barn yards belonging to [the]
rebels, or in the hands of any person or persons for their behoof & laying
up of the same in Magazines at such places & under the care of s[uch]
persons as the Lord Lieutenant shall think fit, To be disposed of for
the use of his Majesties forces. And for your so doing this shall be y[our]
Warrant. Given at the Camp at Stirling this 16th Nov.r 1715

To the Rt Honoble: The Lord
Polwarth Lord Lieutenant &
Deputy Lieutenants & Justices of
Peace of the Shire of Berwick

Argyll

Argyll's circumstances had certainly consolidated through the presence of a number of Dutch as well as Swiss troops.[13] When all his reinforcements arrived, he would be able to count a total strength of 10,000 men. Nevertheless, he had anxieties which set a severe strain upon him.

In the first place, the arrival of Lord Cadogan[14] who had come not to take over his command but rather to act as a Government 'agent' was displeasing; they had never been on good terms.

Secondly, the weather continued bad and virtually halted progress. Yet ministers at Westminster seemed blind to the fact and pressed for an offensive. The following letter addressed to Lord Townshend is an example of how he had to justify himself:

My Lord,

The weather is here extreamely severe; the frost is great; and there is deep snow upon the ground, so that the roads are the most frequented, excepting that between the Town and Edinburgh are pass'd with great difficulty.

My Lord, as to our having little occasion for the Artillery on account of the frost. It is with great submission that I offer it as my opinion that the frost will not make it necessary to have the Artillery. But, my Lord, if Mr. Cadogan who I expect will be here to-night, thinks it is practicable to attack Perth without Artillery, I'll march. In short, my Lord, the moment Mr. Cadogan thinks it practicable to move, even tho' I shall be of a different opinion there shall not be a moment's delay.

My Lord, I thought it my duty not to mention the arrival of the Pretender as absolutely certain, so long as neither I nor any of the General Officers under me find cause to believe it so; if I have been faulty, my Lord, in that matter, I can only say that I mean'd it well.

My Lord, I shall obey all His Majesty's Commands with the utmost readiness that I am capable of, and shall march to the enemy the moment that either I or any of His Majesty's General Officers here, think it possible in nature to do it.

I have the honour to be with the greatest respect,

Your Lsp.'s most obedient and most faithful humble servant,

Argyle

News which had started as rumour and deterred Argyll from proclaiming it was confirmed as true on the eve of Christmas. The Chevalier had indeed landed in Scotland[15] and joined the 'Duke'[16] of Mar at Perth, now the final stronghold of the Rebellion.

The English statesmen reacted by exerting even stronger pressure for an attack on the enemy. Argyll could only repeat his view – shared by colleagues – that to march under the conditions which prevailed would be too hazardous. To judge, however, from a letter written to Lord Townshend on 19 January, his opinion was twisted in a manner calculated to incur the King's displeasure.

My Lord,

I have received your Lsp.'s of the 12th and am extremely concerned that I should have made any observation or given any opinion that is displeasing to His Majesty. I have, my Lord, alwayes made it my chief study, however I may have failed to better do and say every thing that I thought for His Majesty's service, and shall continue to do so in which ever station I am, and my present misfortune that made me so cautious for the future that I hope I shall offend no more.

My Lord, I perceive some people have been so happy as to have their services and sufferings set in a very strong light before His Majesty. I wish I had had the same good fortune.

My Lord, I hope and most earnestly beg that His Majesty will be persuaded that it never entered into my head to impute the continuance of the Rebellion to any act of His Majesty. I take God to witness that it never entered into my thoughts and it is the extreamest mortification to me that I should have explained myself so ill as to make His Majesty think me capable of so high an insolence as finding fault with anything that he does; and since your Lsp. believes what you are pleased to tell me as from His Majesty. It is my duty not to presume to explain these words which had the misfortune to offend, but only most humbly to beg His Majesty's pardon.

My Lord, if my salvation depended upon it, I could do no more towards forwarding this Expedition to Perth than I do, So that if the delay is imputed to me, I am very unfortunate . . .

A week later – 25 January – found Argyll writing again to Lord Townshend :

My Lord,

The day before yesterday I went with a detachment of 200 Dragoons as far as Auchterarder to view the Country and the Roads in order to our march. From the other side of Dunblane we found a vast depth of snow in so much that we were obliged to march the whole way one horse after another, and for the most part up to the horses' bellies, which made Mr. Cadogan and all of us of opinion that it was impossible to encamp, for which reason when we returned, we consulted in what manner it would be practicable to put the Troops under cover in our march and Colonel Dubourgay proposed a method which is most likely to succeed and which we have agreed to put in practice, it carries as far as the River Ern, from when we have about five miles to Perth. If the Rebells upon our arrival abandon the Town, or that we find it such as may be carried soon it will be verry fortunate, but indeed I cannot answere that we shall be able to lye before it, because that cannot be done without encamping and Mr. Cadogan and everybody here agree that it is not practicable to encamp in this depth of snow.

I have, my Lord, disposed of everything so as to be able to march on Saturday and am then determined to pass the River if we are not prevented by a considerable fall of snow, or delayed some dayes by a thaw.

I humbly hope, my Lord, since you see no body here thinks there is one moment left, I shall not suffer in His Majesty's opinion on account of delay which Providence only is able to prevent.

Argyll wrote one other letter. It was for the Duke of Marlborough, by way of Lord Townshend:

My Lord,

The condition in which I found Mr. Ecklyn's Regiment when I lately reviewed it in Scotland is so extraordinary that I think it my duty to give you a short account of it in writing, which I hope Your Grace will lay before His Majesty that it may appear to him how ill he is served in that Corps.

The men, my Lord, are many of them old and little; the Horses generally wrong trimmed and ill-sized; the cloathing the very worst I ever saw tho' not old. The accoutrements both of men and horses unfit for service, and as I am informed have been worn these six years; the Arms very bad, and the numbers uncompleat, to the best of my memory not above twenty-four men a Troop the strongest Corporals included.

This, my Lord, according to my judgement is the true state of that Regiment to which I will only add this short observation that if His Majesty continues his Corps in the hands of persons who serve him in this manner, I am afraid the Brittish Troops will in a very little time, lose the reputation they have so long enjoyed in the world.

    I am, my Lord,
       Your most obedient and most humble servant

                                 Argyll

After the dispatch of these communications Argyll turned to preparations for the march.[17] As Commander-in-Chief of an army now ten thousand strong, he was in a position to achieve his objective.

ARGYLL EXECUTES HIS OWN COMMAND

In the last days of January, Argyll's army marched out from Stirling to face a test of endurance. Besides the fierceness of the cold and ice-bound roads, villages presented a mournful aspect as houses had been ravaged by fire[18]. When evening fell and halted progress, the troops were forced to be in the open and shiver throughout the long night. At length they came to the frozen River Ern. The hazards of crossing it with horses, baggage and cannon cost them severe strain as well as exhaustion. Yet their approach to Perth went unchallenged. On arrival in the town the reason for the enemy's absence became known.

    The Chevalier had chosen to flee the country rather than risk the consequences of another battle which must surely end in defeat. The 'Duke' of Mar and certain other captains had accompanied him. Meanwhile the rebel forces were in full retreat northwards.

    After allowing his weary men a few hours to recover, Argyll ordered pursuit.[19]

    The 8th February found him, with most of the cavalry, in Aberdeen[20] where he established headquarters for the last phase of operations. These began with the issue of an Order – dated the 14th – to the Lord-Lieutenant, Deputy-Lieutenants, Justices of the Peace and Magistrates of the northern counties:

    'It being probable that the rebells are separated, that many of the gentlemen concerned in the rebellion may seek for shelter in their own houses or among their friends, you are hereby desired to make diligent search for all such persons who you are to use your utmost endeavours to apprehend and retain in custody.'

    Nevertheless, he intended to be lenient to those unfortunate Chiefs who had been deserted at the crucial hour.

The Marquis of Huntly was one of the first to 'own myself much obliged to the Duke of Argyle'.[21] Lord Lovat was another who had occasion for the Duke's clemency. To him Argyll wrote on 17 February: 'It is with the greatest pleasure I inform you that last night I received a letter from Lord Townshend acquainting me that he has received His Majesty's commands to make out your pardon, and that I may depend on his losing no time in doing it. When this is over, be persuaded that no man can wish more heartily that you receive further favours. I well know you have honestly deserved them . . .'

Finally, General Alexander Gordon, the Noblemen and the Clans, held a meeting at Ruthven in Badenoch. Impressed by Argyll's chivalrous attitude, they decided to address a letter to him about a general indemnity.

The unfortunate circumstances our country is reduced to by our late divisions must move the pity of any true born Scotsman, and we have just ground to expect that the generosity which every man allows to shine so bright in your character, will make it very disagreeable to you to see your country in that situation. The many and great hardships we groaned under since the last Union were not the least motives of making us take arms and however our judgement may have been mistaken in the way of procuring redress, our intentions must, we think, be allowed to be honourable, and what became a people who have for so many ages preserved their independency. Whatever hardships and un-expected accidents have attended, we see the more easy that we were always resolved to keep the worst, and were willing to hazard our lives in a cause which seemed to us so just, but were our lives the consideration, we would not have given Your Grace the trouble of this letter. That which troubles us more sensibly is the melancholy view we have of so many old and worthy families as must fall with us, which makes us wish for the good of our country that peace and tranquility may be restored and that once more we should all return to that Love and affection to one another that ought to be entertained by a people linked together by so many ties of blood and relation.

This reflection we are confident will touch Your Grace as much as it does us, and make you use your endeavours to obtain so happy an end which would be best effectuated could we expect the Government would grant an indemnity to such as are willing to live peaceably at home and liberty for those to go abroad who are desirous to pass the rest of their lives beyond seas. It may not perhaps be unworthy of the Government to accept the acknowledgement of so many noblemen and gentlemen as have appeared here in arms, and the experience of all ages shows what a body of men reduced to despair may do, and we should consider it as the greatest hardship that can be imposed on us were we forced to act a part of that nature which must prove so fatal to our country. Your Grace has now an opportunity offered you of showing your affection to it and at the same time doing considerable service to the Government by securing the obedience of so many noblemen and gentlemen by the ties of gratitude, which must be considered very strong by men of honour, and we hope those motives will prevail with Your Grace to give us speedy answer; and let us know what are the resolutions of the Government concerning us, and whether we may expect our indemnity for what is past and protection for our lives and fortunes in time comeing which we consider the only means of obtaining the end we now aim at, the peace and welfare of our country, by preserving so many honourable families as are engaged in this affair . . .

Letter from :

General Alexander Gordon, the Earls of Linlithgow and Southesk, T. McDonald, Robertson of Struan, J. Dougal, Alexander McKenzie, C. McDonald, Clanronald, and James Ogilvie – to the Duke of Argyle. (All Jacobite gentlemen).

Although the glow of revolt would linger for some time among Highlanders whose allegiance could only be to the Stuart cause, the campaign was over for Argyll. Affairs of greater importance claimed him in London.

With the letter from the Chiefs of the north in his pocket, and the resolve that so far as it lay in his power mercy would be shown to those who had suffered through their loyalty, he set out from Aberdeen in the last days of February. He was aware of trials awaiting him; but at least he could once more assert: 'I have served my monarch with all the zeal in my heart.'

Chapter III

ARGYLL VERSUS THE KING

AFTER the receptions and praises the feuds of politics: Argyll met the two extremes when he returned to London. As soon as the hero's hour was over and he resumed the statesman's role, the duel of words and clash of ambitions began in earnest.

First were the 'shaped personal heats' between the Earl of Notting-ham and the Duke, when the Septennial Bill[1] was debated in the House of Lords on 10 May 1716. The point of controversy occurred over Nottingham's declaration that the 'Rebellion in Scotland was at an end, but if any ferment yet remained, this Bill was a very im-proper way to allay it'.

The Duke of Argyll, rising to speak immediately after his rival had concluded, announced emphatically 'that he could, by no means, agree with the noble lord that spoke last either as to the beginning or end of the rebellion'.

It has been suggested that the king has been received with the general acclamations of his people; but it is certain, and has since manifestly appeared, that whatever arts were used by the last Ministry to blind and deceive the people, designs had been laid to bring in the Pretender long before the King's happy accession to the throne. The disappointment of these designs was entirely owing to Providence, for had the conspirators thrown off the mask sooner, and improved the ferment their emissaries had raised in the nation at the election of the last parliament, 'tis very probable their wicked schemes for setting aside the Protestant Succession had taken place.

I wonder therefore that my Lord can be puzzled to find out the cause of the present disaffection; for it is plain it proceeds from the false representation of things and persons that have been industriously spread abroad both before and since His Majesty's coming in. As to what has been suggested that the rebellion is at an end –

The Rebels have only shifted their headquarters from Perth to Paris or St Germains. Their emissaries are still as busy and insolent as ever in Great Britain, and want only an opportunity to renew the Rebellion, and favour an invasion. As to what has been hinted that this Bill will rivet the Jacobites in their opinions, There is no good argument against it, for I have seen some persons often shift sides, and change their opinions and be very zealous for both.

At Whitsuntide – towards the end of May – it was announced that a thanksgiving for the successful conclusion of the northern rebellion would be held in St Paul's Cathedral on 7 June. Seven days afterwards the King intended to visit Hanover where he discerned a storm brewing from the direction of Sweden. The Prince of Wales was to have charge of affairs in Great Britain.

In Jacobite circles, news of the King's proposed departure aroused keen speculation. They foresaw an explosion of fireworks between the Dukes of Marlborough and Argyll.[2] If the outcome went against the latter, perhaps he could be induced to contemplate a change of camp; the Chevalier would generously reward an ally of such power. Always in the depths of Jacobite hearts there had glowed the hope that Argyll might be won. In the summer of 1716, that hope waxed strong. Consequently, Jacobite agents were actively vigilant and kept exiles on the Continent almost daily posted with the course of events which, after Cadogan's arrival in London, soared to a climax. The story is best told in the words of John Menzies writing, on 3 July, to Lord Inese:

> Things grow more and more inflamed every day betwixt Argyle and Cadogan who, in effect, succeeds Marlborough and heads the Party in the State and in the Army. Cadogan came on Thursday last to kiss the Prince's hand with his 'green ribbon'.[3] Argyle was there, the Groom of the Stole. Cadogan took no notice of him, though his post is to introduce, but went on directly and fell on his knees. Immediately as he went out, Argyle sent a gentleman to him to demand satisfaction of the affront he had put upon him, and that he must meet him immediately. Cadogan excused it and protested it was mere ignorance, in short begged his pardon.
>
> So there was no fighting with swords, but all this heightened the rancour and the Court struggle to a greater degree, and it was pushed with that heat and assiduity that on Friday a letter was

obtained of the King, the father, which Argyll received in the evening, dismissing him from all his employments and Lord Islay the same. Next morning the Secretary was sent to the Prince to desire him to remove Argyle from his post with him as Groom of the Stole. The Prince said that the Duke of Argyle had served him faithfully and given him no occasion to disgrace him; and in short, excused himself. Many other messages have been sent to him since and we have been gaping every moment to hear what would be the result; but he has stood his ground . . .

. . . if Argyle fall many men will fall with him[4] and we shall see a strange new face of the prevailing Ministry, if the father will send him to the Tower.

Argyll took a firm stand. He requested an audience with the King. It was refused. Then he went into the country for three days; but returned at the end of that week to attend at St James's. 'The Duke appeared in the crowd with the rest to wish His Majesty "good journey". He acts the philosopher and courtier, mightily pretending to vast submission whatever remains *alter mente repostrum*.'[5]

There was indeed reason to act a part. On the one hand stood his enemies of the Marlborough faction; on the other, Jacobites ready to take advantage, by all manner of means,[6] of his breach with the King. Between the two was the Prince of Wales reluctant to part with his favourite courtier and most able adviser. Yet pressures were brought to bear. According to James Murray in a letter dated 13 July to the 'Duke' of Mar:

Mr. Ashburnham [Argyle] and his brother have been turned out of the family notwithstanding their great services to it, with all the circumstances of contempt and ill-usage possible, and this upon the representations of some of their fellow-servants . . . to that extremity were matters carried that, the son having for some days showed a desire to continue Ashburnham [Argyle] in his service, he at last received a message importing little less than that both should go to gaol if he did not dismiss him. This was not to be withstood and accordingly he was dismissed.[7]

When news of these events reached the Dowager Duchess of Argyll in remote Kintyre, she wrote her thoughts to the family lawyer – Mr Anderson.

I think I am as good a giver of affairs though I am not acquainted with the new way of politicks . . . but such a treatment after such signal services would provock [provoke] a slur to resentment,

and I hope their enemies shall discover their error in judgement.
My sons goe off with honer [honour], and they are the contemp
[contempt] of the nation and will as they began over their countrie
perish in the ruins . . . I am confident a little time will put an
end to these things for I am persuaded after the Duke of Marl-
borrow's death that parties will fall, soon.

Jacobite leaders naturally exulted over Argyll's disgrace. This
might well be their greatest opportunity to win the Duke. In the
strong confidence that Argyll, with his love for power, could be at
last secured, they set themselves to that purpose. 'I hope it may be
thought fit on this occasion to make some application to Aylmer
[Argyle]. A line from Patrick [James] if it could be conveyed by a
fit person, might produce good effects . . .' wrote Lord Inese, on
22 July, to the 'Duke' of Mar who was himself addressing letters on
the same subject.

He wrote to Lord Inese on 23 July: 'It is thought yet too soon
a while to make any applications to Aylmer [Argyle] but in a little
time I hope it may be done with success, though I'm afraid as long
as he finds himself so well with the son he'll hardly look our way . . .
and to Sir John Erskine on the 25th: 'I would fain hope that
what has happened to Jennings [Argyle] may make him think
another way than he formerly did and were it not for the hopes he
may have in Grafton [Prince of Wales] I would think it sure.'

In the first days of his exile from Court, Argyll acted in a manner
calculated to inspire Jacobite hopes. As that great writer of gossip –
Fanny Oglethorpe – told the Duke of Mar: 'The Duke of Argyle
makes violent court to all the reformed officers and has a greater
levée than ever any general did. It's rather like an assembly of
mutineers than visits . . . He does not go to Court. There is to be a
camp on Hounslow Heath and several more . . .'

The fact was that as in the days which followed Malplaquet
officers disgruntled with Marlborough's revived dictatorial power
rallied to Argyll's side.

Thus encouraged, the Duke of Mar communicated with James
Murray:

Friday – August 7th –
We will long to hear from you again of that matter[8] and how
Anton [Argyle] behaves. So long as he thinks himself so well with
the Gentleman[9] you mention, Killigrew [James] has nothing to
expect from him directly; but by his other way of working it may

do a great deal of good service. If Anton finds that his interest with that Gentleman fails, or not what he would have it, he'll never bear it, and in that case Killigrew may expect something of him. I wish with all my hopes the last may happen, for I value and esteem him, and would be overjoyed he were that way. Killigrew would do anything to gain him; but till it be seen a little more what happens in my opinion 'tis too soon to make any application to him. It is of consequence for us to know how that affair goes on from time to time and nobody can do it better than you, so I regret your being oblidged to leave the place where he is, but before you go I hope you may be able to say something more of it and to let us know the judgement you make of him.

To this letter James Murray replied from London on 16 August: 'As you know I was formerly on a pretty fair foot with Mr. Anton [Argyle] and his brother. I have lately visited them of purpose to keep a door open there, in order if I find any opportunity, to use it for Mr. Killigrew's [James's] service, and yet I don't know how this may be construed by some people . . .'

Further on, however, he emphatically stated: 'I think you may depend that Mr. Anton is the last man you can expect any friendship of, for he is in a most entire confidence with the Gentleman I formerly mentioned [the Prince of Wales], and seems to build all his prospects upon that bottom, so there is no manner of encouragement to talk with him or his brother on that subject.'

The statement was true. The friendship between the Prince of Wales and Argyll persisted despite efforts of enemies and conspirators to separate them. The Office of Groom of the Stole remained vacant, and during the month of August, which found Marlborough at Bath and the Prince and Princess of Wales at Hampton Court, Argyll passed much of his time in the Prince's company. The strength of a loyalty which pre-eminently belonged to the Duke could not fail to create an impression. A letter written by Sir John Forrester to the Duke of Mar made this apparent.

At the time of Lord Argyle's disgrace, I had all the hopes imaginable, considering his ambition and temper, that some good might have been made of him, having known from a very good hand at London as you saw by my letter to Mr. Nairn, that the view of being generalissimo of the British Forces was then his, which now he ought to believe will go by him, unless (as God forbid) the Electoral Prince should one day come to play. But

being here in the road from Brussels to Paris[10] where English
gentlemen are daily passing, and having made it my business to
be well informed of Lord Argyle's late steps, I find he will neither
belie nor amend the race he is of . . .

For the rest of that year and on into the turn of 1717, malicious
reports about Argyll flooded the Jacobite world. One spoke of his
going to the tower; another that he had been ordered to leave the
country and positively refused to; yet another that the King was
highly provoked against the Duke of Argyll and his pupil (Prince of
Wales), and drastic measures were foreseen when he returned to
England.

Meanwhile, the Churchill (Marlborough) party had their own
plans which, according to Jacobite interpretation, were to 'bring the
Prince into the same lurch with their enemies and as it is certain
they hate him because of his constant attachment to my Lord
Argyle, so they have not been wanting to insinuate that Townshend
and those folks that made too much court to the son in his father's
absence certainly were in a good understanding at bottom with
Lord Argyle whom the old man does not like as being fully persuaded
he designed to set up his son in opposition to him . . .'

Assuredly, these trials demanded of Argyll extreme perseverance
and control of temper in order to stay his ground beside the young
Prince. Bereft of all his state offices, including the most valuable
one – the Colonelcy of the 'Blues'[11] – he could only depend upon
three personal assets – defiance, ingenuity, supreme resolve.

'Lord Argyle may meet with many hard dealings from his
prevailing enemies. He may assume several shapes and characters
for to be even with them, but I question whether they ever can
vex him into loyalty; the name of Argyle and the principles of a
King's man appear to me very incompatible.'[12]

There was truth in those last words. Argyll's independence and
pride as the most powerful Chieftain north of the borders could
never allow him to adopt the principles of a King's man and
remain always subservient. At this hour he had only one objective –
conquest over his enemies. He had been largely responsible for
King George's accession. The dearest person in his life – Jenny
Warburton – was a Maid of Honour to the Princess of Wales.
Therefore, he must, at all costs, rise above the shades of defeat and
emerge victorious.

Chapter IV

DUKE AND DUCHESS OF ARGYLL

ON a morning of the year 1716, a fever of excitement prevailed at Leicester House. Among the feminine members of the Household the atmosphere was particularly animated. They might have been observed pausing amidst their duties to whisper to one another. If Jenny Warburton happened to be in the vicinity, curious glances were cast at her. The Princess of Wales, informed by Mrs Howard[1] of what was afoot, replied: 'How I pity the poor Warburton. Her agitation must be great and she must so dread appearing in public when everybody will be whispering, every eye watching her looks. Go and tell her I excuse her from attendance; she need not wait to-day, nor indeed till all the tittle has subsided.'

Mrs Howard hurried to deliver the kindly message. She expected to find Jenny more agitated than anyone else. To her surprise, the Maid of Honour was perfectly composed and busy with service.

'Not wait to-day!' she ejaculated in response to Mrs Howard's words. 'Why must I not wait? What's the matter? Is the Princess angry with me? Have I done anything?'

'Done!' Mrs Howard's voice became shrill. 'Bless me no!' Astonished, she renewed the Princess's solicitude.

'My dear Mrs Warburton, it is Her Royal Highness's kind consideration for you. She concludes you cannot like to wait; she is afraid of your being distressed.'

'Dear!' exclaimed Jenny, 'I always like waiting exceedingly, and I a'n't in distress; who told her I was?'

Mrs Howard persisted. 'Oh! she is sure it must overpower you; you will never be able to stand it.'

'Not able to stand!' came the retort in surprised tone. 'Why, does she think me sick? Pray tell her I am as well as ever I was in my life, and perfectly able to stand'.

Highly amused, Mrs Howard returned to describe the interview to the Princess and assure her that 'there was no need of uneasiness about Mrs Warburton's emotions'.

The cause of all this flurry was the Duke of Argyll. It had just become known that the estranged wife, so long an invalid, was dead.[2] The news immediately awoke the gossips of society to the question – 'Now that His Grace is at last free, will his interest in the plain Jenny Warburton continue?' It was well known that he desired power and had an inclination for money. In the light of these facts the answer seemed apparent: 'Surely he will look to some quarter where there is more advantage to be found than with the daughter of a country squire.' Women who thought along these lines probably nursed hopes that the eligible Duke might cast an eye upon one of them. Their surmises proved incorrect.

Argyll did not seek a new direction. He hastened to Jenny to offer her, with the utmost ardour, both his love and great name. They must be married at once.

Influenced most probably by superstition rather than sentiment, she positively refused with the words: 'No, indeed, I shall never marry a man who has a wife above ground – not I.'

Even so, he entreated her with every manner of argument. Yet she remained adamant. At length, he was forced to yield to her will; but declared that as soon as the mourning period had passed he would make her his wife.

Six months later, in June 1717[3], the year when Handel's 'Water Music' enchanted London, Jenny Warburton became Duchess of Argyll.

1717 – June – Whitehall.
The Duke of Argyle has declared his marriage with Mrs. Warburton – one of the Bed-Chamber women to the Princess of Wales.
George Tilson to Lord Polwarth – With Office Circular[4]

After their marriage she meant even more to him. He doted, faithful and adoring, far more lover than husband. Whenever she entered the room he would gaze fondly upon her and then, advancing, clasp her in his arms. Jane's response did not match the strength of his ardour. She loved; but in an indifferent fashion. The capacity for a depth of understanding was absent from her character. She could not rise to the heights of an adoration that made her so beautiful in his sight.

On a certain day when a portrait of her had just been delivered at the Bruton Street residence, a kinswoman happened to call. Following the usual courtesies, he led her to the picture, and she heedlessly remarked that it was 'very like'.

'Like?' he repeated in affronted tone. 'No, not like at all; how can anybody think it so? It does not do her justice in any respect. But step this way, my dear, and I will show you another sort of likeness', and from his pocket he withdrew the miniature of a lovely face which did not in the least resemble Jenny. Yet that was how she always appeared in his mind, and nothing could destroy the illusion.

At Number 27 Bruton Street, their first child – a daughter – was born.

According to a 'News Letter' dated 14 November 1717: 'The Duchess of Argyll was three days in labour. Dr. Chamberlain was sent for but being pre-engadged to Abingdon and Herefor he declined to wait on her, whereupon the Duke of Argyll wrote to the Prince for Dr. Hamilton who was with the Princess and he went and in a few hours after she was brought to bed; she and her daughter are well.'

Argyll had lately acquired one of England's great houses – the seventeenth-century mansion of Adderbury in Oxfordshire – and started to plan its development on an eminent scale. Days during December found him there with Jenny; but they were back in London for the Christmas season. 'The Duke of Argyll came to town with his Dutchess and family on Tuesday. The report of his going to Holland has been without any ground but it is confirmed that he has not been with the Prince.'

Thus the announcement in a 'News Letter' dated 19 December.

Their other residence – and the one which became the principal home – was at Sudbrook, on the west side of Richmond Park between Richmond Hill and Ham Common. The house stood amidst park-land where everything charmed the eye: the glades of magnificent trees – sanctuary for birds of every kind; the broad expanses of verdant wilderness – play-ground for the fallow deer; the stream – nursery of ducklings; the pond – breeding-place of mallards from the Thames. For Argyll it represented a haven from the warring world of politics and intrigue.

LIFE AT SUDBROOK

The passage of time brought its changes. In 1726, a new house at Sudbrook, designed by the architect James Gibbs, came into

o

being. Although small in comparison with others of that age, its architecture reflected Argyll's taste for elegance and dignity. Between the red-brick wings loomed the whiteness of the main facade with a splendidly pillared portico of Portland stone.

There was but one shadow across the sunlit path of husband and wife. Instead of the much desired son, five daughters had been born.[5] Perhaps the anguish was even greater for Jenny. It meant that the title would pass to the Earl of Islay who despised her as much as she disliked him. For Argyll, too, was the cutting thought that the brother with whom he had never known real accord must be his successor. To minimize a humiliating position, he arranged for the eldest child – Lady Caroline – to have the rights of a male heir in so far as his English titles of Baron Chatham and Earl of Greenwich went.

As a natural result of these distressing circumstances, the children were kept much in the background. Their education was the mother's charge, so it followed the same pattern as her own: a scant one of learning to read, write, and keep accounts and, of course, needlework. The first three subjects were taught by the steward; the latter by a superior housekeeper. The single intervention on the father's part was to forbid them learning French. 'One language is enough for a woman to talk', he declared.

The sore feelings that the girls aroused within her, coupled with a naturally complacent temperament, prevented Jenny from displaying maternal affection. She was quite content merely to be informed of their progress. Thus the rollicking gaieties of girlhood rarely touched the drawing-room where the reigning favourites were Pug and Puss. Upon these two who 'did not live together like dog and cat' (as Jenny told her visitors), the mother bestowed the fondness which she could not bring to her offspring. Before the great fireplace, designed by Rysbrach, they always had their places.

As Lady Caroline grew up to show charming looks, a slight privilege was granted her. On Sundays she dined with the parents. Otherwise, the sisters had their own province. At Sudbrook, this was an annexe especially built for them and known as the 'Young Ladies' House'. There, they could romp in complete freedom and sometimes young relatives or friends would join them. Perhaps, on occasions, when their gay, carefree laughter echoed across the park, the disappointed parents might have caught the infection of youth and felt almost softened. As it was, they were unable to resist a change of sentiment as the daughters came to teenage years and claimed more attention either through appearance or character. Argyll was

London march ye 27

I hope this will find dear Lady Bute
perfectly recover'd, I cant console with you
that the child was not a son, you haveing
one already have reason to be
satisfy'd & he that has had the smallpox
may be reckon'd as good as 2, so mortal is
that distemper has been this year in town as
ever was known, Lady Dorset has just lost
her eldest daughter of it, she was eleven
yr old, the rest of the children have it, but
are like to doe well, I am I live in a good
deal of uneasiness about mine, I wish them
to have it while they are children but not
this year, I believe we shall be thinking
of the country in less then a month, tho'
tis not believed the parliment will be
up so soon, my Ld Bute thinks the business
will be so much over that if he comes now
& then for a day at a time it may serve

Letter from the Duchess of Argyll to Lady Bute

to become aware of an hour which would find him captured by the youngest child – Lady Mary.[6] In her he discerned his own fearless spirit and impetuous will.

Meanwhile, a pattern developed in the lives of 'John and Jenny'. Always she was the centre and he never ceased to applaud her. He gathered round him a circle of friends with mutual interests: old party colleagues, Scots kinsmen – should they happen to be in town – Army officers who had been his companions in war.[7]

She was usually surrounded by a host of Warburton relations and retainers. They made her salon a 'court' through display of a homage such as she had been incapable of offering either to the late Queen or the Princess of Wales.

There were also visits from those who might be described as her particular acquaintances. While possibly superior to her in manners, language, and deportment, they were social contemporaries, and that fact created common ground. The only people whom she could not tolerate were 'Your clever women', and despite John's remonstrance that 'they should be esteemed' she closed her doors against them.

Only one person in the category of 'your clever women' was accepted as a privileged visitor – and this by order of the Duke. He held a high opinion of Lady Suffolk's[8] capacity of wise judgement and believed that her counsel could, on occasions, be an asset to his wife. He was not mistaken. Lady Suffolk had a measure of influence.

Although his adoration for Jenny caused him ever to show indulgence, he never allowd himself to be ruled, and in matters of importance took the onus of decision. A single word spoken in his tone of command was sufficient. It would neither be resisted nor artifice employed in effort to modify the point in question. Jenny might be stubborn in affairs of her own; but she too had great respect for John and was far too straightforward to seek any method other than obedience. Consequently, arguments did not disturb them. Even in matters touching finance, so often the cause of matrimonial friction, there was no contention. A strict sense of thrift belonged to them both, though John could be as generous[9] as she was, at times, charitable.

The eloquence that distinguished his attitude towards society found reflection in those things which counted most with him. The splendour of his equipage, the excellence of his table – indeed the whole of Sudbrook – bore the mark of the Duke of Argyll.

In the domestic sphere, Jane recalled her Cheshire home where economy had to be practised. On the other hand, she was well aware of her status as wife of one of the greatest noblemen in Britain.

At their magnificent dinner-table, two beloved companions were always present: Pug and Puss.[10] Sometimes guests looked askance at Puss and the situation became awkward. Such an occasion occurred when, to break a guest of his dislike for cats, she placed Puss on the back of his chair. After futile efforts to protect the unfortunate man, Argyll was forced to laugh it off 'as a joke not worth minding'. Jane must have her favourites at hand!

As time passed, intimate friends remarked a change in him. He seemed to prefer the days at Sudbrook to those in the outside world. 'His Jane now stands first with him' – they whispered among themselves. It was true. Most of all the things in his great and varied career, he loved to bask in her company.

Chapter V

HE WHO PLAYS BEST HAS BEST CHANCE

ARGYLL well knew that pressure had been brought to bear upon the King by the Duke of Marlborough and the Earl of Sunderland. Thus, at the turn of the year 1717/18, when, in his opinion, the Earl of Sunderland's political weight was becoming too heavy for the common weal of affairs, he wrote to his brother-in-law the Marquess of Bute:

London – 7 of Jan.
    1718/17.
My Dear Lord,

I am informed that the Earl of Sunderland who seems at present to have more power than I am afraid is consistent with the welfare of the King and Country, designs to try if he can hurt him by calling me to account in parliament. My cause I know to be good but that does not prevent its being necessary to have my friend's consent, so I must beg my dear Lord that you will not fail to be here by the meeting of the Parliament and prevail with all who you take to be friends to justice and their country to be here also. I believe I need say no more but that.

    I am,
        Your most faithful servant

                        Argyll

The sequel – some months later – was Argyll's restoration to royal favour. At the turn of the year 1718/19 came the appointment of Lord Steward of the Household. Then, on 27 April 1719, Argyll was created Duke of Greenwich.

Meanwhile, his place was Parliament.

The twelfth day of February found him in the Lords to attend the debate on 'An engrossed Bill from the Commons for punishing Mutiny and Desertion.'

His first 'skirmish' occurred when Lord Stanhope remarked that 'He was not like some persons who changed their opinions according as they were in and out of places.'

Argyll took this reflection to himself and smartly retorted – 'For my own part I follow the Ministry when I think they are in the right, but go a contrary way if I think they go astray.'

The second reading of the bill came a week later (the 17th) and on the 18th it was 'resolved to address His Majesty that the Articles of War and other Papers relating to discipline and payment of the Army might be laid before the House.'

The Duke of Argyll, who backed the Earl of Oxford's views against the bill, said: 'That besides the 16,000 and odd men of regular troops there was another considerable body maintained under the denomination of Invalids, and that they ought to inquire into their numbers and where they were quartered.'

Two days afterwards, a committee of the whole house debated for five hours. Again Argyll's voice was heard in opposition to the bill.[1] His moment of contest came when the Earl of Sunderland urged 'That among the ancient Romans – the wisest people in the world and the greatest lovers and aspirers of public liberty – martial laws and discipline were invigorated by decrees of the Senate and were in force in times of peace as well as in times of war.'

Argyll promptly arose with the remark spoken in forceful tone, 'It is much better to attend domestic than foreign examples.' He then showed, by several instances drawn from the history of Great Britain, 'that a standing army in time of peace was never fatal either to the Prince or to the nation.'

It was in 1719 that the people of Great Britain were plunged into a spate of speculation. The source was Paris where John Law, the son of a Scottish goldsmith, had launched an enterprise known as the Mississippi Company for the purpose of colonizing those territories of America washed by the Ohio and Mississippi Rivers. Following purchase of the French East India, China, and African Companies, the new Company undertook to pay off France's public debt through Mississippi stock. The result was the soaring of stock to high pressure and almost every prominent person[2] in Britain invested. For a year, Law's financial success governed the political as well as the Banking worlds of Paris and London. Then, in May 1720, credit, strained to a peak, crashed. Law, ruined in the sight of the French Government, went into exile. His quest for aid led, through Mrs Howard (Lady Suffolk), to the Duke of Argyll: 'Can you not prevail on the Duke of Argyle to help me something more than the half-year, or is there nobody that could have good nature to lend me £1,000 . . . ?'

Of Argyll's reaction to this appeal, it is only possible to surmise. To judge by the reputation that Alexander Cunningham gave him for generosity to persons in dire need,[3] he probably assisted his fellow-countryman in this misfortune.

The spring session of 1721 brought a political issue of importance to Scotland. A bill was introduced 'to limit the Peerage in such a manner that instead of the sixteen elected Peers in Scotland twenty-five[4] be made hereditary as part of the ration . . .'

The way the proceedings went caused Argyll the question which he put at the end of a letter to Lord Grange – the eminent Scottish judge and politician. '. . . What party have I to take in relation to the Peerage Bill or other matters, if notwithstanding the usage the Peers of Scotland have met with from the Squadrone, they are still determined to elect humbly by their direction.'

By 1722, the Duke's weight at Court was so far regained that he could influence the King on behalf of the Marquess of Bute. In sequel, he wrote, on 7 April, to his brother-in-law :

London
April 7th 1722.
My dear Bute,

I send you enclosed the letter I received from Lord Sunderland yesterday morning and to-day the King commanded me to acquaint you with the contents of it. I have a reason why I would not have it as yet known who you are to succeed, but only that you are to be in the Bed Chamber. There is one thing good in this, that the payment is very exact, which can be said of few offices at present. It will be necessary that you come up to take the oaths though you stay but a day because you cannot receive pay till you have taken them. I am now to acquaint you that my brother and I have had our thoughts upon the office of the Election and we think Lord Eglinton the person in whose favours we shall make one effort. I have writ to him to-night and I could wish you would see him in your way and let all our friends know our intentions. My brother is in a day or two to have Lord Annandale's post as I am told and have reason to believe it, that we shall very soon gain more ground on the Gentlemen of the Squadrone.

Give my service to my sister dear Bute
Yours
Argyll and Greenwich.

London Ap: y.e 4
                                    1722

My dear Bute

    I send you Inclos'd y.e letter I receiv'd from Lord [...]
yesterday morning, & to day the King Commanded me to acquaint
you with y.e Contents of it, I have a Reason why I would not have
it of y.t known who you are to succeed, but Only that you are to
be in the Bed Chamber, there is One thing good in this, that the
Payment is very exact, which can be said of few Offices at Present
it will be Necessary that you come up to take the Oaths that
stay but a day because you cannot receive pay till you have [...]
them, I am now to acquaint you that my Brother & I have had [...]
thoughts upon the affair of y.e Next, & we think Lord Eglinton
the Person in who's favour we should make our efforts, I
have writt to him to Right, & I could wish you would see him [...]
your way, & let all our Friends know his Intentions, My Brother
is in a day or two to have Lord Arundel's Post, & I am told, &
have reason to believe it, that we shall very soon gain more
ground on the Gentlemen of the Squadron, give my service
to my Sister dear Bute yours

                              Argyll & Greenwich

The next years were to witness Argyll and his brother combining their remarkable energies in Parliament when Sir Robert Walpole was the principal figure.[5]

Their political attitude is brilliantly described by the Earl of Islay:

> . . . All little under-favourites leaving their trade would cease by giving of interest or distribution having the reins entirely in their hands, continually intimate that we are dens of genius if we have too much power, that it is better to make creatures. I give them credit, interest and power that support them who by having interest of their own are more independent; and their politicks is a continually petty war and game and as at all other games one will sometimes win and sometimes lose and he that plays best and has the best shoot has the best chance.

Chapter VI

TO THE HEIGHTS

BETWEEN 1725 and 1740, the Duke of Argyll advanced in his military ambitions. The army and its reform was the chief concern of the King; himself a fine soldier. A system based upon sound discipline, economy, and more honourable methods than those practised in the disposal of Commissions was demanded. Argyll emerged to champion his policy.

In March 1724, the Mutiny Bill[1] again came before the Lords sitting in a Grand Committee. Upon a motion made by Lord Trevor for 'Leaving out of the number of Land Forces to be continued the four thousand additional men raised the year before' – there opened a debate.

'I shall contract within a narrow compass what I have to say.' Thus began Argyll when he arose to reply to a long speech by Lord Townshend. Then he went on to give his reasons for opposition to the proposed reduction of armed strength.

> If I saw the nation unanimous in opinion that our Laws, Liberties, Properties and Holy Religion, entirely depend on the present happy settlement and on the Protestant Succession in His Majesty's Royal Family, I would readily give my vote for reducing the Army; but I am afraid some people so strenuously insist on the disbanding of the additional troops with no other design than to weaken the Government, and thereby have an opportunity of involving their native country in new troubles . . . therefore those noble lords who have spoke for the reduction will do well, when they go down into their several countries, to assure the people with whom, no doubt, their reasons will not fail having great weight, that their liberties and properties are entirely safe under His Majesty's auspicious Government.

In 1725, Argyll was rewarded with the appointment that the late Duke of Marlborough[2] had once held: Master-General of Ordnance.

The following year his name figured twice in the 'London Gazette':

John, Duke of Argyle, appointed to be Colonel (and Captain) of a Troop 2nd Dragoon Guards.
St James's – 22nd February 1726

and a few months later,

John, 2nd Duke of Argyle, appointed to be Colonel of Lord Londonderry's late Regiment of Horse.
St James's – 26th August 1726

It was characteristic of Argyll's chivalrous spirit to engage himself in adventures if such were demanded. The early summer of 1726 brought an occasion.

The call for help came from Mrs Howard (Lady Suffolk), then in the throes of crisis with a husband threatening drastic action to procure her return to him. In a matter of hours, she was faced by a journey alone from Leicester House to Richmond whither the Prince and Princess of Wales had gone for the holiday season. Fear that the violent-tempered Mr Howard (later Lord Suffolk) might seize this moment as an opportunity to capture his unwilling wife impelled her to seek the aid of two dear friends – the Duke of Argyll and the Earl of Islay. The appeal did not go unanswered. At eight o'clock in the morning of the day when, at noon, the royal couple were to travel, an equipage engraved with the Argyll crest appeared before Leicester House. Mrs Howard, who had been anxiously vigilant for its arrival, lost no time in joining the occupants – Argyll and his brother. Under their escort, the road held no terrors. They arrived at Richmond without incident, and Mrs Howard had the shelter of Sudbrook until such time as the Prince and Princess reached their residence.

At the end of June, Argyll left for Scotland to attend to business affairs. The fact that he declined lavish entertainment and adopted such an aloof attitude towards his hosts, even dissuading them from opening bottles of wine, caused remark.

During his stay in Edinburgh he received a visit from the Provost of Glasgow, who assured him that Glasgow's reputed unfriendliness to his family was untrue; on the contrary the citizens had a very real affection for the House of Argyll. He went on to say that they did not think much of attachment to any great men and only valued themselves on loyalty to King George. Argyll's reply, in somewhat frigid tone, was to the effect that 'he did not reckon himself a great man and wished the town would not attach themselves to small men who could not be of much use to them.'

Argyll was on the road to Inveraray when news of Earl Cadogan's death reached him. In consequence of this he stayed only a day or so and then returned to London.[3]

In 1727, the Prince of Wales succeeded to his father. At the time of that event, the Duke and Duchess of Argyll were on a visit to Edinburgh. According to a letter addressed to the Duke of Atholl by a certain Mr J. Douglas and dated 12 April 1727, 'The day after the proclamation of the new King, the Duchess of Argyle had a splendid ball in Her Majesty's own house in the Abbey (Holyrood), where she herself danced a reel with Baillie John Campbell who is a great politician and general informer . . .'

That Argyll always maintained a strong influence upon the politics and politicians of Scotland is proved by a letter which he had occasion to write to the Earl of Saltoun:

London – 7th January 1729.
My Dear Lord,
    I find by John Montgomery that a letter of mine to your Lordship in relation to the Clidsdeal [Clydesdale] Election must have miscarried which makes you have the trouble of this. Your Lordship knew very well when James Stuart first was set up in Clidsdeal, my Lord Duke of Hamilton was out of England, no thoughts of his return for some time, Lord Archibald behaved himself as disagreeably to His Grace as to the rest of those who would not submit to the Squadrone, whi'st James and his Relations pass'd for devoted friends to him; these considerations led many of us to think James the fittest Person to represent the Shire, many stepps were taken in consequence to these reasonings, and no reason was left to dout [doubt] of success, 'tis then possible now at last for me with the least honour to give him up. My Lord there are those who are witnesses of the Regard I have for the Duke of Hamilton, I have taken every method I could to express it, and in other Elections of Clidsdeal my Lord may command me, but in the circumstances I have mentioned 'tis

impossible for me to abandon my friend who you know is as much a man of honour as any of us. I should hope if my Lord would consider the State of Affairs cooly he would think of it as I doe, but however my Lord determining himself to act in it, I hope it needs not interrupt the friendship I desire to cultivate with His Grace . . .'

August of that year found Argyll at Inveraray where Mr Forbes – the King's Advocate – was a guest. On his way south towards the end of the month, he stayed with Sir John Shaw at Greenock, and then continued to Glasgow. The Provost had prepared entertainment for him; but he excused himself on the grounds of having drunk too much during the days passed in Sir John Shaw's company. He stayed overnight and the Magistrates took the opportunity of asking his help to alleviate their economic distresses. Argyll replied by expressing his regret; but so far as he understood – 'They would have none of the name of Campbell to represent them.'

They repudiated this as being a 'hellish lie'. The only Campbell to meet their opposition was Mr Campbell of Shawfield – and that for just cause. In the last election they had given full support to the Laird of Blythswood and he would confirm the fact. Argyll turned to the laird standing by his side: 'Colin, was it so?' The reply came in the affirmative. 'Then,' said Argyll, 'I have been abused.'

With friendship thus established between the City of Glasgow and the House of Argyll, the Provost requested permission to place a memorial of grievances in the hands of Argyll's secretary. 'No, Provost, I'le take it as a favour if you'l lodge the memorial in my hand, and I'le take a care of it.'[4]

Because it was the Duke of Argyll's policy to be on as good terms of understanding with fellow Scots as circumstances would permit, Jacobite vigilance was ever pinned to him.

Away in Rome, the exiled James III (Chevalier St George) still entertained hopes of Great Britain's crown. A new reign fostered these to an activity of correspondence. He sat down to write letters to figureheads in the affairs of Britain. All of them were English; with one exception: the Duke of Argyll. To him who could be the most valuable ally, the Chevalier addressed two communications, the first in 1731[5]: 'Whenever it shall please God to restore me to my kingdom, it is my intention to continue the Duke of Argyle in the employments he now enjoys, or to do for him what may be otherways agreeable to him, and to give him moreover an additional pension of Two Thousand pounds.' Rome, January 31st 1731.

SG 16
1731

Sudbrook Sept ye 22

My Dear Lord

Since I have seen the House at Bury Inn & considered yr Project, I had for wide more maturely which some Accidents make it Prudent for me to lay aside. I should be glad to be free from that Bargue, as the affair stands I think there can be no difficulty in being off, & I beg it of you to get me clear of it as soon as possible.

If I had it, the Plan I have now determin'd to prosecute, would make me dispose of it as I will do of the fifty Pounds a year I have in didgtown. I am much plas'd with my Scarborough expedition & if I can find time, which I hope to do to pass six weeks there Once in two or three years

I may hope to live as long as my Mother or the Baylist of Jura, as I am Only of the cabinet Councell you can not expect to hear any News from me, make my Complements to Lady Eglington Lady Milton & yr Rest of our friends & beleeve me with great sincerity

Your most faithfull & humble servant
Argyll & Greenwich.

Letter from Argyll to Lord Milton *see page* 214

Rome. July 13th 1733

To Lord Argyle

Tho' you will be sufficiently informed of my sentiments & dispositions by my two Declarations for England & Scotland, Yet I cannot on this occasion but write also to you in particular to assure you that a proper behavior in you at this time, will not only make you partake of all the advantages offered in my Declarations to those who shall return to their duty, but engage me to bestow on you the greatest marks of my favor & confidence; There are few who have it so much in their power as you have to deserve them, & a just & laudable ambition will I hope induce you on this occasion to take the most effectual measures for the success of my Cause, & by consequence for the happiness of Great Britain; And I cannot doubt, but that you will prefer the glory of signalizing yourself in the service of your lawful King & Country, to the maintenance of an ill understood point of honor, wch might engage the Kingdoms in blood & confusion. I earnestly recommend . to you

particularly to the giving my ancient kingdoms how many hardships it has lies under

Facsimile letter of James III, the Chevalier St George – the 'Pretender' – written from Rome

P

Two years later – on 13 July 1733 – he wrote a further letter to the Duke of Argyll:

> Tho' you will be sufficiently informed of my sentiments and suppositions by my two Declarations for England and Scotland, yet I cannot on this occasion but write to you, in particular to abjure you that a proper behavior in you at this time will not only make you partake of the advantages offered in my Declarations to those who shall return to their Duty, but engage me to bestow on you the greatest marks of my favor and confidence; There are few who have it so much in their power as you have to deserve them, and . . . [illegible] with ambition will I hope induce you on this occasion to take the most especial measures for the success of my cause, and by consequence for the happiness of Great Britain, particularly for . . . [illegible] my ancient kingdom from many hardships it now lies under, but that you will prefer the glory of signalizing yourself in the service of your Lawful King and Country to maintaining the support of an understood point of honour which might engage the kingdoms in blood and confusion. I sensibly recommend to you duly to consider the consequence of your behaviour in this juncture and then I am persuaded you will soon determine to act such a part as will intitle you to receive the most distinguished marks of my kindness.

The Duke of Argyll was not to be wooed. In public life he had only one alliance; the Protestant Monarchy – now represented by George II.

On 6 August 1733, Argyll was re-appointed Colonel of the Royal Horse Guards (the 'Blues') in succession to the 2nd Duke of Bolton who had joined the Opposition against Sir Robert Walpole's ministry. This established the fact that the colonelcy of the 'Blues' was pre-eminently a political appointment.

Chapter VII

CHAMPION OF THE KING:
CHAMPION OF THE PEOPLE

ARGYLL approached his finest hours in oratory. On 6 March 1733, when a committee of the whole House debated the 'Number of Land Forces' he held an audience of divergent views beneath his spell.

National defence was a question to which he had devoted much study. In his opinion, were the nation not to have a standing army of its own subjects, there could be only three expedients: the fleet, the militia, or an army of foreign auxiliaries; but:

> . . . The main strength of this nation, and that upon which we principally depend, is the superiority of our Fleet; and the bravery of our men in general; Let us continue to preserve the present superiority we have as to our Fleet; let us continue to cultivate bravery and military discipline as much as possible among our men in general; but do not let us, for the sake of groundless jealousie and pretended fears, expose the peace of our country to be disturbed by every neighbouring State who shall take it in their heads so to do, or by every subject who shall be prompted by his resentment or ambition to rebel against the Government of his country.

As defender of the King's prerogative, Argyll was always to the fore in argument. Twice during the opening session of 1734, he had occasion to make a strong plea on behalf of his Sovereign.

The first time was in course of a debate (18 February) relating to the removal of the Duke of Bolton and Lord Cobham from their regiments.[1]

'As to the Address proposed, I really think it worse than the Bill itself;[2] it is certainly as great an attack upon the prerogative of the Crown as the Bill was; for what signifies a prerogative if the King is never to make use of it without being obliged to give an account of his reasons for so doing to either House of Parliament, that shall please to call for such an Account? The Address, therefore, is as great an attack upon the prerogative, and it is a much more direct attack upon his present Majesty's conduct . . .'

Towards the end of March, the Lords debated a message from the King to be 'empowered to augment his Forces by Sea and Land during a Recess of Parliament.' It gave him another opportunity to plead the cause of 'His Majesty, solicitous about the quiet and safety of his people . . . and that power he applies for to Parliament, though he knows it to be vested in him without any such application.'

For Argyll the year 1735 held two events. In its summer he mourned the mother who had dedicated herself to his interests in Argyllshire: on 9 May the Dowager-Duchess died at her Campbell-town home. At its turn, he was honoured with promotion to the highest rank in the British Army. The 14th January 1736 found him gazetted Field-Marshal.

In the spring session of 1737, Argyll emerged as champion of human rights.

'The Nation of Scotland treated with England as an independent and free people; and as that Treaty, my Lords, had no other guarantee for the due performance of its Articles but the Faith and Honour of a British Parliament, it would be both unjust and ungenerous should this House agree to any Proceeding that has the least tendency to infringe it.'

Argyll spoke these words on the day of Wednesday 4 May, 1737, when, 'Three Scotch Judges were called to the Bar [of the Lords] where they appeared in their robes, and some few questions were asked of them.'[3]

The reason for this unique proceeding, censured by Scots' peers as an 'indignity' and upheld by their English contemporaries as being in the tenor of the Union Treaty 'that no distinction should be made between the peoples of the two Nations', belonged to the murder, in Edinburgh, of the State prisoner – Captain Porteous. When report of how he had been seized from the Tolbooth by a rioting mob, and hanged outside the prison, reached St James's, the Queen, in her husband's absence, and Robert Walpole, resolved severe measures to punish the deed. In their anger, they pressed the introduction of a bill of reprisal against the Lord Provost and City of Edinburgh.[4] Meanwhile, as a first step towards this, three Judges of the Supreme Court of Scotland were summoned to London, for the virtual object of 'putting their sentiments in regard to the Porteous affair' on trial.

In the debate which ensued, Argyll's speech, delivered with the eloquence, dignity of manner and force which always distinguished him, proved his dedication to justice.

> I have opposed the present Bill, my Lords, because I look upon it to be an invasion upon property in that part of the kingdom. And on that account, my Lords, were it upon no other, I have more reason to oppose it than any man in this House, nay, perhaps, than any man in the United Kingdom; because there is none whose property is there so extensive as my own. I likewise look upon it, my Lords, as an encroachment upon liberty, and on this account, no man had better reason to oppose it. My family has been always persecuted, and has often bled under tyrants and never had a breathing-time but that of liberty; and should Bills of this nature pass into laws, there is reason to be afraid of their consequences with respect to our liberties.

The majority of peers were so moved by Argyll's oration that they opposed the harsh reprisals for which the Queen and Walpole had pressed. The penalties imposed would be of a tolerant order.

Nevertheless, the bill was sent down to the House of Commons where it caused violent conflict.[5]

From that date, Argyll's dissatisfaction with Sir Robert Walpole sharpened.

'I STAND FOR KING AND NATION'

'The affairs of the English Nation are now in a crisis more important than ever and on your part merit serious attention. Crisis on which depends not only our commerce, our honour and our safety against our foreign enemies; but also the conservation of our liberty.'

These words with which the Duke of Argyll opened a letter written to Sir Robert Walpole in March 1740 aptly describe the development of the international scene during the years between 1737 and 1739.

Queen Caroline's death in 1737 removed the one person who might have been influential to preservation of the constructive foreign policy founded by Stanhope.[6] Almost from that moment began the diplomatic confusions embracing the united Bourbon states of France and Spain and culminating in the Third Treaty of Vienna which, in Argyll's view, constituted the 'parent of all our miseries'. Unfortunately, that Treaty's purpose of pacification was not to be realized.

Britain's commercial relations with Spain were the cause. The Spanish authorities accused her of contravening certain trade privileges which she had enjoyed since 1713.[7] In order to enforce the treaties that governed their system of colonial trade, Spain's government resorted to arbitrary action. The right of search against suspected vessels was instituted with harsh measures against the crews. British national opinion, especially among merchant circles, was aroused. Murmurs of war passed from lip to lip. Members of Walpole's Cabinet were adamant for armed retaliation. He, alone, foresaw the danger not only to the economic system of Britain, but to her growing economic interests overseas, and advised negotiation with the Spanish Government as a means towards arriving at agreement. The Convention of Pardo was the sequel. While, in theory, it might have proved a bridge of understanding between the two powers, in practice it could not placate the temper of Parliament. In the Lords' debates, the Duke of Argyll predominated as one of its chief opponents. He based his reasons upon the principle which dominated him : justice.

> I do not say that we ought to be the judges in this affair, but I think we ought to advise and support His Majesty in defending the just rights and properties of his subjects. And, my Lords, we never can know how the matter stands betwixt his Catholic Majesty and the Company without having a state of the affair from the Company themselves . . .[8] When we have these informations, we shall be able to judge whether this declaration is founded on justice, or whether it is no better than a shift to avoid performing their part of the Convention.

These 'informations' came and the debate resumed. Again, and on this occasion with even greater vigour, Argyll denounced the convention, describing it as 'disgraceful' and 'deformed'. '. . . My Lords, everybody who understands what trade is, knows that if this Convention is approved of by Parliament, our trade must be irretrievably ruined.'

In the House of Commons the Convention was approved. The Opposition then emerged with loud outcry. Its leader – Wyndham – condemned Walpole's policy as 'treacherous'.

Outside Parliament, the clamour became more intense. Even the Prince of Wales was heard in the popular uproar for vengeance against a nation who had insulted the British flag.

Although declaration of war loomed so near, the word could not be spoken without certain diplomatic preparations.

On 16 March 1739, a Treaty of Subsidy with Denmark was debated in the Lords.

'My stock of wonder is at an end', Argyll's opening words when he rose to speak.

> I shall wonder at nothing unless the same measures that have almost brought us to ruin should set us up again. The hardship should not be put on this House of having a message from the King, and not being able to pay it respect. Denmark hath a treaty with Russia, and could not treat with France without breaking that. Besides, Sweden was come in to France, therefore Denmark must come in to us. Denmark will have the help of Russia against Sweden, and was glad of ours. It is necessary to be prepared; but not in a manner that shocks the Constitution. All countries have been enslaved by the necessity of trusting extraordinary powers. Necessities are first created and then pleaded. Let a reasonable number of troops and ships be proposed, and more afterwards if wanted. The administration must have some plan in these four months; and the nation will not sink if this vote doth not pass, which is proposed more to make such sort of powers common than with intent of using it. What good hath it done when such powers have been asked? We did nothing in 1734. If you will come into no other method, I will not be against this. We might have prepared the day after the Convention. For Spain will not give us satisfaction. But if we were sure that France would support Spain, let us not be slaves; let Providence decide the event.

At a later stage of this most controversial debate, Argyll delivered an impassioned challenge: 'For God's sake, my Lords, what are we afraid of? To live freely, or die bravely, has been the resolution of our ancestors in all ages past; I hope it is the resolution of the present generation. I hope it will be the resolution of our posterity in all ages to come.'

The crucial debate on the Spanish Convention came with the question, put to the House of Lords on 4 June – 'Whether it shall be voted that the Convention be broken?'

'I believe it was never before known that every Lord of this House owned a matter of fact to be true in a debate.' Opening with these words, Argyll went on to say:

> This, my Lords, looks very mysterious, and I do not love mysteries. When people follow mysteries, they are apt to fall into

bigotry. I am, my Lords, for our treating in the plain road of truth, nor can I see the least inconveniency that can ensue, if we should put the main question, – Shall it be said, my Lords, that this House was afraid to speak the truth? What power on earth should we be afraid of, while we have a just cause, a gracious Sovereign, and a brave people to support us?

The debate concluded on a resolution being adopted. 'The Ministry will act a part becoming Britons. They will amply revenge wrongs we have already suffered and provide for honour and safety of the kingdom.'

Sir Robert Walpole was left with no other option than to submit to the pressure of colleagues, opponents, court and nation. Britain declared war upon Spain. Yet he remained as Prime Minister.

The period that then ensued found the House of Lords 'no less the theatre of contention than the House of Commons'. The number of speakers on the side of the Opposition was great and formidable. To their ranks the Duke of Argyll gave allegiance.[9]

According to parliamentary records of that era – 'It is still undecided whether his accession to the side of opposition was derived from the quick gift which he is said to have possessed when it was time to leave a Minister from disgust and disappointment, or from disapprobation of measures. But whatever were the motives which influenced his conduct, his defection was a severe blow to the Minister.' (Sir Robert Walpole.)

As sequel to this change he was compelled, for a second occasion, to relinquish the appointment which then ranked among the most important in the state on account of its political character: Colonelcy of the 'Blues'.

In opposition Argyll displayed a fresh zest and energy. His speeches became even more fiery and probably achieved the object for which they were intended: to make a mark upon the public mind. The reason for that great sparkle of brilliance and fire might have belonged to the fact that for the first time in their parliamentary careers, the brothers were separated. The Earl of Islay remained a Government supporter.

A new session came into being and soon days of crisis ensued.

Argyll discerned forces working against national interests. The circumstance to which he took strong exception was advising His Majesty to make the declaration that 'The unhappy Divisions amongst my Subjects are the only hopes of the enemies to my Government.'

War, my Lords, was what the whole nation, except a very few, long since desired. The few that were against it have done what was their duty; they have yielded to the general voice of their country; and the war is now declared . . .

It is hardly possible the event should be unfortunate for this nation, unless we render it so by our own conduct, and as an incorrupt and independent Parliament is the best check upon a Minister's conduct, I shall look on it as a bad omen of our future conduct, if we should, in this first Session, shew so much complaisance to our Ministry as to confirm a misrepresentation made by him to the Crown, especially as that misrepresentation is of such a nature that if it be believed, it must render our enemies more obstinate, and our friends less ready to join in any alliance with us.

The strongest proof that Argyll's sole thought during these days of crisis was for the interests of his King and Country must surely lie in his letter of March 1740, to Sir Robert Walpole. He was an opponent and would soon emerge with speech of censure. Meanwhile, he wrote these words:

Consider, sir, in what crisis our affairs actually are. They afford us the right to decide whether we wish to bequeath to Our children that liberty which our Ancestors conserved for us by deluges of blood; or to leave them a perpetual and ignominious slavery. When we are entirely at the mercy of our Kings, we are as much slaves as the lowest subjects of the great Turk. The Romans were no less slaves under Augustus than under Nero.

To friend as well as foe Argyll personified loyalty in its highest altitude.

The aversion which the anti-ministerial party had conceived against the Duke of Argyll was now converted into respect and love. He who was bitterly arraigned for political versatility, was now applauded for his virtue and patriotism . . . He suddenly became the idol of the party.[10]

Chapter VIII

IN OPPOSITION:
LIGHTS AND SHADES

A NEW horizon faced Argyll when he joined the Tory Opposition. As he grew in their esteem the entertainments which prevailed among them lay open to him.

It was at those dinners and drawing-room parties where, for reasons of policy, everything of the most agreeable order reigned, that he saw women in another perspective.

Hitherto, he had been oddly prejudiced in his views of the feminine sex. Perhaps it was the effect of experience – a first marriage which had ended abruptly on the distasteful note of revulsion; the coarseness met among the 'camp followers'; the discovery that ladies of his own rank, whether foreign or otherwise, had only one design in radiating their charms either intellectually or through play of looks.

To him a virtuous woman was one who made the home her province; gave herself entirely to domestic duties, and never emerged. Those who sparkled amidst their fellow-beings were courtesans; and the majority entered this category.

It was therefore a shock as well as a pleasant surprise to find himself in the company of women whose reputations were untarnished and who could discourse intelligently on a variety of topics with only one aim: the Party cause.

'Have I been deceived in my judgement of the opposite sex?' The question occurred and he voiced it in conversation with the men around him. The conclusion reached was that throughout forty years of life, amidst all ranks of society, he had been wrong.

The day was too late for change; yet what a difference it might have made to that brilliant mind. True, he had discovered a great love; though devoid of qualities which could have led him to even nobler heights.

In contrast to those Tory gatherings effervescing with the wit, grace, and illumination of talk set towards national goals – was the Sudbrook salon filled with 'toadies', prosy 'hangers-on' who dwelt on a sentence from 'the great Argyll' merely to repeat it in other circles, and females who indulged in housewives' gossip ranging from the latest scandal to kitchen affairs. The chatter was such that his beautifully eloquent voice could scarcely be heard. At rare moments when there came a lull and he began to tell a story in a manner which had the power to hold an audience enthralled, Jenny would shrilly intervene:

'No, no, it was not so; No, no, my lord, you don't tell that right; let me.'

Instead of holding his own, he gave her the right of way. While she made a discord of what must have been a delightful narrative, he walked up and down the room, head lowered and hands clasped behind his back. Only when she spoke the final word, would he pause to say placidly: 'There – Jane has told it you.'

If he knew frustration, no sign of it was manifest. At home he was always the congenial companion of his Duchess. In the world outside, the finest orator of the age.

THE CROWNING YEARS OF STATESMANSHIP

The year 1740 opened to find Argyll prepared to play a notable part on behalf of the Opposition against Sir Robert Walpole's policy. In consequence, he was again called upon to resign the colonelcy of the 'Blues'. On this occasion, Algernon Seymour, Earl of Hertford and 7th Duke of Somerset, became Colonel. Summer took him north, for the purpose of influencing Scots' public opinion against Walpole's ministry as the hour of a general election approached.

'My Lord, Of all our friends I thought I might be of some service in the Election of Edinburgh.' From Caroline Park – the Edinburgh country residence named after his eldest daughter – Argyll wrote to the Earl of Marchmont.[1] 'I am doing all that an honest man can doe in that affair, and being informed that your Lordship has interest with Mr. Purves, am to beg the favour of you to let that Gentleman know your thoughts of me and my friends. I am with great sincerity . . .'

During those days when Argyll was so busy among his country-men, Lord Lovat paid him a visit, and afterwards described the occasion in a letter to a friend:

I went the next day to wait on my worthy friend, Generall Guest
who was mighty kind and offered me his charriot to go and
wait on the Duke of Argyle at his country house as oft as I
pleased. I accepted of his compliment, and went and waited on
the Duke at his country house which is two miles from Leith. He
received me very graciously and embraced me after his ordinary
manner. I was very merry with him about my breaking[2] and
made him laugh most heartily. There is one – Doctor Charles
Stewart – with him who travelled with the Duke of —'s children,
he has been my friend for many years. The Duke out of joke
would fain have put us by the ears because he said we were both
Jacobites and that we would learn something of our quarrel. I
told him that the Doctor and I knew one another too well to be
bit that way. He told me laughing very heartily, that was con-
fession enough. I told the Duke that the Doctor was the happiest
man in the world; that he always was a Jacobite, always will be a
Jacobite while he lives; and yet he is a favourite with all the
great men of the Court and of the Government, and if a lying
scoundrell said my Lord Lovat was a Jacobite, he was prescribed
for it without any more enquiry. The Duke told all the next day
to my Lord Glenorchy, who told it to my Lord Islay.

. . . I have been severall times with the Duke of Argyle before
I fell indisposed, and I own that his charming way with his
friends and acquaintances, and indeed with all mankind, gains
the hearts of all who see him, and I own frankly to you for my
own part, that I would rather serve that worthy man without fee
or reward than others with fee or reward. He certainly is one of
the finest gentlemen now in the world . . .

The Duke's wealth of language was heard as never before, when,
on many occasions during those critical years of 1740 and 1741, he
addressed the House of Lords.

Whatever their views on the subject in question, it was an inspiration for everyone present to listen to that melodious voice ringing
with enthusiasm and clashing his points home in a persuasive style.[3]

At the core of most of his speeches was a theme. For example, the
debate on the Pensions' Bill (March 1740) afforded him opportunity
to make 'Corruption' the mainspring. His words are memorable.

Corruption, my lords, has always hitherto been allowed to be
vile, to be dangerous. I have, for my own part, discouraged it in all
stations: I shall always disdain the obedience, or the parasitical

sort of assent that is to be gained only by corruption; and I have always been sorry, when I observed it was not equally discouraged in others; for if it were no way encouraged by those in high stations, it would never be possible for the mode in any country to cover that infamy which naturally attends the corrupted; nor would the quality of the offender ever atone for the wretched meanness of the offence . . .

If a prince or his sole Minister should ever have it in his power to have always a corrupt majority in each House of Parliament, a British Parliament will be no more than a Turkish divan.

He knew, too, the value of introducing phrases which would capture the memory of his listeners. 'I disdain being influenced by hope or fear in this administration or the next. I wish all my thoughts upon public affairs were written upon Charing Cross; my only aim is to be reputed a man who speaks and acts what he thinks right.'

Thus the words that introduced what he had to say when the Lords debated the question of not sending land forces to Admiral Vernon in America.

As the days passed, the Government's conduct of affairs took an appearance of catastrophe in Argyll's opinion. He cited the 'tedious and perplexed negotiations', the 'addresses that were drawn up and presented by Parliament upon the repeated complaintes of our merchants'; and now 'these addresses made an excuse for the most dishonourable negotiations that ever an unconquered nation submitted to carry one'.

There was only one man in the realm to whom he would wholeheartedly give his support: the King. His words in the debate on the address of thanks are evidence:

My Lords, I am for standing by His Majesty against all his enemies, whether they be Spaniards, or French, Irish, Scottish, or English; nay even against those, if there be any such, that are in his Privy Council. These last have always been found to be the most dangerous enemies to the kings of this country; and against whom our sovereign has nothing to depend on, but the wisdom, the honour and the integrity of his assembly.

For the Duke as a soldier, the most important debate of that year, 1740, was on 9 December: The State of the Army and a Resolution against augmenting it by Regiments. His views subscribe insight to him as one with a profound comprehension of his profession.

An army should be rightly proportioned of every species of officers fitted to do service. A hundred general officers for 100,000 men would be an improper proportion. It must be under military direction. The general officers must advise in military affairs, and none but military men must advise in the military part. There must be the very strictest military subordination, on which must be founded the strictest discipline. And so long as you have officers who have seen service in time of war, which alone is service, you ought not to have recourse to others.

There may be exceptions to this and distinctions shewn to persons of the first rank. But it ought to be a general rule. The rest of the places must be filled up with people that have such talents as experience will ripen. And all these must be preferred for their military merit, and punished only for military faults, as breach of the laws . . .

I have been twenty years the third officer in the Army, eight or nine years the second, several years the first. Therefore I may be a good evidence as to fact. And ever since this Ministry hath mounted into power, military methods have been laid aside, the chain broken between the Crown and the Colonel; general officers have had Commissions, as a man of great wit hath said, only to intitle them to call one another names; the general hath been only colonel of his own regiment . . .

No discipline hath been kept up, for reviews and exercises are not discipline; but the ABC of service, of which it is necessary to know a little and no more, the general officers have had no power of acting or advising about the placing so much as an ensign sometimes not even in their own regiments. The same methods have been pursued since the war began. General officers have not been employed or consulted, excepting the lowest; such as were not general officers in the war time; and no man hath been consulted in a proper way. It was necessary last year to augment the army, and it might have been very usefully employed; we might have ravaged the whole coast of Spain as France will do ours if ever they break with us and are masters at sea. But this was not done by additional men to each company which it was my opinion formerly, as well as now ought to have been done, but six regiments of marines were raised in order to erect new offices, and out of above 200 half-pay officers, not above 36 were put into those regiments. I spoke well of one youth who had distinguished himself in two Russian campaigns; yet neither his own desert, nor my patronage, could advance to a Commission. Numbers paid for their Commissions; tradesmen from the counter were made officers; numbers taken from school looked as if their cockades would tumble over. And these may be of use if their brothers, cousins, or cousin's cousins are members of Parliament . . . The dross of the nation has been swept together to compose our *new* forces, and every man who was too stupid or infamous to learn or carry on a trade, has been placed, by this great disposer of honours, above the necessity of application, or the reach of censure.

Argyll counselled that the most reasonable method to follow was not by the raising of regiments which, among other things, would increase the charge of the nation already loaded with taxes; but to add a hundred men to every company.

'We shall not only save the pay of the officers, but far more important, shall form the new forces with expedition into regular troops; for, by distributing them among those who are already instructed in their duty, we shall give them an opportunity of hourly improvement; every man's comrade will be his master, and every one will be ambitious of forming himself by the example of those who have been in the army longer than themselves.'

These words led him to consideration of the foreign military scene in regard to command.

. . . The only troops of Europe that swarm with officers are those of France; but even these have fewer officers in proportion to their private men, in time of war; for when they disband any part of their forces, they do not, like us, reduce their officers to half-pay, but add them to the regiments not reduced.

To the spirit of these men, my lords, are the French armies indebted for all their victories, and to them is to be attributed the present perfection of the art of war. They have the vigilance and perseverance of Romans, joined with the natural vivacity and expedition of their own nation.

The Duke concluded his long and fervently spoken oration by reiterating, with great stress, that: 'Augmenting the army by raising regiments, as it is the most unnecessary and most expensive method of augmentation, is also the most dangerous to the liberties of Britain.'

The problem so vital to Britain, both in times of war and peace, was again debated in February 1741. On this occasion the purpose was to advise the King against augmentation. Once more Argyll predominated.

It was ten days after this debate that Lord Carteret introduced a motion for the removal of Sir Robert Walpole. A Prime Minister whose beginning had shown such promise stood suspected by the majority in Parliament as well as a greater part of the general public, of 'having solely engrossed the ear of his Sovereign; of having endeavoured to destroy the independency of Parliament and the freedom of Elections'; and with regard to Foreign Affairs, 'of having sacrificed the interests of his country, and the interests of Europe, to the cultivation of a dangerous friendship and correspondence with France; besides having exposed both the honour and the trade of his country to the insults of Spain.'

The speech delivered by the Duke of Argyll was the last and undoubtedly the finest of his statesman's career. Into it he introduced all the ideals that had ever governed him in Parliament. Indeed, in essence and in spirit he more than fulfilled Alexander Pope's famous lines —

> Argyle, the State's whole thunder born to wield,
> And shake alike the Senate or the Field

If I were convinced of his innocence, as a friend to him, I should advise him to resign, in order that he might have his character vindicated by an impartial, a strict, and a fair enquiry; and if he refused my advice, I should, from that very refusal, begin to suspect his innocence, and, consequently, should agree to the address now proposed.

This, I say, my lords, should be my behaviour as a friend to him, if I were convinced of his innocence; but as I have my own suspicions, as well as other people, and have perhaps more reason than most other people, therefore, as a faithful counsellor to my Sovereign, which I have the honour to be, by my having a seat in this House, and as a sincere friend to my country, I must be for agreeing to the address proposed.

There was not a detail omitted from Argyll's survey of Walpole's conduct. When he touched the foreign scene and the Spanish conflict which embraced America, his words must have penetrated deep, not only for the emphasis that attended them, but for the fact that they threw more vivid reflection upon his character as a commander.

This is not a war to be carried on by boys; the state of the enemies' dominions is such, partly by situation, and partly by the neglect of that man whose conduct we are now examining, that to attack them with any prospect of advantage will require the judgment of an experienced commander, of one who had learned his trade, not in Hyde Park, but in the fields of battle, of one that has been accustomed to sudden exigencies and unsuspected difficulties and has learned cautiously to form, and readily to vary, his schemes.

An officer, my lords, an officer qualified to invade kingdoms, is not formed by blustering in his quarters, by drinking on birthnights, or dancing at assemblies; nor even by the more important services of regulating elections, and suppressing those insurrections which are produced by the decay of our manufactures.

My lords, those whom we have destined for the conquest of America, have not even flushed their arms with such services, nor have learned what is most necessary to be learned, the habit of obedience; they are only such as the late frost hindered from the exercise of their trades, and forced to seek for bread in the service . . .

Nor are their officers, my lords, extremely well qualified to supply those defects, and establish discipline and order in a body of new raised forces; for they are absolutely strangers to service, and taken from school to receive a Commission, or, if transplanted from other regiments, have had time only to learn the art of dress . . .

To their commander-in-chief, my lords, I object nothing but his inexperience, which is by no means to be imputed to his negligence, but to his want of opportunities; though of the rest surely it may be said that they are such a swarm as were never before sent out on military designs; and in my opinion, to the other equipments, the Government should have added provisions for women to nurse them.

Had my knowledge of war, my lords, been thought sufficient to have qualified me for the chief command in this expedition, or had my advice been asked with regard to the conduct of it, I should willingly have assisted my country with my person or my counsels . . .

Argyll drew the curtain on the scene of the nation in all its relations and circumstances, by turning to the word – 'administration', a 'term without a meaning, a wild indeterminate word, of which

Q

none can tell whom it implies, or how widely it may extend; a charge against the administration may be imagined a general censure of every officer in the whole subordination of government, a general accusation of instruments and agents, of masters and slaves; my charge, my lords, is against the Minister, against the man who is believed by every one in the Nation, and known by great numbers, to have the chief, and whenever he pleases to require it, the sole direction of the public measures; he, to whom all the other Ministers owe their revelation, and by whose smile they hold their power, their glories, and their dignity.'

With the weight of national opinion against him, Sir Robert Walpole had no chance of survival as Prime Minister.

After his resignation which occurred in February 1742, came Argyll's final triumph in the army. Besides restoration to his Colonelcy of the 'Blues', he was appointed Master-General of the Ordnance and Commander-in-Chief of all forces in southern England. At the same time, he retained the command in Scotland.

'Two men wish to have command of the Army – the King and Argyle – but by God neither of them shall have it . . .'[4] He might well have recalled those words spoken by rivals in the days after George I's accession. He had virtually gained his ambition. Unhappily the reward came too late.

A profound disillusionment in his domestic life; a rebuff from the new political chiefs[5] who positively refused his demand that the Tory partisans with whom he had formed league should be recognized in the coalition (or 'Broad-bottom' administration as it was known): these two events affected him so deeply that he could not, as in the past, kindle the fires of battle.

'I have liv'd so long in the great world not to have any faith in Ministers'.

On 16 March 1742, the Duke of Argyll resigned all his appointments, including the Colonelcy of the 'Blues'.

Then he turned back to the home into which sorrow had crept. Broken in spirit – yes; but not defeated in the ideal which had been the lode-star of his career: To serve my sovereign and through him my country.

Chapter IX

SUNSET

THE movement of time had brought the 'unwelcome' daughters to a stage where they could no longer be ignored. Lady Caroline Campbell made her debut, and on that occasion her two sisters, Anne and Elizabeth, were admitted to the drawing-room. It could not have given them much pleasure as they held their father in the greatest awe. With the fourteen-year-old Lady Mary it was different. She had no fear of him and he returned that attitude by lavishing her with affection. Instead of curbing her impetuous whims which influenced flights of temper, he indulged them. 'Look at Mary, look at Mary!' he was wont to exclaim as she screamed and raged until appeased with his reward of a sugar-plum and caress.[1]

Of the five sisters, Lady Anne predominated in looks which bore resemblance to her father's exquisite features. So it was not surprising that she quickly made a conquest. Lord Strafford, eligible both in years and wealth, met her when he dined with the family on his return from travel abroad. Without hesitation he requested a betrothal and was accepted.

Anne's marriage brought liberation to Caroline and Elizabeth. Previous strictures were removed, and they burst upon the London social scene as the 'most noisy hoydening girls.'

Among the younger set of the Tory opposition was one for whom Argyll had a high regard. In Lord Quarendon[2] he discerned abilities which promised well for the future. He made much of the youthful politician and, with expressions of praise, introduced him to the home circle. Thus, he admitted a fate destined to bring distress to himself.

Lord Quarendon and Lady Caroline discovered a mutual admiration for one another. A friendship blossomed and from it the fruit of an attachment grew. Yet she must have known that union with him would not meet her father's sanction. As heir to his English titles, she was expected to marry someone able to provide great estate and dowry. Lord Quarendon could not qualify in either of these ways.

Instead of taking the honourable course, Lady Caroline allowed self-will and sentiment to govern. She prevailed upon her mother to assist the affair. From that hour, an element of plot tarnished Jenny's straightforward life.

Argyll was the only one in the dark. He probably saw the young couple often together; but he never gave it serious thought. Caroline knew his wishes and, besides, was far too proud.

Then Francis Scott, Earl of Dalkeith,[3] appeared upon the scene. He lacked Lord Quarendon's handsome looks. On the other hand, he possessed qualities of more enduring value. Absolute sincerity, a solid sense of righteousness, and a manner which displayed a kind heart. For these points alone, Argyll approved him as a husband for his daughter. There was also the fact of his rank and wealth.

Caroline's first reactions to Lord Dalkeith's request for her hand were tears and rebellion. Gradually, however, she yielded to the father whose word was command and could not long be resisted. At Bruton Street, on 2 October 1742, the marriage took place.

The satisfaction which Argyll gained through seeing the future Baroness Greenwich married to so excellent a man as Lord Dalkeith was swept away by Lord Quarendon's revengeful act. He publicly announced that 'Lady Caroline Campbell had jilted him', and as proof presented the Duke with her letters which could only have been written by one virtually engaged.

This, in itself, inflicted a profound hurt to Argyll's deep-rooted sense of honour as the highest virtue in man.[4] Far more awful though, was the fact that his Jane had allied herself with the deception. The towering edifice of truth which he had so long created around her fell in ruins. He could never know her again in the same glorious light. As a result his health waned. A paralytic disorder afflicted his nervous system. The evening of a great life was closing on a broken heart.

Because the inward part of him still felt an abiding love, he could not admonish Jenny. Yet his manner towards her altered. Instead of the warmth that he had always shown, he became cold, silent, melancholy. While remarking the change, she did not attribute it to any cause other than ill-health. The notion of herself as perhaps to blame never occurred. Her simplicity of mind and essentially virtuous nature prevented realization of the harm which she had unwittingly brought to their lives.

Therefore, she continued to be Jenny – the wife who had ever been watchful of him and attentive to his needs. The fact that he was ill and needed more care kept her busy fussing around him throughout the days when his thoughts were so tragic.

'Now, my lord – do eat this!' 'Now, my lord, don't eat that!' 'Now pray put on your great-coat.' 'Now be sure you take your draught.' 'Now you must not sit by the fire; it's too hot.' 'Now you should not stand at the window; it's too cold . . .'

He did not attempt to remonstrate. In silence he would allow her to help him on with his great-coat; or take the draught that she offered him. Almost mechanically he would obey the voice that was so persistent with orders useless to his state of mind and heart. In the rare moments when he raised his head to look at the face which had been so precious to him that he beautified it in his imagination, only the flicker of a smile would momentarily light the sad countenance.

Summer had indeed gone from the Sudbrook circle. Even the high-spirited laughter of his darling Lady Mary could not restore the past to him. Nevertheless, an echo of the old Argyll thunder was to resurrect itself for one final occasion.

Chapter X

'AWA TAE HELL'

SUMMER days of 1742 found Argyll at Adderbury wounded in heart, ailing in health, saddened by his break with State affairs; he faced the fact that nothing remained save the monotony of retirement.

One morning a name was announced: 'My Lord Barrymore.' A visit from one not seen for a number of years came as an unexpected pleasure. He cordially welcomed the man who had been on his staff in Spain. The next hours were to figure among the happiest and yet the most tragic of his life.

As he and Lord Barrymore strolled through the gardens, dined, and over wine recalled former times, all sense of weariness left him. At length there arrived the moment for farewell.

Argyll, accompanied by his daughter Lady Betty,[1] attended their guest to the equipage; Lord Barrymore prepared to enter, but paused on the steps as though reminded of something. From an inner pocket he withdrew a sealed packet and thrusting it into Argyll's hand, said in lowered voice – 'By the way, I had orders to give you this'.

An instant later he had leapt into the carriage and the horses, stimulated by the driver's whip, sprang to the gallop.

When Argyll broke the seal the reason for that abrupt departure was clear. The letter[2] which he unfolded bore the signature of the man who had sought, by all means, to win him: James III – Chevalier de St George.

May 25th 1741.
R. [Rome]. I received in due time the letter or paper written by your friend in March last, with another short paper in the same hand that accompanied it. I have perused both with attention and satisfaction, and can easily remark in them a fund of experience

and good sense and affection for our country and my family. I
am no way surprised that my character and principles should be
so little known where he is. Neither I nor my children have many
occasions of declaring our sentiments . . .

We have now been more than fifty years out of our country.
We have been bred and lived in the school of Adversity, unacquainted with flattery and power, which always attend Princes
on the Throne, and equally unacquainted with certain ambitious
views which are common to them. If long experience teaches us
how little we can depend on the friendship of foreign Powers,
whatever the view of a present interest may have formerly, or may
hereafter induce them to undertake in our favour, our restoration
no doubt would be much more agreeable both to our subjects and
to ourselves were it brought about without foreign assistance. I
am far from approving the mistakes of former reigns. I see and
feel the effects of them, and should be void of all reflection did I
not propose to avoid them with the utmost care, and therefore I
do not entertain the least thought of assuming the Government
on the footing my family left it. I am fully resolved to make the
law the rule of my Government and absolutely disclaim any
pretensions to a dispensing power. I am sensible that the ruin and
oppression with which our country is distressed may make the
generality of people desirous of a change at any rate, but for my
part, as natural, as just as it is for me to desire that I and my
family should be restored to our just rights, I am far, at my age
especially, from desiring that should happen but upon an
honourable and solid foundation, cemented by mutual confidence
between King and People, by which the welfare and happiness of
both may be effectually secured. It is manifest that not only
justice but the interest of the nation requires my restoration,
because I can never have any interest separate from that of my
country, nor any hopes of peace and tranquility for my family but
by cultivating the affections of my people, and having only in
view their honour and happiness. I am persuaded there are many
persons of great talents and merit who would be of this opinion
were my true sentiments and dispositions known to them, though
they are not at this time looked upon as well-wishers to my cause;
neither can I wonder they have prejudices against it – they have
been bred up in them from their youth, and constantly confirmed
in them by all the artifices imaginable. But I hope the time is not
far distant in which they will see things in a true light; and if
they lay aside all unjust prejudices against me, and lay as much

to heart as I do the happiness and prosperity of our country, I make no doubts we shall soon be entirely satisfied with one another. It is fit your friends should know I have by me a draught of a declaration, which there never hath as yet been an occasion to publish. This declaration was in consequence of the sentiments and reflections expressed in letter. It contains a general indemnity, without exception, for all that has passed against me and my family; a solemn engagement to maintain the Church of England, as by law established, in all her rights, privileges, and immunities whatsoever; and as I am utterly averse to all animosities and persecutions on account of religion, it also contains a promise to grant and allow a toleration to all Protestant Dissenters. I also express in it an aversion to the suspending of the Habeas Corpus Act, as well as to the loading my subjects with unnecessary taxes, or the raising of them in a manner burthensome to them, and especially to the introducing of foreign excises, and all such methods as may have hitherto been devised and pursued to acquire arbitrary power, at the expense of the liberty and property of the subjects, and besides, there is a general article of my readiness to settle all that may relate to the welfare and happiness of the nation, both in civil and ecclesiastical matters, by the sincere advice and concurrence of a free Parliament. In fine, were I known, and were justice done to my sentiments, it would, I am convinced, make many alter their present way of thinking, and induce them to concur heartily in measures for my restoration, as the most effectual means to restore peace and happiness to our country . . .

After reading this letter Argyll recognized the significance behind Lord Barrymore's words – 'I had orders to give you this . . .': It echoed his challenge to the arbitrary measures of the Walpole administration. By proposing the same standard of patriotism, the Chevalier had presumed successful conclusion to the mission.

Argyll's response could be only one: 'Awa tae Hell.' Besides the fact that no persuasion, however strong, would corrupt his principles as a 'faithful counsellor to my Sovereign', the papist exiles owed his family two heads.

Consequently, he addressed a note to the King and enclosed the Chevalier's letter. Once more he had proved his life's dedication.

I have served my Prince with my tongue. I have served him with any little interest I had, and I have served him in my trade, and were I to-morrow to be stripp'd of all the employments I have endeavoured honestly to deserve, I would serve him again to the utmost of my power and to the last drop of my blood.'[3]

At the same time he was troubled in conscience. He had named the Chevalier's emissary. Despite the realization that the wound now in his heart had been dealt by Lord Barrymore, he could not forget the bond once between them : a soldier's friendship with its peculiar bond of honour. The element of betrayal existed in a mind which had never before carried that guilt. It would strengthen when he learnt of the King's action : a command that Lord Barrymore and two others[4] found to be associated with him as the Chevalier's envoys, be committed to the Tower.

Loyalty to nation, loyalty to brother officer : which of the two claimed the strongest obedience? The question would haunt him to the grave.

4 OCTOBER 1743

On a couch in a ground floor room of Sudbrook lay the Duke of Argyll. Beyond, the park was bathed in a mellow sunlight which enhanced the glory of the autumnal colours. Silence reigned. Even the roe-deer grazing in the glades seemed reluctant to move. The whole scene reflected respect for the man whose life's breath was fast leaving him.

In those final moments of the great tenancy he had enjoyed on Britain's soil, when his body was dying, his thoughts must still have been active.

Once more he stood on the floor of the House of Lords with all his friends and enemies around him. The eloquent voice was raised in impassioned declarations :

How we in this age come to have so much political faith, for I do not think we have improved much in our religious, I shall not pretend to account for . . .

In my opinion the best thing you can do is to convince the world that there is a perfect harmony subsisting between His Majesty and Parliament, that the British nation will concur with His Majesty in a vigorous prosecution, not only of the present war, but of any other war His Majesty may be necessarily engaged in, for maintaining the balance and liberties of Europe . . .

I have lived long enough in the world to see Great Britain glorious, triumphant and terrible abroad, her government loved, respected, and envied at Home . . .

The light of vision faded. He was away to greater, wider domains.

The British nation mourned the warrior-statesman – chieftain of Scotland – as he was borne through London to his final abode on this earth, Westminster Abbey.

> His worthy conduct did resolv'd appear
> Untaught the little vulgar vice to fear,
> Ah, now no more! his Sword the warrior draws,
> No more the Patriot in his country's cause
> Rife and assert her Liberties and Laws:
>
> Thy toilsome race is now victorious run
> And now all sorrow to a center's come.[5]

EPILOGUE

INSCRIPTION by
SIR THOMAS FERMOY
on the
MONUMENT to
JOHN, 2nd DUKE OF ARGYLL
in
WESTMINSTER ABBEY
. . . .

'IN MEMORY OF AN HONEST MAN
a CONSTANT FRIEND, JOHN – the
GREAT DUKE OF ARGYLL & GREENWICH.
A GENERAL AND ORATOR EXCEEDED BY
NONE IN THE AGE HE LIVED.'

LINES ON ARGYLL MONUMENT IN WESTMINSTER ABBEY

BRITAIN BEHOLD IF PATRIOT WORTH BE DEAR
A SHRINE THAT CLAIMS THY TRIBUTARY TEAR,
SILENT THAT TONGUE ADMIRING SENATES HEARD,
NERVELESS THAT ARM OPPOSING LEGIONS FEAR'D.
NOR LESS A CAMPBELL THINE THE POWER TO PLEASE,
AND GIVE TO GRANDEUR ALL THE GRACE OF EASE,
LONG FROM THY LIFE LET KINDRED HEROES TRACE
ACTS WHICH ENOBLE STILL THE NOBLEST RACE.
OTHERS MAY OWE THEIR FUTURE FAME TO ME,
I BORROW IMMORTALITY FROM THEE.

(The monument is the work of Roubillac)

ELEGY

On the much lamented death of His Grace the Duke of Argyll &
Greenwich who departed this Life on Monday the 4th of this
instant October at His Grace's seat at Sudbrook near Petersham in
Surrey in the 63rd year of his age.

(Printed for T. Davis in Fleet Street)

Ye Muses Nine, put on your Sable Dress,
And joyn with me in sorrow to rehearse
The loss, the greatest loss we ever had.
'Tis such a loss will make all England sad,
But still a Comfort we obtain,
That his Departure is his Glorious Gain.

A finer Patriot, surely ne'er was mis't
Than brave Argyle whose gone to heavenly Bliss.
No golden Idol, e'er could sway his Mind,
But steady to his Trust he was inclin'd;
His Country's Rights from which he never swerv'd.
His Courage bold, and from Corruption free,
He valued not the Threats of M . . .
Their Gaudy Titles he did still disdain,
And always spoke his Mind both free and plain.
When he was jogg'd by an brother P . . . r,
To vote against his Mind, he would not hear;

He scorn'd to Falter from his Noble Mind,
Which only to do justice was inclin'd,
By which He gained his Country Peoples' Heart,
And seem'd displeas'd when'er he did depart.
But when their welfare called him away,
They parted with him shouting loud huzzays;
With Acclamation of his safe Return
For which their Hearts most ardently did burn,
No sooner had he trod the English shore,
But there was still Rejoycings more and more.

O! had there been but Issue of his Loins
A noble Heart had then been left behind
That we might have had a second brave Argyle

Which would have caused the People still to smile,
But now alas! all Joy and Comfort's fled
Since our Defender brave Argyle is dead:
And now there is none left to take their part;
They must with Patience bear the Yoke at last.

An epitaph

Within his Urn, Lyes one whose Soul is Blest,
Crown'd with Eternal Glory, heavenly Rest,
When living bore a firm and . . . Mind.
And to his Country prov'd a Father, Kind.
Who while on Earth made it his only Care
His Country of his Labour should take share,
O! may his Name in lasting Mem'ry be,
From Age to Age, to all Eternity.
Intrepid in the Field, in Senates wise,
You set with Honour and with Honour rise,
Not the least cloud obscured your downward course,
Not the least spot checks your meridian Force.
Pure as the Light we feel the clearing ray
And happy Britons hail the glorious Day;
Rejoice my Country, sing my native Isle,
No longer shall the Hounds of Rapine spoil,
Our Fruitful Fields, and reap the farmer's toil,
Corruption sneaks away, dark fraud retires
Both sunk disgraced to their infernal Sires,
Tell me, my Friends, which most shall me admire,
The Patriot's eloquence or the Hero's fire;
When list'ning Senates with attention hung
Upon each pleasing accent of his tongue.
Or when the Routed Gaul before him fled
Nor the deep French contain'd the copious Dead;
He on each stage acted the noblest part,
Here Caesar's arm prevailed, there Cato's heart.

– To the Duke of Argyll by William Somerville Esq.

NOTES

Chapter I

1 The Earl of Peterborough resigned in order to take up the post of Ambassador to the Italian States.
2 Queen Caroline, as she would become on the accession to the throne of George II.
3 Memoirs of Lady Louisa Stuart.
4 Residence of the Prince and Princess of Wales.
5 The elections at the turn of the year 1714/1715 proved a signal success for the Whigs.
6 Halifax — First Lord of the Treasury, Lord Cowper — Chancellor, The Duke of Nottingham — Lord-President, Lord Townshend — Secretary of State, Earl Stanhope — Secretary of State, Earl of Sunderland — Lord-Lieutenant of Ireland, The Duke of Marlborough — Commander-in-Chief and Master of the Ordnance, Robert Walpole — Paymaster (but to become, in 1716, First Lord of the Treasury and Chancellor of the Exchequer).
7 The soldier — irrespective of rank — was treated with scorn. This fact had its repercussions upon the whole service. Discipline, morale, and order suffered a 'dry rot'.
8 The Pretender, as he was commonly known.
9 As reports from agents at Versailles reached England, war-like preparations were set on foot. The reason was not disclosed, yet citizens observed the Foot Guards encamped in Hyde Park. The Horse were also called out; several regiments received orders to march nearer London, and five or six regiments, among them the 'Buffs', were recalled from Ireland.

'Tis said pairt of Horace Walpole's errand to Holland is to take care the Dutch boatmen be in readiness upon the first notice from home. These things look like no joke.
'Tis not to be expected the Ministry should publish the reasons of thus putting things into the posture of defence. The towne says they have some discovery of ane immediate insurrection so soon as the King should be gone and that the rebells abroad with the late Duke of Ormonde and such as the zeal of priests in Spain and France could influence, were to land in England, which was to be the signall for other desperate associates and correspondents here to take arms and pursue their wild attempt. This, my Lord, is the towne's talk for the true source and spring of our fears and preparations . . .
. . . I heard from a pretty good authority that the precautions taken would not only secure us from reall danger but even crush the making of any attempt to disturb our quiet. 'Tis thought by many now that the King will not go over this summer, so far is certain he does not go before the first or second week of June . . .

10 French Foreign Office Archives.
11 The Duke of Argyll to Lord Townshend.

Chapter II

1 Argyll to William Stuart — third son of James, Earl of Galloway.
2 All the noblemen, gentlemen and other persons who favoured the Chevalier issued a manifesto to support the incontestable right of their legitimate Sovereign — James VIII [the Pretender] by the Grace of God — King of Scotland, England, France, and Ireland, Defender of the Catholic Faith, and to deliver his ancient Kingdom of Scotland from the Oppression with which it is overcome.'
3 Lord Townshend was then Secretary at War.
4 Argyll.
5 French Foreign Office Archives.
6 A report dated 7/8 October, sent by Monsieur d'Iberville to the French court, states: 'After having garrisoned places with about 1,200 regular troops, the Duke of Argyle assembled the Militia. These people are nearly all Presbyterians and for this reason regarded as enemies of the Pretender and strongly attached to the Duke of Argyle whose forbears have always been the Chiefs of this Sect. They vulgarly call themselves "Cameronians" . . .'
7 The first order went to Lord Polwarth:

> John, Duke of Argyle — Generall & Commander-in-Chief of His Majestie's Forces in North Britain.
>   You are hereby required to send sixty of your Militia with proper . . . from their present Quarters . . . to Edinburgh and to take . . . prisoners Sir Thomas Hope and . . . whom they are to deliver to the Lieutenant Governor of Edinburgh Castle, and to take a Receipt from him for their being put into his custody: they are likewise to take charge of what stores shall be delivered them from the castle of Edinburgh and conduct the . . . to Falkirk, there to be relieved by another party to bring the same to this place, and all Magistrates, Justices of the Peace and others concerned are required to be assisting to them in providing Quarters, in preparing carriages or otherwise as shall be requisite.
> Given at ye 5the Camp at Stirling 3 October 1715.

> To the Rt. Hon. my Lord Polwarth or the Officer Commanding the Militia of the Shire of Mers at Falkirk.

Another order read: 'Protection for houses of David Graham of Fintry — from John, Duke of Argyle — Generall & Commander-in-Chief His Majestie's Forces in North Britain.' (Reference: Sir John James Graham of Fintry, K.C.M.G.)
    Argyll also sent a number of orders to have 'all the Boats, Ships, and other Vessels lying in the Forth, to be sent over to the Lothian.'
8 A kinsman, John Campbell, wrote to Lord Townshend:

Edinburgh — November 1715.
    We are all too sensible of the great service the Duke of Argyle did to this town in preventing the danger it was in, of falling into the hands of the enemie, and how absolutlie necessary it is for the King's

service to preserve it that we have been at the expense of making such works at all the avenues of it as may render it defencible, without giving His Grace the trouble of a detachment from the little army he has to employ against the designs of the enemy at Perth which, Your Lordship will judge, is of as great importance as Stirling to His Majesty's service . . .

9   In a certain respect, the Earl of Mar's position resembled that of Argyll. With an initial strength of 12,000, he, too, had need of reinforcements as the troops were disorderly and ill-provided for both in food and ammunition. Yet the forces which he had requested and expected from abroad failed to arrive. Thus frustrated, he preferred to remain in the neighbourhood of Perth while an Expedition commanded by Mackintosh of Bordun proceeded to northern England where support might be raised. It was doomed to failure, and resulted in the loss of 2,500 men.

Without news from Mackintosh, Mar decided on the bold tactics of taking the offensive.

10 'When the Duke ordered drums to beat "The General", the signal of preparation for advance, they beat a considerable time without action on the part of the men whose orders had been not to stir from their Arms of the previous night. Despite the efforts of Officers to assemble them, an hour or more elapsed before they were ready to march.' 'But that not being a fit time to punish for breach of Order, the Duke was forced to pocket up the matter till a more convenient season.' (Rae.)

11 The 'Buffs' lost their colonel, Lord Forfar, who died of his wounds ten days after the battle.

12 Argyll lost about 600 men: Morrison's, Clayton's and Orrery's Regiments suffered heavily in killed and wounded. Mar's losses came to about 800.

13 *London Gazette* and contemporary 'news-letters'.

14 The French agent in London reported in a note dated 17 December: 'Le General Cadogan et le General Wightman etoient arrivés dans cette Capitale le jour aupararant de Stirling, après avoir visité avec le Duc d'Argyle le Terrain entre Perth et Stirling sur tout les environs de Dumblain et le Champ de la dernière bataille et consulté quel etoit le passage le plus propre pour faire marcher . . .'

15 The Chevalier St George ('The Pretender') landed at Peterhead.

16 The Chevalier had conferred the title of 'Duke' upon his Commander-in-Chief.

17 According to a report sent by M. d'Iberville to the French court: 'Le Duc d'Argyle en consequence des ordres qui luy ont esté envoyés se disposait à marcher contre les Rebelles vendredy passé, mais faute des chevaux pour l'artillerie et pour les vivres qu'il attendait d'Angleterre, sa marche a esté remise à 28 . . .'
        (Janvier).

18 According to a letter dated 30 January from James Campbell to Lord Bute: '. . . They [the rebels] have burnt Crieff, Auchterarder, Blackford, Muthill, and such places this side of Perth as could accommodate an army. The weather is most unfavourable for the Duke especially when all places of shelter are demolished.'

19 'The Scots rebels, after the Pretender left them, marched in a body
northward, first to Aberdeen, then further north towards Strathspey
and Badenoch. Argyle did not pursue them much further than
Aberdeen, but sent detachments to Peterhead and Fraserburgh.
Clemency is expected for the prisoners.' Report to the 'Duke' of Mar
from Captain H. Seaton.

20 Captain Seaton also sent a report to Clanronald: '. . . Upon certain
information of our reconnoitring party commanded by Captain
Cavanagh, we began our march from Aberdeen about 10 o'clock on
Tuesday morning, being the fifth day. The Foot quartered that night
at Inverury and the Horse at Old Meldrum, and late that same night
the Duke of Argyle, with most of his cavalry, came into Aberdeen . . .'

21 On 14 February, the Marquis of Huntly writing to Lord Lovat stated:

> . . . I have submitted to the Government and my friends, but could
> not in particular to anybody unless the Duke ordered me, who gave
> me assurances of life and fortune for myself and friends before I
> cam from Perth by allowance of the Government.

Some days afterwards, he sent news to Lord Seaforth:

> General Wightman, Brigadier Grant and his brother, and some horse
> and foot arrived to-day at Gordon Castle. The General sends me word
> if I surrender to him he will only put two sentries on me in the
> house . . . I send you the paper and hope it will please you, since
> in it, as on all occasions, I will own myself much obliged to the
> Duke of Argyle.

Chapter III

1 The purpose of the Septennial Bill was to impose a seven-year period
for the holding of elections. Hitherto, these had been held every three
years in accordance with the Triennial Act; but as the Duke of Newcastle represented in opening the debate, 'Triennial elections of Parliament had inconveniences – "particularly that they serve only to keep
up Party division and raise and foment feuds and animosities in private
families." '

2 A certain Hugh Thomas wrote to Lord Inese: '. . . His Majesty designs
for Hanover and is resolved to leave the Government entirely to the
Prince. If so, Argyle will certainly ruin Marlborough to prevent which
Marlborough has advised His Majesty to appoint the Prince a Council
for his guide, and has hastened up Cadogan from Scotland to blacken
Argyle that it may not be said of Marlborough.'

3 The Order of the Thistle.

4 Besides his brother – Lord Islay - Lord Selkirk, Lord Orkney, and
Lord Orrery, were also dismissed from their official appointments and
Lord Orrery's regiment was given to Macartney.

5 J. Menzies to Lord Inese.

6 It was even inferred that he had been closely involved in Jacobite

affairs. Anthony Hammond writing to Lord Stair stated: 'The con-
jectures here about the Duke of Argyle are various. Some of the Dutch
officers who were in Scotland do not stick to say that he had a criminal
correspondence with the enemy and that he might have reduced them
sooner, and this I speak only to your Lordship.'

7 The Whigs had another reason to give for Argyll's dismissal. According
to their explanation, a Council was called for approving the Act of
Regency. On account of limitations in the Act that displeased him, the
Prince refused to attend. The Duke argued against the limitations.
Then the King ordered the whole Act to be destroyed, whereupon
Argyll asked permission, which was granted, to go to the Prince. After
their discussion, he informed the Council that the Prince accepted the
Commission as it stood. After the Council broke up, the King sent word
to Argyll that there was resolved 'None should be about his son that
had more interest with him than he had.' Therefore he had 'no further
service either for Argyle or his brother.'

8 A scheme to win Argyll's support for James III (the Chevalier of St
George).

9 The Prince of Wales.

10 The letter was addressed from Cambrai.

11 In March 1717, Argyll was superseded as Colonel of the 'Blues' by
Charles Paulet, 8th Marquis of Winchester and 3rd Duke of Bolton.

12 Owen O'Rourke to the Duke of Mar.

Chapter IV

1 Afterwards Lady Suffolk.

2 The first Duchess, who died at the age of thirty-six, was laid to rest in
Westminster Abbey.

3 A query may arise in regard to both events happening in 1717, particularly as the peerage states that the first Duchess's death occurred in
1716. It must be remembered, however, that the 'old style' calendar
when the New Year began in March and not in January was still in
force.

4 Polwarth Papers.

5 One died in infancy.

6 Afterwards Lady Mary Coke.

7 Among them was Colonel Jack Campbell – a future Duke of Argyll.

8 Formerly Mrs Howard and future mistress of the Prince of Wales when
he became George the Second. Both the Duke of Argyll and the Earl
of Islay were on terms of great friendship with her. They made the
arrangements for the purchase of her house – Marble Hill – and acted
as her trustees.

9 According to Lady Louisa Stuart, a kinswoman through the Bute
relationship, Argyll's reputation for 'mean-ness' was erroneous. He
was 'strictly just, habitually regular and careful, maybe somewhat too
careful – in his expenses; but never mean; very capable of generous
actions and when he gave, giving nobly.'

10 The Duchess pronounced their names alike.

R

Chapter V

1 The Duke of Argyll considered that a court-martial court was inconsistent with the rights and privileges of Englishmen. He also opposed the 'keeping up so great a number of Forces, which being altogether useless in time of profound peace could not but raise just apprehensions that something was intended against our happy and ancient Constitution.'

2 The Earl of Islay was one of the principal investors.

3 To quote Alexander Cunningham – 'When he [Argyll] found any man desperately in debt, involved in distress, and without any prospect of relief; if he perceived him to be a man of courage, he would receive him in to the number of his particular friends, and load him with rich favours and hopes, and infallibly attached him to his person.'

4 The Duke of Somerset represented that the number of peers being of late years very much increased, especially since the union of the two kingdoms, it seemed absolutely necessary to fix the same lot to preserve the dignity of the peerage and present inconveniences that may attend the creation of a great number of peers to serve a present purpose of which they had remarkable instance in the last reign. He moved: 'The bringing in of a Bill to settle and limit the Peerage in such a manner that the number of English Peers be not enlarged beyond six above the present number, which upon failure of male issue, might be supplied by new creations; that instead of the sixteen elected Peers in Scotland 25 be made hereditary as part of the Kingdom whose number upon failure of one being male, be supplied by some other Scotch Peers.'

 The Duke of Argyll seconded the motion which was backed by the Earls of Sunderland and Carlisle.

5 Sir Robert Walpole's era as Chief Minister opened in 1727 and lasted until 1742.

Chapter VI

1 Second reading.

2 The Duke of Marlborough's death occurred in 1722. Since then, until 1725, Cadogan had held the appointment.

3 After Cadogan's death, Argyll had expectations of being made Generall of the Foot. However, he only received the Duke of Bolton's regiment, offices and pension, either £10,000 or £14,000 per annum.

4 There is a doubt about the dispatch of these letters, copies of which are in the Royal Archives at Windsor. They may not have been sent.

5 Source of reference – Woodrow, *Analecta*.

Chapter VII

1 In the Commons, Mr Sandys had presented a 'Motion for Address to H. M. the King to know who advised His Majesty to remove the Duke of Bolton and Lord Cobham from their Regiments.'

2 In the Lords, Lord Morpeth had put in a 'Motion for a Bill to prevent any Commissioned Officer not above the rank of Colonel of a Regiment

being removed, unless by a Court-Martial or by Address of either House.

3 Timberlake's Parliamentary Debates.

4 These were to take the form of revising the City Charter, abolishing the Town Council, and banning the Provost from employment in Great Britain.

5 'The Lord Provost and the City of Edinburgh having been admitted to be heard of their Counsel against the Bill, upon its being read a second time in the House of Lords, that Hearing began on Wednesday, May 4th, and was continued every day till Saturday the 7th, and then the Bill was committed to Monday when repassed in the Committee and on Wednesday May 11th was read a third time and passed in that House on a Division — 54 Content to 22 Not Content.'

6 As Foreign Minister after King George's accession, he elevated Great Britain from the isolation and disrespect into which she had descended, to a place of strong prestige among the nations.

7 Britain had been allowed the privilege of supplying Spanish colonies with Negro slaves and sending annually a merchant vessel either to Carthagena or Portobello.

8 The South Sea Company, who, it was claimed, stood indebted to Spain for £68,000.

9 As a result, the Duke of Argyll was dismissed from his state offices.

10 Parliamentary Records — 1739.

Chapter VIII

1 Letter from the Marchmont Papers.

2 The 'chariot' (carriage) in which Lord Lovat had travelled from Inverness-shire had broken several times on the journey.

3 He won several Government members over to the Tories. Among them was Dodington.

4 Spoken by the Earl of Orford in the year 1740, after Argyll had resigned all his military appointments.

5 Lord Willingdon headed the 'Broad-bottom' administration; the Duke of Newcastle remained Secretary-of-State; Hardwicke was Lord Chancellor; Henry Pelham, Paymaster-General; Sandys, Chancellor of the Exchequer.

Chapter IX

1 In after days, as Lady Mary Coke, she had the reputation of having the most ungovernable temper.

2 Son of the Earl of Lichfield.

3 Heir to the Duke of Buccleuch.

4 'A soldier's honour is his virtue Gownmen
Wear it for show, and barter it for gold,
And have it still: a soldier and his honour
Exist together, and together perish.'

Florian H. Walpole
[Horace]

R*

Chapter X

1 Afterwards Lady Betty Mackenzie.
2 On 25 May 1741, James Chevalier de St George issued a circular letter for a Scottish friend and Argyll. The original is, or was, in the Charter Room at Cullen House, Banffshire.
3 Spoken in reply to the attack made upon him during the Porteous murder Debate in the House of Lords – 1736.
4 Colonel Cecil and D. Beaufort.
5 Lines from epitaph to John, Duke of Argyll and Greenwich, 4 October, 1743.

Appendix I

JOHN, 2nd DUKE OF ARGYLL
as
LANDLORD

1 Projects for Inverary
2 Instructions to his managers
3 Letters on business affairs
4 Residences
5 Lands in the Parish of Kilblain
6 The 'Old Faithfuls'

PROJECTS FOR INVERARAY

On two occasions Argyll had the desire to make his ancestral seat a great and stately mansion. The first one belonged to the years between 1717 and 1720.

As a result of the Rebellion, the castle had fallen into a disorder which compelled works of restoration.[1] 22 October 1718 found him at Sudbrook and writing to Lord Bute :

'. . . I am at no such loss for want of the plan at Inveraray which Your Lordship promised to send me and without which I am not able to provide materials for the repairs which I project next summer. May my good Lord let me have it. I am astonished to hear that you have at least laid the foundation of a house, having, I confess, taken it for granted we should never see it but in black and white. Pray give my service to my sister and believe me your most faithful slave – Argyll.'

Because of this work he decided to visit Inveraray the next summer season. Due to the slowness of communications, preparation began far in advance. So early in January 1719, his kinsman, John Campbell, wrote to Lord Bute :

'. . . The Duke of Argyll being fully resolved to be in Roseneath this season and from thence His Grace goes to Inveraray and to leave his Dutchess at Roseneath while he is in the Highlands, has desired me to write to your Lordship to provide him a couple of hogsheads of good wine and he will repay you at meeting . . .'

At that time, Argyll proposed the castle's reconstruction as a palace. Architectural plans were prepared;[2] but there was no further progress.

After he became Master of Ordnance (1725) and advanced to other military rewards, his ambition revived. He appointed Dugald Campbell to prepare a plan for the castle rebuilt in the style of a Spanish fortress.[3] The project did not go beyond an elaborately composed design.

The only development that took place was building of the house[4] to which Argyll had alluded in his letter to Lord Bute. Completed by 1723, it stood in the castle's vicinity. He lived there occasionally; and during those times entertained his Highland friends.

JOHN, DUKE OF ARGYLL'S INSTRUCTIONS TO HIS MANAGERS, 1704

(Argyll's duty as landlord dated from his inheritance of the Dukedom. One of his first missions was to address instructions to his managers.)

Be it known to all men by thir (their) presents (presence) us – John Duke of Argyll – and for as much as albeit We by our Commission by the date of His present.

Did nominate and apoint James Campbell Younger of Ardkinglas, Colonel Alexander Campbell of Fanab, Campbell of Minie, John Campbell, Merchant in Edinburgh, and Ronald Campbell, Writer to the Signet – To be Manadgers of our Estate both personal and real containing most ample powers therein mentioned. Yet nevertheless it is hereby declared that the said Commission is burdened with the Instructions after mentioned and are holden as therein repeated and are to be faithfully observed by our Manadgers in time comeing.

Primo. That there be an exact and true rentall made of our whole Estate and for that effect that Baron Courts be held in the severall places of our Estates and the persons liable in payment examined upon oath and their Tacks and Charters produced and this rentall once made up That the same be recorded and signed by our Manadgers. And that any addition or alteration that may happen may be yearly added and recorded, and that one dupplicat of the said rentall and of the additions and alterations as often as they shall happen signed by the Manadgers and the Chamberlains be transmitted to us as soon as the same are made up. *Secundo.* That the Estate be divided in two districts and that the Chamberlain of each District have a coppie of the rentall of his own District signed by himself and the Manadgers. And that the factor leave in the Manadger's hands, one Dupplicat of the rentall signed by himself with an oblidgement to compt (account) accordingly. *Tertio.* That the factors be pressed to transmit to our Receiver such money as comes to their hand with all convenient speed. *Quarto.* That the accomps for the crop one thousand seven hundred and three years and precedings be made in October next by the Factor to the Manadgers of their Quorum. And that there be yearly accomps made in October for the year preceding that current year in all time comeing. And that Dupplicats of these accomps signed by the Manadgers and Chamberlains be transmitted to us yearly immediately after they are stated and discharged. *Quinto.* That these accomps be faithfully audited and the manner of Instruction marked on the margins of the discharge, and that when money is payed in to his Receiver that his receipt be marked in the article, and that there be ane Responde marked in the margine in these words – 'Responde to the Receiver', and that the Chamberlains of the severall Districts give bonds for their balances and rests. *Sixto.* That the Charge of these accomps be made not only conform to the Rentall, but that the preceding balance be charged even the bond be granted for it. *Septimo.* That the Chamberlain's accompt being fitted and cleared the Receiver doe also compt in January or February yearly and that his charge be made up of the Respondes drawn from the Chamberlain's discharges and such other articles as he shall receive either for debts or compositions, And that upon fitting of the accompt he get up his rents and that Dupplicats of the Receiver's Accompt signed by the Manadgers and Receiver be also transmitted to us yearly. *Octavo.* That all fitting of the Chamberlain's accompts especially at the fitting of the Receiver's accompts the extraordinary Commissioners of a quorum of them if they can be conveniently made to be present. *Nono.* That there be ane Exact book of Debit and Credit keeped (kept) for clearing of the generall Receiver's and : a second book wherein the Chamberlain's accompts may be recorded. A third book of the sederunts of the Commissioners con-

taining the Minutes of the proceedings, the coppies of letters written
to them and by them and a fourth book containing the doubles of
all Charters and Tacks which shall be signed by the Vassals. *Decimo*.
that the Chamberlain's accompts being fitted be keeped by the
Manadgrs until the Receiver's accompts be fitted and then the
Receiver getts the keeping of the Chamberlain's accompts, and the
Receiver's own accompts be delivered to ane of the Manadgers to be
appointed by the other Manadgers or their Quorum. *Undecimo*.
That there be an exact list of the debts and their bygone resting
annual rents and the rents, be applied with the greatest care and
prudence (so far as it is not exhausted by liferents or applied to our
own use) for clearing the debts. *Duodecimo*. That before the
receiving of vassals or selling the compositions and before turning
out of Chamberlains or selling of Tacks or Discharges of accompts
and generally in matters of greater concern, the Manadgers are to
transmit the state of the case with their opinion to us, before concluding – That we may give direction unless some pressing and
necessary require the contraire (contrary), and if the cause be
pressing that we may be immediately acquainted. And we the said
Manadgers doe hereby accept of the aforsesaid Commission with
and under the burden of the aforsesaid Instructions and by our
acceptative thereof bind and oblige us to observe the same in all
points.

In witness whereof we have subscribed their presence (written by
George Gordon, servitor to Ronald Campbell – Wryter to the Signet)
at Canongate the eleventh day of September one thousand, seven
hundred and four years, before their witnesses – Sir Alexander
Cumming of Coulter – Advocate – David Campbell – Merchant in
London and Daniel McNeill our Servitor. E. Argyll – David
Campbell – Witness – Donald McNeill – Witness – George Gordon –
Witness.

LETTERS WRITTEN BY HER GRACE THE DOWAGER DUCHESS OF
ARGYLL AND HIS GRACE JOHN, DUKE OF ARGYLL, ON BUSINESS
AFFAIRS DURING 1704

His second task after being Duke was to address a series of letters
on business affairs.

Extracts from two letters written by the Dowager Duchess of Argyll.
'I receiv'd yours of the 28th this evening'; thus opened a letter
which the Dowager Duchess wrote to the family lawyer, Mr
Anderson, on 12 February 1704.

Good news my son's designing to be so soon home. There is nothing I desire more or would be a greater satisfaction to me. All things remaining as you left it at Stourton but threatened with great disorder. I can do no more than I have done both to preserve it and to satisfy just creditors; but if my son will lose it I can't help it. It will be lost to him, not me. I could have wished you came with him and let him see all things. When he does I suppose he will think them fitter for Inveraray than they are.

She also turned to the Duke of Somerset to ask for 'what is proper to be done and execute by authority of any of your Lordship's Court of officers. I entreat the favour of justice and dispatch, for I shall, I hope, make my sons and my title very clear . . . My brother Dysart and my son will wait upon Your Lordship at London and make my compliments of thanks to your Lordship for his trouble.'

Letter written by His Grace, John Duke of Argyll, to Ronald & John Campbell.

I receiv'd yours and am glad you have made an end of Lord Montrose's affair. I do not understand it positively but doe not in the least dout but that you have made the best out of so what you advyse me of referring this thing to my Lord Montrose doe in it as you think fitt, pray take cair I have my money pay'd me at the time for I shall need it.

I am your servant

Argyll

London,
September the 28 – 1704
To Ronald & John Campbell

Letters addressed to Ronald Campbell in Edinburgh
Ronald,

I wonder you should make any difficulty as to my being paid my thousand pound in November. I thought when I did so much towards the standing of the Family it was by no means the way to make me proceed to pay me ill, the little I have receiv'd for my own mentenance I dont desire to put my selfe out of houmer (humour) by inlarging on the subject; but I doe expect to be pay'd punctually by the beginning of November. If I do not, I must alter mesures (measures) for want I will not on any account.

I am yours

Argyll

4th October

Ronald,

I would know from you when I shall send you that bill if by
Lord Montrose because you avow it may be dangerous if lost. I
must own I think he might have acted more prudent than he has
dun and more civilly towards me but be depend on't, I shall not
forgive it and I order you who are my manager to show all the
resentment of it that lys in your power upon all occasions. I doe
not know what I can doe more than to write to Arkinglass to lett
the Gentlemen of the Shire know I incline they fall on such
methods as may prove effectual for that purpose.

Argyll

London Oct: ye 20 1704

Ronald,

I believe the Queen is sattisfied to discharge me my Feu dutys
during my life-time, it will be need full to consult laws in what
manner it may be dun most justly for me. I desire you may take
advice and by next post send a draft of a Paiper such as may be
good in Law, the Beginning of November now draws near and I
expect my Money without faill for I can't live on air, you may
tell Sanders Campbell I desire he may stop monthly of those
gentlemen whom have not as yet paid for their Horses what they
can be supos'd reasonably to spair towards the paiment of the
Horses, I believe I shall be able to lett you know in some little
time of sumthing dun for me in England which will please you,

I am yours

Argyll

Lon: Oct the 24
    1704.

The middle of November came and the thousand pounds he had
so urgently requested was not forthcoming. On the 11th went an
even more emphatically worded letter.

Ronald,

I receiv'd yours with the Draft of the paiper, you tell me you
desire to send me the thousand pound so soon as you can. I must
own Ronald I am much surprised I have it not before now. I
cant imagine whow (how) you can think I live here and I dair
assure you if I havena that thousand pound with the answer of
this letter and am not for the future pay'd, surely to a day I shall
alter my method *for by God Allmighty I will not starve for the
saik of my Family or any thing on earth.* You know their will be

five hundred dew me again at Candlemass. I expect not to have the saim trouble about that which I have had about this, I shall make euse (use) of but one argument to persuade you to this which is that if I can not be eazy (easy) otherways (when I have two thousand pound a year clear) I shall sell and make myselfe easy that way.

I am yours

Argyll

London, ye 11 Nov. 1704

That month drew to a close and found him still without satisfaction.

Ronald,

I receiv'd Mr. Dugald Stuart's letter and send you here one for him inclos'd, pray let the letter thatt is sign'd either by the King or Queen, 1 dont know which, be laid before the Commission as other matters so that I may not be oblig'd to pay that – I am much surprised I have not receiv'd my thousand pound.

Argyll

London, ye 21st Nov: 1704

Four days later, he wrote again.

Ronald,

I receiv'd your's with ye bills which I was very glad to see and I hope for ye future you will order matters so that I may have my munny [money] pun[c]tually, for since I take so little I can not afford waiting for it, after ye time of payment I shall write to you more fully in a Post or two so say no more now.

I am yours

Argyll

His next letters were written during the month of December.

Ronald,

I would have sent you the Bond by this post but could not find anybody to fill up the blank, but you may assure your selfe I shall send it by next post. I must Ronald put you in mind that I must be pay'd my next five hundred pound very punctually for if I cant bye things with reddy money they are shure to cost a third more which you know what I spend wont alow (allow) of, so I hope you will be sure not to disappoint me.

I am yours

Argyll

London Decr. ye 9 1704

On 16 December he addressed a long communication to certain gentlemen who were engaged in the management of his affairs.

Gentlemen,

I receiv'd yours and shall writ to my Mother as you desire me for my Uncle John I understand you would have called him to an account for his intromitions and that he had no more to doe with my part of the Esteat for I never desir'd he should. As for the methods you propose for dyscharging the Debt, I leave all this matter entyerly to you, but there is an expression in your letter which I can not understand which by that you would have me transfer no more money for the year that ends this month. I agree with you but if you will you would have me draw for no more money for a twelvemonth. I am afraid you have given your advice without much thinking for you know I have had but a thousand pound since my father's death and when he dy'd he was in arrear to me thirteen hundred pound so that this two years I have receiv'd but forteen hundred pounds and I can assure you every body that knows the affair is astonished how I have been able to live on so little, and now you would have me live another year on the air so that in these years you would alow me forteen hundred pounds, in short I wont believe you mean it in this sense, you know I told you I proposed to live on my post and a thousand pound a year paid out of my Esteat which considering that I have my feu Duty from the Queen I have but four hundred out of the Esteat. I think this is doing extremely much for the family as if nothing will satisfie but my starving myselfe that is what no consideration will oblige me to, upon the contrary if my friends beant satisfied in the hyest manner of the straits I put myselfe in for the preservation of the family I shall hereafter have not regard for my own ease which I shall find a very easy way to accomplish so that to shun all inconveniences that may follo I hope you will take cair to remit me the thousand pound I . . . myselfe . . . at the usual terms of the year by then things will go well.

I am Yours,

Argyll

London, Decr. ye 16 1704

I send inclos'd the Bond for my Lord Bute

RESIDENCES

Besides his town house – 27 Bruton Street – Argyll had three other residences.

Before 1714, he acquired Sudbrook House by Richmond.

In 1717, he obtained the lease of Adderbury – a property situated on the east side of the main road to Banbury in Oxfordshire: with it went a seventeenth-century mansion. Once the home of Anne, Countess of Rochester, this had been classified by Dr Plot (1676) as 'One of our most stately buildings' and among the most eminent in the country. Yet Argyll was not satisfied with either the architecture or scale, and made plans for re-building. According to Horace Walpole, these were carried out in several stages.

Drawings now in Dalkeith House Charter Room 'show that the existing south front, originally surmounted by six Jacobean gables, was remodelled probably in 1722, the date on the rain-water heads.' At about the same time, the north front was constructed to suit the fashion of the new age – the Georgian – although traces of the seventeenth-century masonry were retained. Soon after 1731, Roger Morris, whose work bore the influence of Sir John Vanbrugh, designed the arcaded wings. The southern wing, distinguished by a great gallery nearly eighty feet long, with a coffered ceiling and other decorative features, was in the Palladian style; but the arcades pointed to Vanbrugh.

The grounds, of approximately 224 acres, showed a wealth of flower gardens and park-land enclosed by a verge of ever-greens and forest trees. There was also a 'fine serpentine stream of water in full view of the house.'

In all its perspectives, the Estate of Adderbury provided evidence of Argyll's taste for splendour merged with beauty. It constituted a noble heritage for his eldest daughter – Lady Caroline (Countess of Dalkeith) and her son – Henry – (3rd Duke of Buccleuch). During the year 1768 he 'carried on great works at Adderbury.'

In 1739, Argyll acquired a property in the parish of Cramond, Midlothian. From the owner – Lord Roystoun – he bought the Barony of Granton and Granton House (Roystoun Castle). To these estates[5] amidst a hundred acres of wooded park-land he gave the name Caroline – in memory of the late Queen.

Caroline Park[6] then became one of his principal residences and he endowed it with the magnificence which distinguished him as head of great establishments.

His armorial bearings are still to be seen in a room in the west tower of Caroline House.

Above one of seven large mural paintings the Coat-of-Arms of the Argyll Campbells has its place. Surmounting it is a ducal coronet encircled by *'Honi soit qui mal y pense'* and guarded by two lions. Beneath is scrolled the family motto – *'Ne obliviscaris.'* Over an adjacent panel a boar's head represents the Arms of Argyll, while inscribed below is the motto which he chose when created Baron Chatham and Earl (afterwards Duke) of Greenwich: 'Vix ea nostra voco.' The ducal coronet together with the Garter legend (*'Honi soit qui mal y pense'* and two guardian lions) are present.

The estate of Caroline Park was an inheritance for the Countess of Dalkeith. As Dowager-Countess[7] and Baroness Greenwich she had her day there: In 1793, it passed to Henry – 3rd Duke of Buccleuch and continued the heritage of the Buccleuch family. Today, it is still in their possession.

LANDS – ARGYLL v. the DOWAGER-DUCHESS

Lands in the parish of Kilblain were the cause of a prolonged legal dispute between Argyll and his mother. It opened with a letter which he addressed to his Commissioners:

> Sudbrook 4 1/17
>
> Gentlemen,
> T'is long since I beg'd the favor of you to settle the account standing out with my Mother. I am certainly uneasy that it is not as yet finished, and longer I will by no means have it delay'd on any account whatsoever, I desire you will let her know you have my positive orders to put an end to that matter with the utmost despatch, upon which if she endeavours at further delays, I absolutely order you to proceed to oblige her by law, I hope upon this subject I have fully explained myself and that I shall never need to trouble you upon it again who am
> Your most faithful servant
>
> **Argyll.**

He added a post-script

to beg the favor of you to have those lands which my Mother
has possessed ever since my Father's death under the mistake of
their being part of her joynter no longer in her possession. I have
ever had the greatest respect and duty for my mother, but I am
so fully satisfied that in order to continue the friendship and
good understanding which is fully between us, it is absolutely
necessary we neither medle or make with one another's money
that I will on no account whatsoever either delay settling the
Account with her or leave those lands any longer in her hands
and therefore in this as in the matter of the Account; if she is
advised to make any delay, I absolutely order the making use of
the law to procure me justice, and pardon me to say to you,
Gentlemen, who have been long in my affaires, that you might
have prevented me this trouble. However my Orders are now
plain and positive, and I depend upon their being truly
observed . . .

'Gentlemen,

I received yours, but I was so long by the way I cold [could] not
sooner answer it. You desire me put other in possession of the
parrish of Kilblain . . .'

Thus began a letter that the Dowager-Duchess wrote, on 6 July
1718, to the 'Duke of Argyll's Commissioners for managing his
affairs.' In the course of it she stated – 'I have nae inclination to
have any dispute with my son.'

It must have been a matter both complicated and painful to both
parties. Writing in August 1719 to the lawyer – Mr Anderson – she
gave her version of the dispute :

. . . What you writ of the signing? I did not pretend any right to
Kilblain parish but for security of the other two is a great mistake,
for you may remember when for it they disputed my right I told
you and Bute before my Lord Islay that had the late Earl survived
my Lord I had more right, but they know that did not happen
and I shall make that appear as so whenever I come to town.
What I hate most is to find a report that I abstracted any con-
tracts to cheat my son. My son next betrayed my trust in making
them sign a rental wherein those lands were to which I had no
right or knowledge. Had they ever had a ground to believe I
possessed anything I had no right to but it had been discovered at
first; but sich a precedent in the most barbarous part of the
Highlands was never used as against me and they cant deny but I

have adverted the rent of this country more than I possess, first and last which is the reason so great paine and underneath means is used to get me out of the country. I regret my son should be made the instrument of such unjust proceeding; but when he is better informed he will do me justice. I claim the making good my contract with I will insist on and let the world know how I have bestowed my jointure which though the world will condemn me yet it will appear how much I have laid out on my son's interest and how much I have been used first and last.

Later, she was to inform Mr Anderson –

I must let you know how I am situated. In the first place, the Duke's servant, though mine formerly, serves him better than he ever did me, for not only the Duke's rent, but he borrowed up all the money in the country to make him a gain, and though while he was my chamberlain he could never pay the feu duties of the lands he bought, yet in this year he lifted it, and the feu claim is paid, for when I called for these tenants they produced dated receipts, so you see there was a design of letting me run in a maze, but I see and not see at present . . .

By the turn of the year 1719/20, Argyll had received memorials from his mother as well as a report from the Commissioners. They presented their views in such a manner that he judged it prudent for them to adopt a more moderate course. On the other hand, he was firm that 'they should lose no time in taking his Mother's accompts.'

In one direction, development of the countryside, the Dowager-Duchess had her eldest son's interest sincerely at heart. She exploited the Campbelltown lands for coals and the shore for salt; but the creation of plantations was her supreme pleasure.

'All my delight is to plant great trees as may be useful to the country and when it can be done in pretty figures, I think it noe great odds in the expense.'

A certain day in the year brought truce to her administrative energies.

'To-morow being my son's birthday we are to be as merry as we can. Long life may he have and be blessed with imaginable happiness.'

'THE OLD FAITHFULS'

Argyll was constantly reminded of the fact that he had followers who would never forsake him. Time neither wore the patience nor diminished the well-phrased memorials from Tradesmen.

John Tavish, Mason,

Humbly sheweth –

That when the Memorialist contracted for the building of the Bridge over Garron water near the Duloch, the Estimate he gave in amounted only to £11. 14/-. But as the work as it now stands amounts to £173. 8/- owing to the lowness of the ground on the one side of the water and the difficulty that attended making both sides of the Bridge equale. The Memorialist also begs leave to mention that £9. 10/- for the flank wall was neglected to be charged in the calculation of the first Estimate and £9. 5/- of difference between the measurement by the plan and the work as it now stands.

Which is humbly submitted to His Grace by

John Tavish.

26th October 1706.

Unto His Grace the Duke of Argyle,

The Petition of James Johnstoun, merchant in Edinburgh –

Humbly Sheweth

That where Robert Forman – Baker in Leith, did in 1698 and some succeeding years furnish to Your Grace's Father – Archibald, Duke of Argyle, severall Batches of Bread and other particulars for the use of his horses at sundry times according to a particular accompt given as instructed by the hands of His Grace's Master of horses and Grooms – extending to £19. 14. 10 Sterling.

This poor man – Robert Forman – being under a great many difficulties, your Petitioner did not only Relieve him Twice of our Prison, but is daily supplying him in his necessitys, being his friend and Relation – for which reasons the said Robert Forman hath given your Petitioner a full and ample right to the foresaid ground of Debt and he is informed by his Credent that some years agoe, Your Grace was pleas'd to order Commissar Ronald Campbell to pay Forman his Accompt, but when he went to the Commissar he refused to pay unless Forman could produce Your Grace's written order, so that hitherto neither Forman nor any for

him have ever gott one shilling of the soume, the verity whereof
the Commissar will attest.

May it Therefore Please Your Grace to consider this poor
man's condition and according to Your Grace's distinguishing
character of doing Justice to all, Order Your Petitioner's Payment,
and Your Petitioner shall ever pray –

James Johnstoun.

Unto the Honourable the Commissioners for the Manadge-
ment of the High and Mighty Prince, Duke of Argyle, and his
Estate in North Britain.

The Petitioner was a certain Charles Ramsay – resident in
Edinburgh – who 'having had the honour to serve His Grace the
late Duke of Argyle for the space of four years most faithfully
and honestly – There became due to me thereby a certain soume of
money for the said services.' Then followed a long account of his
'pinched circumstances.'

On 15 August 1720, there arrived a 'Memorial to His Grace the
Duke of Argyle from John Spreull – Merchant in Glasgow.'

The said John Spreull having furnished some wines to the late
Duke of Argyle all two severall times, the first by ane order from
His Gace in September 1699 and another quantity in August and
September 1703 when the late Duke was indisposed for which last
he gott not the Duke's signed order but only two receipts from
Phillis Walker, then His Grace's housekeeper (thereafter Countess
of Cromarty).

In November 1718, Mr. Spreull applyed to His Grace's
Manadgers and Commissioners for payment of his accompt
extending together to 462.8/ Scots, and produced what instructions he had, being considered by the Manadgers They ordered
him payment of the first part of his accompt extending to 213.8/
Scots. In respect Mr. Spreull produced the Duke's signed order
for furnishing thereof : But delayed to order the payment of the
last. Mr. Spreull gott payment of the first part of the accompt in
January 1719. But the other part remains yet unpaid.

Mr. Spreull has therefore ordered a coppy of the last part of
the accompt and the Vouchers thereof to be laid before His
Grace that orders may be given for payment thereof also, and
expects the want of the late Duke's signed order will occasion no
demurr ; Because His Grace was lying indisposed all the time.

Besides it is informed that some part of the wines last furnished were found in the Duke's Cellars at his lodging in the Cannongate and also some that were sent in bottles to his house in England after his death and intramelled with and disposed of by the Dutchess Dowager or others by her order upon that occasion which Her Grace cannot remember.

It is therefore humbly expected His Grace will order the payment of the last part of the Wines furnished by Mr. Spreull to the late Duke on Phillis Walker's receipt extending to 245 Scots conform to the accompt whereof ane coppy and of the receipts therefore are on the other side.

And your Petitioner shall ever pray –
Memoriall to His Grace of Argyle.

1703

Accompt of wines furnished to the late Duke of Argyle by JOHN SPREULL – merchant in Glasgow.

August 8th

Imp. 8, Gallons, 2 pints, i, Mutchkinen Canary all clear wine 14s. 8 pence Ster. pr. Gallon . . . 119. 5

Imp. 2 Caskes thereto as pr. Receipt . . . 2. 16

September 16th

Imp. 8 Gallons, 2 pints, 3 Mutchkins Rich Canary . . . 120. 3

Imp. 2 Caskes thereto . . . 2. 16

Summa Js. . . . 245. –

Follow the Coppy of the receipts granted by Phillis Walker then His Grace's housekeeper (now Countess of Cromartie) for the wines above mentioned.

August 8th – 1703 –

Received from Mr. John Spreull – Merchant at Glasgow – Two Caskes of Sack containing 8 gallons, 2 pints, i, Mutchkine for the use of His Grace the Duke of Argyle – By his orders by me Subscrived thus

Phillis Walker – September the 26th 1703

Received more two Rubbers of Canary Sack for the use of His Grace the Duke of Argyle from Mr. John Spreull by me Subscrived thus –

PHILLIS WALKER

NOTES

1 During the Rebellion and for some time after, the Dowager-Duchess could not visit Inveraray to inspect its condition. When eventually she was able to go there, 'I found it so in disorder within and without that I was obliged to stay till I put things in order which took so much time I laid aside thoughts of returning here [Kintyre] again before winter.'

2 Two sheets of these plans*, together with a plan for the old castle, are at Inveraray (No. 50 and dated before 1720).

3 The plan* is at Inverary (No. 41 and dated between 1725 and 1743).

4 The plan* is at Inverary (No. 18). This house became the home of the Earl of Islay when, as Duke, he was planning the modern castle.

5 The estates of Caroline Park brought with them the islands of Inchkeith and Inchmickery in the Firth of Forth, and also the oyster fishings in the estuary.

6 Formerly Roystoun Castle built by George, Lord Tarbat, in 1685.

7 The Countess of Dalkeith's husband — Francis, Earl of Dalkeith, died before succeeding to the Dukedom of Buccleuch.

*These three Plans were reproduced in the book *Inverary and Old Town* by Mary Cosh and Ian Lindsay, published in 1972.

Appendix II

TITLE AND ORDERS
held by
JOHN, 2nd DUKE OF ARGYLL

Knight of the Thistle, 1704
Created Baron Chatham and Earl of Greenwich, 26 November 1705
Knight of the Garter, 22 March 1710–11
(Then resigned the Order of the Thistle)
Created Duke of Greenwich, 27 April 1719

CALENDAR OF MILITARY APPOINTMENTS
held by
JOHN, 2nd DUKE OF ARGYLL (1680-1743)

Colonel – 4th Troop Horse Guards, 1703–15
Colonel – 3rd Regt. of Foot (or 'Buffs'), 1707–11
Colonel – Royal Horse Guards, 1715–17, 1733–40 and February
to March 1742
Master General of Ordnance, 1725
Colonel – 3rd Horse (later 2nd Dragoon Guards), 1726–33
Brigadier–General, 1704
Major-General, 1706
Lieutenant-General, 1709
General, 1711
Field-Marshall, 14 January – 1735–36

S

CALENDAR OF CIVIL APPOINTMENTS
held by
JOHN, 2nd DUKE OF ARGYLL (1680–1743)

Privy Counsellor (G.B.), 3 February 1708–9
Ambassador to Charles III, 1710–11
Governor of Minorca, June 1712 to April 1714, and 5 October 1714
to July 1716
Governor of Edinburgh Castle, 1712–14
Lord-Lieutenant of Surrey, 1715–16
Lord-Lieutenant of Argyll and Dumbarton, 1715–43
Lord-Steward of the Household, 1718–19, 19–25
Governor of Portsmouth, 1730–37

Bibliography

Boyer, Abel, *Political State of Great Britain*, London 1711

Campbell, Robert, *The Life of the Most Illustrious Prince John, Duke of Argyle and Greenwich*, London 1745

Caroline Park House, published by A. B. Fleming and Co.

Chamberlayne, Edward, *Angliae Notitia* (*Magnae Britanniae Notitia* from 1707), London 1669

Churchill, Sir Winston, *Marlborough*, London 1947

Clerk, Sir John of Penicuik, Bart, Memoirs of, from his own Journal, 1656–1755, Scottish History Society Publications 1892

Colbert, J. B., Marquis de Torcy, Memoirs of, 3 vols, London 1756–7

Complete Peerage (ed. V. Gibbs)

Coxe, W., *Life of Walpole*, London 1798

Cunningham, Alexander, *The History of Great Britain from the Revolution of 1688 to the Accession of George I*, London 1787

Dictionary of National Bibliography

Douglas's Scottish Peerage

Knight, C. R. B., *The Historical Records of the 'Buffs' (East Kent Regiment) 3rd Foot*

Macaulay, Thomas Babington, *History of England from the Accession of James II*, London 1849–61

Macray, W. D. (ed.), *Correspondence of Colonel Hooke 1703–1707*, London 1760

Miège, Guy, *New State of England (Present State of Great Britain and Ireland* after 1707), London 1691

Minto, Earl of (ed.), Baillie of Jerviswood, *Correspondence*, Bannatyre Club, 1842

Packe, Edmund, *Historical Records of the Royal Regiment of Horse Guards*, London 1834

Strickland, Agnes, *Lives of the Queens of England from the Norman*

Conquest to the Death of Queen Anne, 12 vols, London 1840–8
Stuart, Lady Louisa, *Memoirs of*, London 1899
Sutherland, John Douglas, 9th Duke of Argyll (ed.), *Intimate Society Letters of the Eighteenth Century* (includes the Godolphin correspondence), London 1910
Trevelyan, G. M., *England under Queen Anne*, London 1930–4
Walpole, Horace, *Memoirs of the Reign of George II*, London 1846
Wilcock, J., *A Scots Earl in Covenanting Times*, Edinburgh 1907
Woodrow, *History*, vol. II
Woodrow, *Analecta*, vols I, II, III, IV
Wortley-Montagu, the Rt Hon, Lady Mary, Letters and Works of, introduction by Lady Louisa Stuart, London 1893

Edinburgh Courant, 1705
English Historical Review, 1904
The Flying Post, 1705–6
The London Gazette, 1725
St James's Post, no. 100
The Observateur 24–7 October, 1706
Contemporary news-letters

Unpublished Sources

Acts of Parliament of Scotland, 1702–7
Correspondence Politique – Ministère des Affaires Etrangères, Paris, folios 222, 237, 242, 260, 264, 270, 274, 279
Parliamentary Papers supplementary
Privy Council Minutes, 1705
Register of Privy Council of Scotland, 4th series, X176
State Papers, Domestic, Public Record Office
State Papers, Scotland, Scottish Record Office
Timberlake's Parliamentary Debates

Correspondence and documents from His Grace the Duke of Argyll's muniments at Inveraray Castle
Complete correspondence of John, 2nd Duke of Argyll, when Commander-in-Chief, Spain, 1711 (discovered at the Bedford Record Office)
Correspondence and documents from the private muniments of His Grace the Duke of Atholl

Letters from the private muniments of His Grace the Duke of Buccleuch

Correspondence and documents from the private muniments of the Marquess of Bute

Hitherto unpublished correspondence from His Grace the Duke of Marlborough's muniments at Blenheim

Correspondence from the hitherto unpublished Seafield Papers at the Scottish Record Office (by courtesy of the Countess of Seafield's instructions to the Curator of the Scottish Record Office)

Culloden Papers, Historical Manuscripts Commission

More Culloden Papers, Historical Manuscripts Commission

Dartmouth Papers, Historical Manuscripts Commission

Harley MSS calendared in vol. V of the Historical Manuscripts Commission Report on the Portland Papers

Leven and Melville Papers, Historical Manuscripts Commission

Lockhart Papers, Historical Manuscripts Commission

Lothian and Morton Papers, Historical Manuscripts Commission

Mar and Kellie Papers, Historical Manuscripts Commission

Marchmont Papers, Historical Manuscripts Commission

Polwarth MSS, Historical Manuscripts Commission

Rawlinson MSS, A.169, fol. 16; D.1145, fol. 66b; D.919, fols. 82–101; D4, fol. 70

Bodleian Library, Oxford

Stuart Papers, Windsor

Index